PENGUIN ⓟ CLASSICS

THE LETTERS OF THE YOUNGER PLINY

PLINY was born in late A.D. 61 or early 62, the son of Lucius Caecilius of Comum. He probably had tutors at home before continuing his education in Rome; there he came in closer contact with his uncle, the polymath Elder Pliny who, on his death in the eruption of Vesuvius which destroyed Pompeii, left the Younger Pliny his estate, having adopted him as a son. Gaius Plinius Luci filius Caecilius Secundus, as he was thereafter known, began his career at the Bar when he was eighteen, and specialized in cases of inheritance. He managed to emerge unscathed from Domitian's 'reign of terror', even being appointed an official at the Treasury, and he held a similar appointment after Domitian's death. In 103 he was awarded a priesthood in recognition of his distinguished public service, and was prominent in several major prosecutions. His final senatorial appointment was to represent the Emperor Trajan in Bithynia and Pontus, where he died probably in 113. He was given the consulship at the very early age of thirty-nine, and was married three times. His nine books of personal letters (a social commentary on his times) were selected by Pliny himself and were published in his lifetime, while his official correspondence with Trajan was published as a tenth book after his death and contains the celebrated exchange of letters on the early Christians. Of his many speeches, only the *Panegyricus*, addressed to Trajan in thanks for his consulship, survives.

BETTY RADICE read classics at Oxford, then married and, in the intervals of bringing up a family, tutored in classics, philosophy and English. She became joint editor of the Penguin Classics in 1964. As well as editing the translation of Livy's *The War with Hannibal* she translated Livy's *Rome and Italy*, the Latin comedies of Terence, *The Letters of Abelard and Heloise* and Erasmus's *Praise of Folly*, and also wrote the Introduction to Horace's *The Complete Odes and Epodes* and *The Poems* of Propertius, all for the Penguin Classics. She also edited and introduced Edward Gibbon's *Memoirs of My Life* for the Penguin English Library. She edited and annotated her translation of the younger Pliny's works for the Loeb Library of Classics, and translated from Italian, Renaissance Latin and Greek for the Officina Bodoni of Verona. She collaborated as a translator in the Collected Works of Erasmus in preparation by the University of Toronto and was the author of the Penguin reference book *Who's Who in the Ancient World*. Betty Radice was an honorary fellow of St Hilda's College, Oxford, and a vice-president of the Classical Association. She died in 1985.

THE
LETTERS
OF
THE
YOUNGER
PLINY

TRANSLATED WITH AN INTRODUCTION BY

BETTY RADICE

PENGUIN BOOKS

Penguin Books Ltd, Harmondsworth, Middlesex, England
Viking Penguin Inc., 40 West 23rd Street, New York, New York 10010, U.S.A.
Penguin Books Australia Ltd, Ringwood, Victoria, Australia
Penguin Books Canada Limited, 2801 John Street, Markham, Ontario, Canada L3R 1B4
Penguin Books (N.Z.) Ltd, 182–190 Wairau Road, Auckland 10, New Zealand

—

This translation first published 1963
Reprinted 1967
Reprinted with Select Bibliography 1969
Reprinted 1971, 1974, 1975, 1977, 1978, 1981, 1983, 1985, 1986

—

—

Set, printed and bound in Great Britain by
Cox & Wyman Ltd, Reading
Set in Monotype Bembo

TO E. V. RIEU

magistro discipula

Contents

Familiar letters written by eye-witnesses, and that, without design, disclose circumstances that let us more intimately into important events, are genuine history; and as far as they go, more satisfactory than formal premeditated narratives.

Horace Walpole to Sir John Fenn, 29 June 1784

Introduction

'There is a bareness about an age that has neither letter-writers nor biographers.' Virginia Woolf[1] was writing about Dorothy Osborne and the seventeenth century when 'the bare landscape becomes full of stir and quiver and we can fill in the spaces between the great books with the voices of people talking'. The Romans are the first letter-writers of the Classical world, or, rather, theirs are the letters which chance has preserved to satisfy our curiosity about people as persons, each one unpredictable and full of contradictions and different from his fellows. Greek literature keeps the quality of bareness: the great sweeps of thought are there, and the magnificent power to analyse human capacity and weakness, but there is no one, with the possible exception of Socrates, whose personal idiosyncracies are known. We pick up scraps where we can – from Aristophanes or Xenophon or Plutarch; and there are the pitiably few undisputed letters of Plato or the touching details of humble persons which survive in the occasional papyrus letter, but no one reveals himself as the true letter-writer never fails to do. So the Greek statue stands aloof with his stylized enigmatic smile, while the Roman portrait bust is recognizably someone like ourselves, and its irregular features speak for a single individual at a point of time.

Roman letters can take many forms. Cicero's poured out freely, without thought of subsequent publication, and the Emperor Marcus Aurelius and his tutor, M. Cornelius Fronto, wrote almost daily to each other letters which are personal and wholly unselfconscious. Horace, Statius and Martial addressed verse letters to their friends; Pliny published his personal letters himself in carefully arranged selections. But it is a fallacy to suppose that only the first type of

1. *The Common Reader*, Second Series.

letter is self-revealing – we come to know Chesterfield and Walpole through their letters, if not as intimately as the Pastons or Charles Lamb. Horace's form of letter-essay, which reappears in Montaigne and Addison, never loses its personal note, and Pliny's letters have a wealth of autobiographical detail to capture the imagination and 'fill in the spaces . . . with the voices of people talking'.

Cicero is generally thought to be most representative of the great writers of the late Republic, and his letters provide the most revealing information about his times. It is 150 years before the Empire has its letter-writer in Pliny. He has left a more faithful and less prejudiced picture of Rome as he knew it than did any of his contemporaries, and in him we can best see how a Roman of his class lived and thought at the turn of the first century. It is also possible to build up a remarkably complete record of his career and his personal life, for which all the facts come from four inscriptions (the most important of which are translated on pages 303–4) and his letters: there are 247 letters in the nine books of the personal correspondence, and 121 official letters to and from the Emperor Trajan published separately in a tenth book.

He was seventeen at the time of the eruption of Vesuvius in A.D.79 (VI:20), so was born in late 61 or early 62, the son of Lucius Caecilius of Comum. Both the Caecilii and his mother's family, the Plinii, owned property in the district to which several letters refer. From the fact that he says nothing about his father, and from an inscription recording the latter's bequests to his two sons and a concubine, Lutulla, it is supposed that his parents were separated and Pliny lived with his mother; after his father's early death he had Verginius Rufus as guardian, the famous Rufus who had put down the revolt of Vindex against Nero in 68 (VI:10 and IX:19), and whose death at the age of eighty-three is described in an early letter (II:1). As there was no school at Comum (IV:13) he probably had tutors at home; a system he recommends to his friends (II:18 and III:3). He mentions with a touch of amusement the 'tragedy' he wrote in Greek at the age of fourteen (VII:4). He came to Rome to continue his education and attended the lectures of Nicetes Sacerdos, a well-known teacher of rhetoric from Smyrna, and those of the great teacher and writer Quintilian, whom Vespasian had appointed as a salaried professor of rhetoric (VI:6). In Rome he came in closer contact with his mother's brother, the polymath Elder Pliny, who died during the eruption of Vesuvius; Pliny and his mother were then staying at Misenum where the uncle was in command of the fleet (VI : 16 and 20).

Under the terms of his uncle's will he inherited the full estate, and a change of name indicates his adoption by will as a son. Henceforward his official title is Gaius Plinius Luci filius Caecilius Secundus. He began his career at the bar at the age of eighteen (V : 8) and mentions an early success before the Centumviral Court (V : 8) – the Roman Chancery Court which specialized in cases of inheritance and which was to be Pliny's special sphere throughout his active life in the courts (VI : 12). About this time he married his first wife, and soon after his senatorial career began with his appointment to a minor magistracy as one of the *decemviri stlitibus iudicandis* who presided over the panels of the Centumviral Court. He was then military tribune of the Third Gallic legion, probably for the minimum six months, and served in Syria as auditor of the auxiliary forces' accounts (VII : 31). There he met the exiled philosophers Euphrates and Artemidorus (1 : 10 and III : 11). After another minor office (*sevir equitum Romanorum*) he was one of the quaestors attached to the Emperor's staff who conveyed his messages to the Senate (VII : 16). This was in 88 or 89.[1] In 91 he was tribune of the people and felt it his duty to suspend his practice at the bar (1 : 23). The Emperor Domitian allowed him to proceed to the praetorship in 93 without waiting for the statutory year's interval (VII : 16), and in the same year he appeared for the prosecution in the first of the four public trials of provincial governors which were to occupy him at intervals for many years. Baebius Massa was convicted in the case brought by the province of Baetica (VII : 33), but then retaliated by charging Pliny's colleague, Herennius Senecio, with high treason. Senecio was one of the leaders of the 'Stoic opposition' to the Emperors, and his conviction and execution mark the beginning of the reign of terror for which Domitian is remembered, and which is so vividly recalled in Tacitus's *Agricola*. The leaders of the opposition were put to death and many of their supporters were exiled, but though Pliny afterwards described himself as surrounded by falling thunderbolts (III : 11) he emerged unscathed. Indeed, he was given a

1. These dates are much debated; as given here they are taken from Chapter 7 of Ronald Syme, *Tacitus*, Oxford University Press, 1958.

three-year Treasury appointment as one of the officials in charge of the military Treasury.

Domitian was assassinated in September 96, and Pliny took the opportunity to vindicate the Stoic Helvidius Priscus by charging his prosecutor Publicius Certus (IX : 13). But the spirit of Nerva's reign was against raking up the misdeeds of his predecessor, and Pliny had to be content with the fact that, though Certus was one of the officials of the Treasury of Saturn, and this usually led to the consulate, he was passed over; and when he died soon after, Pliny succeeded to his Treasury post along with his friend Cornutus Tertullus. This too was a three-year appointment; in Pliny's case from 98 to 100. There had been changes in his personal life; his first wife had died and he had married again at some date unknown; his second wife died just before the trial of Certus. He remained on friendly terms with her mother, Pompeia Celerina, and appears to have managed her investments for her (III : 19). His guardian Verginius Rufus and his old friend and advisor Corellius Rufus had also died at the beginning of Nerva's reign (I : 12 and II : 1).

In a letter written to Trajan soon after his accession in January 98 (X : 3a), Pliny seeks official permission to conduct the case against the governor of Africa, Marius Priscus, while still in his Treasury post, and elsewhere describes the trial in detail (II : 11 and 12). Priscus was found guilty in January 100, and soon afterwards Pliny agreed to conduct a similar prosecution of Caecilius Classicus on behalf of the province of Baetica (III : 4). He was working on this when he and Cornutus Tertullus were consuls together for two months (September to October 100) and Pliny moved the official vote of thanks to the Emperor which he subsequently elaborated and published as the *Panegyricus* (III : 13 and 18). Classicus was convicted in the following year, but Pliny had to wait until 103 before receiving a priesthood, the usual decoration for merit in his day. He was duly elected augur to fill the vacancy left by the death of Frontinus (IV : 8). Trajan's answer to his earlier petition for a priesthood (X : 13) is not preserved. (In a short inscription found in a village near Como, Pliny's official titles include that of priest of the deified Emperor Titus; this must have been an honour bestowed by his native town.) He married his third wife Calpurnia, orphaned granddaughter of Calpurnius Fabatus, a wealthy citizen of Comum who evidently supervised the manage-

ment of Pliny's estates in the district (VI:30). Pliny writes a touching account of this new marriage (IV:19), and his devotion to his
young wife and grief at her miscarriage and subsequent sterility
are undisguised (VII:5 and VIII:10). Trajan's conferment of the
privileges of parents of three children can have been only poor
consolation.

At the end of his Treasury duties Pliny was again active in the
Centumviral Court, though he looked forward increasingly to
honourable retirement (II:14). He also acted frequently as assessor,
either in the City prefect's court (VI:11) or to Trajan himself (IV:22).
Two more big cases involving governors of Bithynia occupied him;
he defended Julius Bassus during the winter of 102–3 (IV:9), and
Varenus Rufus in that of 106–7 (V:20). He accepted another three-
year office in 104 when he was elected president of the Tiber Con-
servancy Board (*Curator alvei Tiberis et riparum et cloacarum urbis*;
V:14) and so was responsible for keeping the river banks in repair to
prevent flooding and for maintaining Rome's sewers. Pliny must
have enjoyed this; practical problems of water supply and drainage
had always interested him and he probably knew the works on civil
engineering of his friend Frontinus.

Finally came his appointment to a special commission as the
Emperor's representative in the province of Bithynia and Pontus, a
post similar to that held in Greece by the Maximus to whom Pliny
addresses a famous letter of advice (VIII:24). The mere fact that the
province had brought charges against two successive governors indicated that something was very wrong with its affairs, both political
and financial, and Pliny was to tour the towns, write reports cn his
findings, and settle lesser problems on the spot. Trajan doubtless
chose him because of his knowledge of Bithynian interests gained
through his thorough handling of the defence of Bassus and Varenus;
he was also a recognized expert on finance. He arrived in time to
celebrate the Emperor's birthday on 18 September 111 (X:17b), and
he was on tour in Pontus when he conducted the annual ceremony for
Trajan's accession on 28 January 113; but as there is no mention of
birthday celebrations for 113, presumably he died before September
113, and evidently with his work unfinished. (His colleague in the
consulship, Cornotus Tertullus, was sent out later in Trajan's reign
with the same powers, and Tiberius Julius Severus was similarly sent

there by Hadrian.) Calpurnia travelled out with Pliny; the letters break off with Trajan's authorizing her return to Italy by the Imperial Post service, so that she could be with her aunt as soon as possible after her grandfather's death. She and Pliny could not have seen each other again.

This was a successful career. It was very rare to hold the consulship at the early age of thirty-nine; Pliny's colleague Tertullus was twenty years older. It was also rare to hold two Treasury posts in succession. It is interesting that none of the letters mentions the first of these, when the only other appointments not recalled are the local priesthood at Comum and the two minor offices held at the onset of his career and scarcely worth a mention after twenty years. It is in fact only from the Como inscription that we know that Domitian chose Pliny to fill the post in the military Treasury, and it may be that he wished his readers to forget that he owed anything to an Emperor whom he presents as a monster of tyranny and caprice. He was friendly with a great many people who suffered death or exile for their political views, and though he says more than once that he took risks on their behalf (III : 11 and IV : 24) perhaps he felt some embarrassment when the exiles of 93 returned to find him prosperous and unscathed. This is not to suggest that Pliny was a time-server; but his interests were not really political, and his professional experience was financial and legal, with the law of property as his special sphere. In a famous outburst in the *Agricola* (Chapter 42) Tacitus quotes his father-in-law's career as an example to prove that 'even under bad Emperors there can be great men'; Pliny too is a witness to the fact that competence and honesty can survive a corrupt régime. Someone must keep the civil administrative machine working, and it is the Plinys of all times and places who form a civil bureaucracy to carry on while governments come and go.

The nine books of the personal letters, carefully selected and arranged by Pliny himself, were certainly published in his lifetime and before he went out to Bithynia. The order is roughly chrono-logical, but very few letters can be firmly dated by independent evidence, especially as the main dates of Pliny's career are also in doubt. The theory that the books were published year by year, start-ing before the death of Verginius Rufus in January 97 (II : 1) cannot be proved, and it seems much more likely that when Pliny says in his

introductory letter 'I have made a collection ...' that he is writing
some time after the date of the letters in Book I though he arranges
them to give an impression of 'taking them as they came to my
hand'. Perhaps Books I–III appeared together, with the letter on the
death of Martial closing this chapter, and the remaining books in
pairs or threes: a single book would have been rather a slender volume
even for an editor as cautious and painstaking as Pliny. His last important public case (that of Varenus) ends not later than the early part
of 107. Between that date and that of his departure for Bithynia in 111
would seem to be a likely time for Pliny to be dividing his time
between Laurentum and Tifernum and spending the retirement he
had long anticipated (IV : 23) in sorting, selecting and arranging
letters which had accumulated over a period of years.[1] Earlier on he
is not sufficiently advanced in his career and too busy delivering and
revising his speeches for publication (V : 8) to consider publishing anything else. On this theory Books I–III cover the years 97 to 102
but are compiled and published some five years later; Books IV–VII
deal with events of 103 to 107; and Books VIII–IX refer to the years
108 to 109 and cannot have been written long before they were made
public.

The earlier letters are in fact far fuller of events and show Pliny
active in Rome, professionally in the Centumviral Court and the
Senate, and personally in many ways; revising his speeches and writing
verse, carrying out social engagements and spending long hours at the
verse-readings of his many friends, and writing tactfully phrased
letters of recommendation for those whose careers he hoped to
further. They also contain the tributes to the great men who had influenced his early years, Corellius Rufus, Silius Italicus, Verginius
Rufus and his uncle. By the end of Book VII our picture of Pliny's
youth and early career is as complete as he is going to make it, and the
last letter expressing his hope to be included in Tacitus's Histories
seems to close a chapter. Books VIII and IX contain only one long
letter on a professional subject (IX : 13), and this refers to his vindication of Helvidius Priscus more than ten years earlier. Book IX is almost
wholly descriptive, literary, or reflective; Pliny is enjoying his leisure
at Tifernum, with plenty of time for reading and contemplation, and
for writing literary criticism or philosophic advice to his friends.

1. For a different view see Syme, op. cit., Appendix 21.

Twice he writes of his pride and pleasure at being recognized as an author and coupled with Tacitus, with the quiet assurance of one who feels he has reached his goal (IX:13 and 24). There is no indication that the series of letters is ended, though one letter (IX:2) may hint that retirement from professional life in Rome may result in a shortage of letters worthy of publication. But whatever Pliny's intentions, his appointment to the special commission in Bithynia and Pontus marks the end of the life of cultivated leisure he had planned in one of the earliest letters (II:14). It is greatly to his credit that the new stimulus and responsibility bring out the best in him.

Bithynia lay along the south coast of the Black Sea and had been left to Rome by the will of its last king in 74 B.C. Nine years later Pompey extended the province eastwards by the addition of the western part of the kingdom of Pontus, and laid down its constitution by the *lex Pompeia* to which Pliny refers in his letters to Trajan (X: 80, 112, and 114). Nicomedia and Amastris were the capital cities of the two halves of the province, but only Chalcedon and Amisus were 'free and confederate' cities (X:92), and there were only two *coloniae* or Roman settlements, in Trajan's time: Apamea (X: 47) and Sinope. Though it was on the European side of the Bosporos, Byzantium belonged administratively to Bithynia (X:77). After Augustus's reorganization of the Empire, Bithynia was governed as a senatorial province by a proconsul. Several of these governors are mentioned by Pliny: Lappius Maximus under Domitian (X:58), Servilius Calvus under Nerva (X:56), and Julius Bassus and Varenus Rufus whom Pliny had defended in their trials for maladministration in 103 and 106.

The problems confronting Pliny were mainly three: political disorder, municipal bankruptcy arising out of unregulated public spending, and irregularities in administration both central and local. That there was a risk of political disturbance in the province is evident from Trajan's reluctance to permit people to form societies even for such purposes as a fire brigade or mutual benefit, and no less from Pliny's doubts concerning the Christians. Though they appeared to do no more than support a 'degenerate sort of cult carried to extravagant lengths' and had ceased to hold meetings since Trajan's ban on political societies, Pliny felt there was a risk of their fanaticism spread-

ing from the towns to rural districts. Trajan's attitude is calm and im-
partial (see x:96–7 and note).

Pliny's reports as he tours the cities have a recurrent theme. Prusa
has large debts as a result of bad contracts and still needs public baths;
Nicomedia has squandered vast sums on two abandoned attempts at
building an aqueduct; Nicaea has thrown away money on a theatre
and gymnasium without having the site surveyed; and Claudiopolis
is busy with an impracticable plan for a gymnasium. Pliny is indefatigable in his efforts to remedy a bad project, to improve the
amenities of the cities, and to ensure that there will be money to
cover expenditure. He asks for authority to provide Sinope with a
water supply and to cover an open sewer in Amastris in the interests
of public health, and he convinces Trajan that communications at
Nicomedia can be improved by cutting a canal from a nearby lake
to the sea.

There are also irregularities of all kinds to report, some perhaps
trivial in themselves, but all indicative of administrative inefficiency
or dishonesty. In one town Pliny finds that slaves have found a way
into the legions, in another that persons condemned to exile are still
at large. He has to seek official rulings to define the legal position of
foundlings or the age of entry to a local senate and the legality of
admitted senators' paying an entrance fee. Pliny writes fluently and
precisely, and Trajan's briefer replies are always to the point and
explicit on principles for Pliny's guidance: good administration must
be in the interests of the people, tradition must be respected, and
nothing is to be gained by retrospective penalties for the deficiencies
of the past. Pliny has often been unfairly criticized for consulting
Trajan unnecessarily. But only sixty-one letters were addressed to
Trajan over a period of not quite two years, and, if the testimonials
and formal congratulations on public anniversaries are excepted, Pliny
wrote not more than forty times asking for guidance on specific
points; and a large proportion of these letters fall into the first year of
his appointment. Today, when cables and long-distance telephone
calls can pass as freely as official dispatches, it does not seem that
Pliny was unduly communicative for a man on a special commission
in a disturbed area. There is no direct evidence for all he did on his
own initiative, which must have been considerable, especially in his
second year. When he obtains instructions to deal with the building

problems at Nicomedia and Nicaea, presumably he deals with them, for he does not raise the subject again; and when the state of a city's finances calls for no comment, evidently he found nothing he could not settle himself. Nor can the letters provide evidence for Trajan's undue preoccupation with routine detail; his secretariat would acknowledge formal messages and draft some of the briefer replies while passing up to him the more important issues. 'Trajan to Pliny' is often a Whitehall formula, of the pattern 'I am directed by the Lords Commissioners of the Board of the Admiralty' in a clerk's letter. Sometimes there is no doubt that Trajan is writing himself, and he may be revealed in a trace of impatience or amusement, but the relationship between the two was one of mutual trust and appreciation, with some real warmth of feeling. Here, too, is not the decline and fall of the Empire, but a living indication of why it stood so long.

Book X as we have it was published posthumously; by whom there is no indication – Suetonius, perhaps, or another of Pliny's literary friends. The correspondence dealing with Bithynia is prefaced by fourteen short letters addressed to Trajan in which Pliny offers congratulations or thanks for honours conferred, or makes requests on behalf of friends and dependants. Most of these seem to date from the early years of Trajan's reign, and it is surprising that no more letters were to be found in the imperial files or among Pliny's personal papers to add to this record of the relations between one of the best of Rome's Emperors and his devoted servant.

More than a hundred persons have letters addressed to them in Books I to IX, and many more are referred to by name. Some are deserving young men, often from provincial Italy, about whom the letters tell no more than that Pliny wished to further their careers, though from other sources we may know that they won distinction. For example, the Fuscus Salinator and Ummidius Quadratus whose early success at the bar gladdened Pliny's heart (VI : 11) both reached the consulship after his death and married into the imperial family; one married Hadrian's niece and the other the sister of Marcus Aurelius. They receive several letters of advice and appreciation. Other correspondents are better known. There are professional colleagues such as Titius Aristo, the jurist, and Calestrius Tiro and Voconius Romanus, two of Pliny's closest friends. There are literary men like

Tacitus and Suetonius and literary aspirants such as Pompeius Saturninus and Sentius Augurinus (I : 16 and IV : 27) of whom Pliny writes in
glowing terms. He is always appreciative of older men like Spurinna,
whose life could be enviable in his late seventies (III : 1), and Arrius
Antoninus, who retained all his literary gifts (IV : 3); and there are
family letters to Calpurnia's grandfather and the aunt who brought
her up, as well as to Pompeia Celerina, the mother of his second wife
in whose relatives Pliny continued to take an interest (X : 51).

Several names show that Pliny never lost touch with his birthplace,
Lake Como, the town and its people.[1] His visits north were rare, but
he remains sentimentally attached to the family property (II : 15) and
can write wistfully to Caninius Rufus about 'our darling Comum'
when he sees no chance of escaping there (I : 3 and II : 8). Calvisius
Rufus is a town-councillor of Comum and is empowered to act for
Pliny (V : 7); Annius Severus (III : 6) is commissioned to have a pedestal
made for a statue Pliny wishes to present; Atilius Crescens is a boy-
hood friend and needs help with his money affairs; and Metilius
Crispus owes his promotion to centurion's rank to Pliny and receives
a substantial sum to pay for his outfit and equipment (VI : 8 and 25).
There is a Maximus from Verona (VI : 34), and Minicius Acilianus
(I : 14) comes from Brescia with a mother from Padua. Verginius
Rufus is a native of Milan, and Spurinna is probably a north Italian:
his wife Cottia has a Celtic name from the region of Turin. These
Italians have the virtues which Pliny most admires: hard-working,
loyal and responsible, they have a genuine simplicity uncontam-
inated by the life of a great city, a simplicity which Pliny never lost
himself.

It was perhaps through their common background that Pliny came
to know several members of what is often called the 'Stoic opposition'; its leader, Thrasea Paetus, was a native of Padua. This opposition to the imperial régime was not truly Stoic in doctrine, for it
opposed rule by a king in any form, whereas the Stoics accepted the
principle of monarchy provided it was put into practice by a philoso-
pher-king. Thrasea Paetus's long campaign against Nero and execution in 66 are described fully by Tacitus in *Annals*, XVI; more than
twenty years previously his father-in-law, Caecina Paetus, had joined
in a conspiracy against Claudius and had been compelled to commit

1. See G.E.F.Chilver, *Cisalpine Gaul*, Oxford University Press, 1941.

suicide.[1] Pliny quotes Thrasea with admiration more than once (VI : 29
and VIII : 22) and pays an eloquent tribute to the devoted life and
heroic death of Caecina's wife Arria (III : 16). Thrasea's daughter
Fannia married Helvidius Priscus : he too was executed for seditious
opposition by Vespasian, but left a son by his first wife, another
Helvidius, to carry on the tradition. This Helvidius was executed by
Domitian in 93 along with his supporters Arulenus Rusticus and
Herennius Senecio; other members of his party were banished and did
not return until after Domitian's death (III : 11). Pliny was then
honoured to be asked by Rusticus's brother to find a tutor for his
orphaned nephews (II : 18) and a husband for his niece (I : 14). Pliny's
natural recommendation for the latter position was the young man
from Brescia and Padua. Fannia and her mother he knew well (VII :
19) and from them he learned about the elder Arria's heroism of more
than fifty years back. Pliny was well aware that he himself was not
cast for the role of hero and martyr, and this may be why he was
attracted to the personalities who championed a cause he did not
actively support. As suggested above, his admiration for their courage
was perhaps tinged with embarrassment when the exiles returned.
But he could recall with pride some years after how he spoke in the
Senate in vindication of Helvidius (IX : 13), and the published version
of his speech was considered one of his best (VII : 30).When Helvidius's
daughters both die in childbirth and their brother is left alone to continue the line, Pliny repeats that 'my love for their father has remained
constant since his death, as my defence of him and my published
speeches bear witness' (IV : 21). This record of four generations of
independence and courage certainly influenced him deeply.

There were few people left at the end of the first century who could
trace their descent from the old families of the Republican and

1.

```
                              Caecina Paetus = Elder Arria
                                            |
                      Thrasea Paetus = Younger Arria
                                       |
        (1) = Helvidius Priscus = (2) Fannia
         |
   Helvidius = Anteia
              |
   _____|_____
   |                     |
Helvidius           2 daughters
```

Augustan nobility, and none of these receives a letter from Pliny. If there was a top set in Rome, evidently his provincial origins and tastes kept him out of it. The absence of certain literary names is more surprising. The last days of Silius Italicus are described (III : 7), but he receives no letter. Statius is never mentioned, though he and Pliny had at least one mutual friend in Vibius Maximus to whom Statius dedicated the seventh poem in the fourth book of his *Silvae*. Juvenal does not appear at all, and the two men cannot have had anything in common except their uncompromising hatred of Domitian; but Juvenal's *Satire* v recalls Pliny's two letters on snobbery and vulgarity at dinner-parties (II : 6 and IX : 17) and the end of *Satire* x deplores time wasted at the Races as Pliny does in another letter (IX : 6). Pliny was a patron of Martial, and Martial knew Juvenal well enough to address a verse-letter to him from Spain (Martial, XII : 18), but in Rome the two poets may have moved in different literary circles. It has even been suggested that in his choice of pseudonyms Juvenal satirizes some of Pliny's correspondents.[1] At any rate it is hard to imagine Juvenal being politely appreciative at Pliny's literary parties.

Pliny was a conscientious friend, indefatigable in his efforts to further the careers of the people in whom he was interested. One may tire of the worthy young men who feature in the letters of recommendation and wonder how many of Pliny's swans proved to be no more than geese, but the Roman concept of friendship retained something of the relations between patron and client, and Pliny's sense of duty towards his juniors is the counterpart of his gratitude to his elders who had helped him in their turn. He was generous and without ulterior motive. Several humble people had reason to be grateful to him: his old nurse for a small farm (VI : 3); a school-friend of Comum for a substantial sum to raise his social status (I : 19); a friend's daughter for a dowry (VI : 32); and a valued freedman for holidays abroad in search of better health (V : 19). To criticize Pliny for mentioning such gifts at all is to misunderstand the Roman attitude to these *officia* and *beneficia*; for services rendered and kindness bestowed, the giver had every right to expect in return society's approbation and a suitable gratitude in the recipient.[2] He was also a generous public benefactor.

1. Gilbert Highet, *Juvenal the Satirist*, Clarendon Press, Oxford, 1954.
2. See A. M. Guillemin, *Pline et la vie littéraire de son temps*, Collection d'Études Latines, Paris, 1929.

Comum had a library built and endowed (1 : 8), one third of a resident
teacher's salary paid (IV : 13), and provision for children in need from
a rent charge on Pliny's property (VII : 18). In all, Comum received
more than two million sesterces by Pliny's will and nearly as much in
his lifetime. At Tifernum on Tiber a new temple was built to house
Pliny's collection of statues of the Emperors (X : 8) and the temple of
Ceres on his own land was restored and enlarged for the use of the
public (IX : 39).

He could of course afford to be generous; his tastes were not extravagant and his capital was solidly invested in land. He might complain about the hazards of weather and failure of crops, but he was
able to reduce his tenants' rents when times were bad (IX : 37) and
make concessions to the contractors who stood to lose when the grape
harvest was a poor one (VIII : 2). Though of necessity an absentee
landlord for a great deal of the year, Pliny's practical interest in farm
management is apparent in many of the letters: as far as possible he
selected tenants and inspected accounts personally, and once seriously
considered introducing the experiment of rent payment by share of
produce (IX : 37). This can still be found as the *mezzadria* system of
Tuscany and north Italy. He certainly was much more than the
'scholar turned landowner' at whom he gives a gentle dig in the
person of Suetonius (1 : 24), although he can laugh at himself playing
the part of proprietor 'but only to the extent of riding round part of
the estate for exercise' (IX : 15). In reality he was very practical, missing
no opportunity of seeing things for himself and working out his own
building plans for his homes in Tifernum or Comum (IX : 7), or for
Calpurnius Fabatus's property in Campania (VI : 30). One wing of the
villa at Laurentum near Ostia he designed himself, and at Tifernum he
could indulge 'the love I have for all the places I have largely built myself or where I have perfected an earlier design' (V : 6). The gardens
there, where the formal terraces were planned in contrast with the landscape garden outside, were watered by a complicated system of pipes
and fountains. Anything to do with water seems to fascinate Pliny, and
his only criticism of Laurentum is that it has to depend on wells for
lack of running water. If we add the scientific problem of the intermittent spring at Comum (IV : 30), the description of the underground
streams and floating islands of Lake Vadimon (VIII : 20), and the
account of the construction of the harbour at Centum Cellae (VI : 31),

as well as all the letters from Bithynia on drains, aqueducts, and canals, we can see that in different circumstances Pliny might have been a civil engineer. He combined a fair share of his uncle's tireless energy with a much more scientific approach to natural phenomena and antiquarian anecdote; for example, the ghost stories (VII:27) and the dolphin of Hippo (IX:33) are recounted respectively as a psychic problem and an instance of animal behaviour. He also had an observant eye and a retentive memory, and rightly remarked that we need not travel to 'Greece, Egypt, or Asia or any other country which advertises its wealth of marvels' if we use our eyes and shake off the besetting habit of postponing a visit at home to what we know can be seen whenever we feel inclined.

A great many of the letters deal with literary topics, advice to young friends, requests for opinions on Pliny's own work, or his views on style and choice of subject. Two at least (I:20 and IX:26) analyse the weaknesses of the pure 'Attic' school of oratory with its rather negative ideals of brevity and avoidance of faults. The language of all these critical letters recalls that of Quintilian and shows how the emphasis on rhetoric and style colours the whole system of Roman education. But if Pliny's preference is for something less arid than the purists allowed, he is none the less aware that speech which is 'fluent, vigorous, and expansive' can degenerate into the rhetorical extravagances of Regulus or the volubility which pours out 'a torrent of long monotonous periods without taking breath' (V:20). What he values most is the sense of fitness combined with versatility which enables anyone to match his style with the subject and the occasion; a gift which Pliny exhibits to a marked degree himself. He is widely read in Greek and Roman authors and at first sight seems wholly typical of his generation, but a closer study of the authors he knows and quotes reveals his personal tastes. He is not interested in philosophy or political theory; he refers twice to Plato and never mentions Aristotle. (His connexion with the theorists of the 'Stoic opposition' was purely personal.) He quotes Euripides twice, but never Sophocles or Aeschylus; and there is no reference to Ovid and only one to Horace whose verse letters one would expect him to enjoy. He shows a knowledge of more than ten Greek and fifteen Roman authors, but apart from his detailed study of the Athenian orators (IX:26), most of his verbal quotations are from the *Iliad* and the *Aeneid*. His remarks on art are no more than conventional – realism in representation is his ideal – but the really disturbing thing is the poverty of his literary judgement, in poetry at least; he quotes four sets of verses, two by himself, one by Martial, and one by Sentius Augurinus, with approbation for their poetic merit (VII : 4 and 9, III : 21, and IV : 27). These verses are so embarrassingly banal that it is impossible not to suspect the qualities of unquoted works we are called on to admire. Calpurnius Piso's *Legends of the Stars* and the plays and poetry of Vergilius Romanus (V : 17 and VI : 21) may well have been no more inspired than Statius's *Thebaid* and Silius Italicus's *Punica* about which Pliny himself has his doubts (III : 7). It is remarkable that Pliny can recognize the weakness inherent in a majority vote 'so long as men have the same right to judge, but not the same ability to judge wisely' (II : 12) without seeing that the collective criticism of the sort of discussion-group assembled in letter VIII : 21 was bound to stifle originality. An independent spirit like that of Tacitus or Juvenal could never have submitted itself to the opinion of lesser men.

The letters are the best source of information we have about the social and political history of Rome at the turn of the first century, when the uneasy years of Domitian were followed by what Gibbon called 'the period in the history of the world during which the condition of the human race was most happy and prosperous'.[1] It has often been remarked that Pliny acts as a foil for his contemporaries; Juvenal's remorseless castigation of the faults of society, Martial's malicious thrusts at individuals and their vices, and Tacitus's searching analysis of corruption in morals and politics are countered by a picture of the times drawn by someone who lives and works in a world far removed from that of the idle rich and the irresponsible aristocrat. The letters are not selected to prove a point or teach a lesson: to that extent the evidence they provide is disinterested. Pliny moves among active professional men who take their responsibilities seriously; many of them owe their position in the Senate to the Emperor's recognition of their merit, and none can afford to squander his capital or neglect his obligations. When Pliny writes sometimes of abuse of privilege in the Senate or improper conduct in a court of justice, it is because he and his correspondents really care about things

1. *The Decline and Fall of the Roman Empire*, Chapter 3.

like right procedure, law and equity, and effective administration. Through him we see both the day-to-day routine of the Chancery Court and something of the work going on behind the scenes, and we learn much about the activities of the Senate at this time: a Senate which may be very different from that of the Republic, but as a deliberative assembly neither sycophantic nor redundant.

But the letters are more than a source-book; they also paint the fullest self-portrait which has survived of any Roman, with the possible exceptions of Cicero and Horace. It has in fact been suggested that Pliny sought 'to acquire literary fame in an original fashion – not history but autobiography, subtly blended with the depicture of contemporary social life'.[1] Like Horace Walpole, Pliny is consciously and unconsciously revealed in his letters until he emerges in the round. He has his faults. He is no more able to criticize his own work than was Wordsworth, and he can be priggish in the same way. The caution and pedantry of the lawyer are sometimes evident, and so is the complacency of the middle-aged; though here he is no worse than Cicero or any other Roman eager to win recognition. It is useless to look to him for any outspoken criticism of the conventions of his day: he accepts without question the employment of slaves and gladiators, the deification on death of the Emperors, and the political necessity of suppressing a fanatical Christian minority. But his qualities are positive and often original. His professional honesty, industry and efficiency are beyond question, and he is totally free from professional jealousy. He may seem self-satisfied, but he is not vain, and he is well aware that his talents are of secondary merit and that Tacitus is his superior (IX : 14). Tolerance in all its forms he always preaches and practises (VIII : 22), whether he is defending a spendthrift son or an erring servant, or writing with true imaginative insight into the feelings of a subject people with a glorious past (VIII : 24). A sceptic himself, he is patient with Suetonius and his dreams, and the simple piety of the votive inscriptions in the shrine of Clitumnus calls for a comment which is amused without being unkind. He is glad to escape from the noise of the Saturnalia, and happy to leave his slaves and freedmen to enjoy their celebrations without the restriction of his presence, and, though a temple is to him no more than a gallery for displaying works of art, when one on his property needs restoring he takes the oppor-

1. Syme, op. cit., page 664.

tunity to provide for the comfort of worshippers. He is a kind and thoughtful master, not only towards the individual members of his household, in whom he feels a special interest, but in his policy of allowing privileges to his slaves in the home and readiness to grant them freedom (VIII : 16). He is also a devoted husband and a considerate son-in-law, and a loyal friend who can appreciate the idiosyncracies of his companions, while remaining wholly genuine and free from affectations. This explains why his tolerance gives place to contempt in the case of his contemporary Regulus, who is everything which Pliny is not: unscrupulous, avaricious, vacillating and superstitious, as well as crudely flamboyant. Pliny dislikes this exhibitionism in Regulus almost as much as his dishonesty; he has sharp words too for the affectations of a rhetorician (IV : 11) and for people who court publicity by a show of superiority (VI : 17), while snobbery in all its forms he detests (II : 6). Neither has he any use for the childish passion of 'adult men' for the Races, because they have no genuine interest in the horses' speed and the drivers' skill.

But to call Pliny genuine and unaffected is not to say that he is naïve. He can laugh at himself as an advocate who welcomes an adjournment 'for I am never so well prepared as not to be glad of a delay' (V : 9), or as a practical landowner who gathers in the grape-harvest 'if you can call it "gathering" to pick an occasional grape, look at the press, taste the fermenting wine in the vat, and pay a surprise visit to the servants I brought from the city – who are now standing over the peasants at work and have abandoned me to my secretaries and readers' (IX : 20); and while deprecating a friend's lavish hospitality he adds, 'I must own I was shameless enough to accept everything.' These are endearing touches which bring him to life: admirable he may be, but he is not dull. It is refreshing, too, to find in him a champion of the rising generation, when it was a convention to look to the past for a Golden Age. Here Pliny's sturdy realism shows itself: 'It is not true that the world is too tired and exhausted to produce anything worth praising'; nor is it true that the simple virtues of a Golden Age are found in the country life idealized by the poets (Pliny's farmers are real peasants who grumble and muddle their affairs and are always a worry to landlords). Perhaps Pliny remembers how he came in his own youth from a northern province to find opportunities for a career in the metropolis; at any rate he is always generous in helping others to do the same and delighted when he finds individuals less casual and mannerless than young people in the mass inevitably appear to their elders. Some of his generalizations also go beyond the conventional. Among so many aspirants to fame, of whom he was one, it was Pliny who wrote that 'I am also well aware that a nobler spirit will seek the reward of virtue in the consciousness of it, rather than in popular opinion' (I:8); it was Pliny too who saw that the proverbial 'reflection leads to hesitation' is true in the sense that 'diffidence is the weakness of right-thinking minds' (IV:7).

There has been no serious attempt at a translation of Pliny's letters as a whole since the one published by William Melmoth in 1746. This was reprinted in the Loeb series in 1915, after revision and compression by W. M. L. Hutchinson because 'judged even by the easy canons of his time in regard to translation, his [Melmoth's] work is extraordinarily loose and inaccurate; a good deal of it is simply paraphrase and in many places the sense is flagrantly wrong'. But enough of Melmoth was left to present Pliny through a cloud of verbiage which was never his, so that the misty figure which emerged was more like an eighteenth-century dilettante than the real man, and the subtle variety of style to match the mood of each letter was lost in the polished phrases of Melmoth's day. Of course, the personal letters are literary in the sense that they are written with care on selected subjects, and are quite different in style and content from the remarkable series preserved in Book X. They are more to be compared with Horace's *Epistles* or Walpole's letters than with the intensely personal letters of Cicero or of Keats. Pliny draws the contrast himself: 'You want me to follow Cicero's example, but my position is very different from his. He was not only richly gifted but was supplied with a wealth of varied and important topics to suit his abilities, but you know without my telling you the narrow limits confining me.' (IX:2). There was nothing in Pliny's life to match Cicero's experience of revolution and civil war. If, as he tells us, Pliny published this revised selection from a larger number of letters, it is not always easy to see why some of the more trivial notes were chosen; to please the recipient, perhaps, to lower the tone between two more important letters, or possibly to give the reader the pleasure of seeing how the virtuosity of the stylist can find expression in a couple of sentences. These brief notes with their puns and allusions recall the conceits of Catullus and Martial as well as the characteristic Roman delight in epigram. Pliny can be elegantly formal, colloquial and conversational, analytically critical or tersely descriptive. He draws on legal language for his jokes with professional friends, quotes the poets in Greek as well as in Latin, and sets himself to describe a scene or a scientific problem in precise terms. No translation can hope to convey such versatility successfully, but a fresh approach may perhaps give a better idea of Pliny's gifts of accurate observation and clear description which put him high among the prose writers of any period.

His detached eye-witness account of the eruption of Vesuvius, recorded long after the event but with no trace of false sentiment to blur those terrifying sober facts, is a masterpiece of writing; scarcely less remarkable are the descriptions of natural scenery at the source of the Clitumnus and Lake Vadimon, or his loving account of his country homes at Laurentum and Tifernum. He can bring an animated scene to life, when senators reveal their nervous tension after Domitian's death or crowds pack the court to hear a *cause célèbre*; the hired *claques* watch for their cue to applaud a speaker; a brutal master's slaves conspire to murder him in his bath. Personalities can also stand out clearly – the ravaged dignity of Julius Bassus facing trial or a Vestal Virgin accepting a terrible death with composure, a soldier with a rambling story of his adventures as a prisoner of war and a father mourning the death of a thirteen-year-old daughter. Regulus cringes or blusters his way through the courts, the elder Pliny lights his lamp to work in the long hours before dawn, Spurinna plays ball to keep himself fit, and an old lady of seventy-nine tries to keep boredom at bay by playing draughts and maintaining a private ballet company. Meanwhile Pliny finishes his day's work before driving out to Laurentum along the Ostia road and then the side-road which is 'sandy for some distance and rather heavy and slow going if you drive, but soft and easily covered on horseback'.

There are still sandy side-roads in Italy, and some of the unchanging features of the country bear witness to Pliny's pleasure in them and his gift for expressing it. The foothills of the Apennines behind his Tuscan home are still much as he saw them, where 'the vineyards spreading down every slope weave their uniform pattern' as far as the cornfields 'where the land can be broken up only by heavy oxen and the strongest ploughs', and the water meadows, bright with flowers. North and south of Rome stretches the sandy, harbourless coast, and along it are the umbrella-pines which gave him an unforgettable simile for the ominous cloud rising from Vesuvius. Pliny can bridge the gulf between the past and present; some of the excavated houses at Pompeii, an estate like the one uncovered at Boscoreale, or the frescoes depicting magnificent villas to be seen in the Naples museum[1] may bring us nearest to his world, for here we can actually see a court-yard where fountains play and a dining-room with 'a fresco of birds perched on the branches of trees', and can picture the life of cultivated leisure where friends meet to discuss the details of a new poem or the fine points of a Corinthian bronze. The great Italian *palazzi* still have the gardens he would recognize – the colonnades and terraces, marble seats and fountains, the cypresses and vine pergolas, and the beds of acanthus, and 'the box shrubs clipped into innumerable shapes'. The shores of the northern lakes are fringed today with villas situated like Pliny's, either high up with wide views or 'on the very edge of the water' where the waves break and you can fish, 'casting your line from your bedroom window and practically from your bed, as if you were in a boat'. Flooded rivers after heavy rain, the dried-up beds of streams in summer, and the hot, dusty roads, the stormy winds of the west coast, and the winter frosts and summer breezes of the Apennines, where the view from a hill-top is like 'a painted scene of unusual beauty rather than a real landscape': these are all in the letters and familiar in Italy today.

Some sites are closely associated with Pliny. The intermittent spring at Comum, which fascinated him as a scientific problem, is to be seen in the grounds of the sixteenth-century Villa Pliniana; Leonardo da Vinci recorded it in his *Notebooks* and Stendhal has left an account of his visit in 1816. Lake Vadimon, round 'like a wheel lying on its side', with its floating islands and sulphurous water which was 'pale blue with a tinge of green' interested him for those very features, and not because it had been the scene of two early Roman victories over the Etruscans; it is sad that the text is corrupt at the very point where Pliny attempts a precise description of colour, so rare in a classical writer. At Lago di Bassano, near Orte, the small lake has shrunk to a

1. See plates III and VIII in Rostovtzeff, *The Social and Economic History of the Roman Empire*, Oxford University Press, 1926.

marshy pool with reeds instead of islands, but it still has its outlet
which disappears underground, and the modern *Guida d'Italia* describes its waters as '*biancastre e sulfuree*'. The source of the Clitumnus,
known to Virgil and Propertius,[1] is the subject of one of Pliny's best
letters. The little temple is in ruins, but the water continues to rise
miraculously from level ground very much as Pliny saw it; Corot was
to paint it, and Byron to pay his tribute,[2] and it inspired Carducci's
patriotic ode *Alle fonti del Clitunno*, where the line '*Ride sepolta all'imo
una foresta*' is an echo of Pliny's words: 'The banks are clothed with
ash trees and poplars, whose green reflections can be counted in the
clear stream as if they were planted there.' It is described and illustrated
in a recent study of the Latin poets,[3] and more than anything, perhaps, it brings Pliny near us. The gift of feeling visual and immediate
delight in a natural scene for its own sake is something which is outside time and place, but tends to be taken for granted since the Roman-
tic and Impressionist movements. Yet it is so rare in the ancient world,
where everything seen was bound up with religious, mythological
and historical associations, that Pliny's unconscious possession of it is
one of the strongest reasons why he should be remembered. 'Whether
posterity will give us a thought I don't know,' wrote Pliny to Tacitus,
'but surely we deserve one. . . .' The verses he wrote are probably
better forgotten and only one of the much-revised speeches survives:
but the letters are there to be read and justify his claim.

*

This translation was originally made from the 1958 edition of Schuster's
text in the Teubner series, but has been revised as far as possible to
follow the new Oxford Classical Text of Professor R. A. B. Mynors.
Most alterations have been made in Book x where there is very fragmentary MS. authority. Professor Mynors has given me generous help
in advance of publication of his text, for which I am most grateful.
I must also thank Mr A. N. Sherwin-White for his help in interpreting
Pliny and for giving me access to his Commentary before publication,
my husband for constructive criticism, and many friends for their

1. *Georgics*, II : 46 and *Elegies*, II : 19.
2. *Childe Harold's Pilgrimage*, IV : 66–8.
3. Gilbert Highet, *Poets in a Landscape*, Hamish Hamilton, London, 1957;
Penguin Books, Harmondsworth, 1959.

interest; notably Miss Marion Pick and Mr T. L. Zinn for advice on special points, and not least Dr E. V. Rieu for his help and encouragement. The members of my family have lived perforce with Pliny in their midst for longer than they may have bargained for, and I am grateful for their support and forbearance.

In translating the personal letters I have consistently omitted the formal beginning and ending, to avoid repetition and artificiality. I have translated geographical features (names of rivers and mountains) into English, but left most towns in the Latin form with the modern name in footnote. Official terms have been left in Latin or given an accepted English form, whichever seemed more natural, and a Key in an Appendix explains the less familiar of these. After long consideration, I have left sums of money in sesterces, but have included a note on purchasing power. Pliny's many Greek quotations appear in English, but all quotations have a footnote giving the source where this is known. Pliny's estate near Tifernum, to which he generally refers as *mei Tusci*, I have spoken of as if it was in Tuscany; in fact it is just over the boundary in Umbria. The ruins of a large villa have been discovered a few miles north of the town (Città di Castello), and tiles stamped with Pliny's initials. Five books of the letters have manuscript authority for a single name only for each recipient; wherever possible I have supplied a second name from information given by Mr Sherwin-White, but where the subject is too complex (there are several individuals addressed only as Maximus) I have left a single name and must refer readers to his researches.

Highgate, 1962   B.R.

BOOK ONE

1. *To Septicius Clarus*

You have often urged me to collect and publish any letters of mine which were composed with some care. I have now made a collection, not keeping to the original order as I was not writing history, but taking them as they came to my hand. It remains for you not to regret having made the suggestion and for me not to regret following it; for then I shall set about recovering any letters which have hitherto been put away and forgotten, and I shall not suppress any which I may write in future.

2. *To Maturus Arrianus*

I see that your arrival is going to be later than I expected, so I am sending you the speech which I promised you in my last letter. Please read and correct it as you always do, and the more so because I don't think I have written before with quite so much spirit. I have tried to model myself on Demosthenes, as you always do, and this time on Calvus[1] too, though only in figures of speech; for the fire of great men like these can only be caught by 'the favoured few'.[2] If I may venture to say so, the subject-matter actually encouraged my ambitious effort; for I had to fight my way most of the time, and this shook me out of my usual lazy habits, as far as anything can shake up a man like me. However, I didn't altogether abandon the 'lavish colouring'[3] of our master Cicero whenever I felt like making a pleasant deviation from my main path, for I didn't want the force of my argument to lack all light relief.

You must not think that I am asking you to be indulgent to my

1. Orator and poet, contemporary of Cicero and Catullus; here taken as a model for the 'pure' Attic style of oratory.
2. Virgil, *Aeneid*, VI : 129.   3. From Cicero, *Letters to Atticus*, I, 14, 5.

experiment. To sharpen your critical powers I must confess that my friends and I are thinking of publishing it, if only you cast your vote for the proposal, mistaken though it may be. I must publish something, and I only hope and pray that the most suitable thing is what is ready now – there's laziness for you! But I want to publish for several reasons, and above all because the books which I have already sent out into the world are still said to find readers although they have lost the charm of novelty. Of course, the booksellers may be flattering me; well, let them, as long as their deception makes me think well of my own work.

3. To Caninius Rufus

I wonder how our darling Comum is looking, and your lovely house outside the town, with its colonnade where it is always springtime, and the shady plane trees, the stream with its sparkling greenish water flowing into the lake below, and the drive over the smooth firm turf. Your baths which are full of sunshine all day, the dining-rooms large and small, the bedrooms for night or the day's siesta – are you there and enjoying them all in turn, or are you as usual for ever being called away to look after your affairs? If you are there, you are a lucky man to be so happy; if not, you do no better than the rest of us.

But isn't it really time you handed over those tiresome petty duties to someone else and shut yourself up with your books in the peace and comfort of your retreat? This is what should be both business and pleasure, work and recreation, and should occupy your thoughts awake and asleep! Create something, perfect it to be yours for all time; for everything else you possess will fall to one or another master after you are dead, but this will never cease to be yours once it has come into being. I know the spirit and ability I am addressing, but you must try now to have the high opinion of yourself which the world will come to share if you do.

4. To Pompeia Celerina, his mother-in-law

What luxuries you have in your houses at Ocriculum, Narnia, Carsulae,[1] and Perusia[2] – even baths at Narnia! I need only send a letter, and there is no need for you to write after the short note you sent

1. All in Umbria [now Otricoli, Narni, Consigliano].
2. In Etruria [now Perugia].

there some time ago. In fact your property seems more mine than my own, but with this difference: I have better service and attention from your servants than I do from mine. Perhaps you will have the same experience if you ever stay with us, as I hope you will for two reasons; you could enjoy our possessions as if they were yours, and my household would have to bestir itself at long last – it is unconcerned to the point of indifference in the way it treats me. Slaves lose all fear of a considerate master once they are used to him, but they wake up at the sight of new faces and try to win his favour by giving his guests the service due to him.

5. To Voconius Romanus[1]

Have you seen anyone so abject and nervous as Regulus[2] since Domitian's death? It has put an end to his misdeeds (which were as bad as in Nero's day, though latterly better concealed), and made him afraid I was annoyed with him, and rightly so; I *was* annoyed. He had helped with the prosecution of Arulenus Rusticus[3] and proclaimed his delight in Rusticus's death by giving a public reading of his speech against him (which he afterwards published) where he used the words 'Stoic ape' 'branded with Vitellius's mark'. (You will recognize his style of rhetoric.) Then he took to abusing Herennius Senecio with such violence that Mettius Carus said to him, 'What are my dead men to you? Have I ever attacked Crassus or Camerinus?' (two of Regulus's victims in Nero's time). Guessing how strongly I felt about all this, Regulus did not invite me to his reading. He must have remembered too the deadly trap he laid for me in the Centumviral Court, when Arulenus Rusticus had asked me to support Arrionilla, Timon's wife, with Regulus against me. Part of our case depended on the opinion of Mettius Modestus, the eminent senator who had been banished by Domitian and was still in exile. Up gets Regulus: 'Tell me, Pliny, what is your opinion of Modestus?' Now you can see the danger if I gave a good one, and the disgrace if I did not. I can only say the gods must have put words into my mouth. 'I will give my opinion,' said I, 'if the court is to pass judgement on this man.' He then repeated his

1. For Voconius Romanus see II : 13.
2. See II : 20, IV : 2 and 7, and VI : 2. One of the leaders of the Roman bar, and the only person whom Pliny consistently attacks.
3. See Introduction, page 22.

request for my opinion. 'Witnesses used to be cross-examined about persons on trial,' I replied, 'not on those already convicted.' 'Never mind then, what you think of Modestus,' he said: 'I want your opinion of his loyalty.' 'I know you do,' said I, 'but I think it is quite improper even to put questions about a man on whom sentence has been passed.' That silenced him. Afterwards I received praise and congratulations for not damaging my reputation by saving myself with an expedient but dishonourable reply, and for not falling into the trap of such a treacherous question.

So then he was terrified by the realization of what he had done, seized Caecilius Celer and Fabius Justus, and begged them to bring about a reconciliation. Not content with this, he called on Spurinna and implored his help – he can be very humble when he is afraid. 'Please see Pliny at his home in the morning – early in the morning, please, I can't bear the suspense any longer – and somehow stop him being angry with me.' I was awake when the message came from Spurinna that he was on the way, and sent back to say I would call on him; so we met in the colonnade of Livia, each making for the other. Spurinna repeated Regulus's request and put in a plea of his own, but being an honest man acting on behalf of a dishonest, said little. 'You must decide yourself what answer to take back to Regulus,' I said. 'I can only tell you frankly that I am waiting for Mauricus[1] to return from exile, and so can't give you an answer either way, since I must do what he decides. The decision must be his, and I shall abide by it.'

A few days after this Regulus and I met on an official visit to the praetor; he came up to me and asked to see me alone. He said he was afraid that something he had once said in court in reply to Satrius Rufus and myself was still rankling in my mind: 'Satrius Rufus, who makes no attempt to copy Cicero, and is satisfied with the standard of oratory today.' I replied that now that he admitted it, I realized that the remark was offensive, but that it could have been taken as a compliment. 'Personally I do try to copy Cicero,' I said, 'and am *not* satisfied with today's standards. It seems to me foolish not to aim at the highest. But if you remember this case, why have you forgotten the one where you asked me for my opinion of Mettius Modestus's loyalty?' He grew noticeably even paler than usual, and then stammered out, 'The question was meant to damage Modestus, not

1. Brother of Arulenus Rusticus.

you.' (See the cruelty of the man who admits he intended to damage someone in exile.) Then he proffered a fine reason: 'He said in a letter which was read out before Domitian that Regulus was "the vilest of two-legged creatures".' Modestus never wrote a truer word!

This practically ended our conversation, for I did not wish to prolong it and have to commit myself before Mauricus arrived. I am well aware that Regulus is hard to come to grips with; he is rich, influential, backed by many people and feared by more, and fear usually brings more support than popularity. However, it is quite possible that these props may collapse and let him down, for a bad man's popularity is as fickle as himself. But, as I said, I am waiting for Mauricus. His opinions carry weight and his wisdom is gained from experience, so that he can judge the future by the past. My own plans for attack or withdrawal will depend on his decision, but I am writing all this to you because, as a good friend, you ought to hear about my intentions as well as anything I have said and done.

6. To Cornelius Tacitus

I know you will think it a good joke, as indeed it is, when I tell you that your old friend has caught three boars, very fine ones too. Yes, I really did, and without even changing any of my lazy holiday habits. I was sitting by the hunting nets with writing materials by my side instead of hunting spears, thinking something out and making notes, so that even if I came home emptyhanded I should at least have my notebooks filled. Don't look down on mental activity of this kind, for it is remarkable how one's wits are sharpened by physical exercise; the mere fact of being alone in the depths of the woods in the silence necessary for hunting is a positive stimulus to thought. So next time you hunt yourself, follow my example and take your notebooks along with your lunch-basket and flask; you will find that Minerva walks the hills no less than Diana.

7. To Octavius Rufus

See what a pinnacle you have set me on, giving me the same power and majesty as Homer gives to Jupiter Highest and Best: 'And part the Father granted him, but part denied.'[1] You see I can use the same mixture of assent and denial in answer to your plea. I can very properly agree, as you ask me, not to act for the Baetici against a single in-

1. Homer, *Iliad*, XVI:250.

dividual; but it would hardly be consistent with the unfailing sense of duty you admire in me to act *against* them, when I have formed a close connexion with their province through so many different services rendered and all the risks I have run on their behalf at various times. I shall therefore have to steer a middle course, and choose from the alternatives you offer something which will satisfy your good judgement as well as your inclinations. It is not your present wishes which I have to consider so much as your high standards for what will have your permanent approval.

I hope to be in Rome round the middle of October when I can explain my position to Gallus in person, with you to support me; but meanwhile you may assure him of my intentions, 'and he bowed his dark brows'.[1] I feel like addressing you in Homeric verses whenever I can, as long as you will not let me quote your own – a privilege I covet so much that I believe it would be the only bribe which would induce me to act against the Baetici.

I have nearly left out the most important thing: thank you for your excellent dates, which are now having to compete with my own figs and mushrooms.

8. *To Pompeius Saturninus*

Your letter asking me to send you one of my recent compositions reached me at a good moment, when I had just decided to do that very thing. So you have spurred on a willing horse and removed any excuse you had for refusing the trouble of reading my work as well as my scruples about asking you to do so; I can hardly be expected to hesitate about availing myself of your offer, nor can you feel it a burden when you made it yourself. All the same, you must not expect anything new from a lazy man like me. I intend to ask you to take another look at the speech I delivered to my fellow-citizens at the official opening of the library at Comum. I have not forgotten that you have already made some general comments on it, so this time will you please apply your usual critical eye to the details as well as to the work as a whole. I can then revise it before committing myself whether to publish or suppress it, and possibly the very process of revision will force me to make up my mind at last, and either show the speech is not yet fit for publication or actually make it so.

1. Homer, *Iliad*, 1: 528.

And yet it is the actual subject-matter rather than my treatment of it which is holding me back in this way. It makes me seem rather carried away by my own praises, and this increases my diffidence even if I limit myself to a few simple words, especially as I am obliged to dwell on my own generosity as well as that of my relatives. This puts me in a very difficult and delicate position, though somewhat justified by being inevitable. Even disinterested praise is very rarely well received, and it is all the harder to avoid a bad reception when a speaker refers to himself and his family. We feel resentment against merit unadorned, and still more when pride publishes it abroad; in fact it is only when good deeds are consigned to obscurity and silence that they escape criticism and misconstruction. For this reason I have often asked myself whether I ought to have written this speech, such as it is, for an audience or only for my own benefit, seeing that there are many features which are essential when a matter is still in the process of preparation but lose their value and power to please once it is completed. To take the present case as an example of this: nothing could have been more valuable to me than to set out the reasons for my generosity. I was thereby enabled first to dwell on noble sentiments, then to discern their virtue by prolonged reflection, and so finally to avoid the reaction which follows on an impulsive handing-out of gifts. Thus too I trained myself to some extent to think less of my riches, for though we all seem to be born slaves to money-saving, my love of liberal giving, long and deeply reasoned, has freed me from these besetting bonds of avarice, and my generosity seems likely to win more praise because I was led to it from principle and not out of mere impulse.

I had also to consider the fact that I was not paying for public games or a show of gladiators but making an annual contribution towards the maintenance of free-born children. Pleasures for the ear and eye need no recommendation (in fact they are better restrained than encouraged in a public speech) but carefully chosen and persuasive words as well as material rewards are needed to prevail on anyone to submit willingly to the tedium and hard work involved in bringing up children. Doctors use persuasion to recommend a diet which will bring their patients better health though they may find it dull; still more must anyone acting in the public interest find attractive phrases to introduce a beneficial service which is not immediately popular. My own special difficulty was to make the childless appreciate the benefits gained by parents, so that the majority would be willing to wait and prove worthy of the privileges granted to a few. At the time, I was considering the general interest rather than my own self-glorification when I wished the purpose and effect of my benefaction to be known, but my present idea of publishing the speech may perhaps make me seem to be furthering my own reputation instead of benefitting others. I am also well aware that a nobler spirit will seek the reward of virtue in the consciousness of it, rather than in popular opinion. Fame should be the result, not the purpose of our conduct, and if for some reason it fails to follow, there is no less merit in cases where it was deserved. But, when people accompany their generous deeds with words, they are thought not to be proud of having performed them but to be performing them in order to have something to be proud of. So what would win a glowing tribute from an independent opinion soon loses it if accompanied by self-praise, for when men find an action unassailable they will criticize the doer for his pride in it; hence either your conduct is blamed for anything in it which is best passed over in silence, or you can be blamed just as much yourself for not keeping silent about your merits.

I have besides my individual difficulties. This was delivered not as a public speech in the open, but before the town council in their senate house, so that I am afraid that it is hardly consistent at this point to court by publication the popular favour and applause which I avoided when I was speaking. I put the doors and walls of the senate house between myself and the populace whom I was trying to benefit, so as not to appear to court their favour; but now I feel that I am going out of my way to display my powers and thus win over those whose sole concern with my benefaction rests in the example it sets.

These then are my reasons for hesitating in this way; but I know I can always depend on your good advice and should like to take it now.

9. To Minicius Fundanus

It is extraordinary how, if one takes a single day spent in Rome, one can give a more or less accurate account of it, but scarcely any account at all of several days put together. If you ask anyone what he did that day, the answer would be: 'I was present at a coming-of-age ceremony, a betrothal, or a wedding. I was called on to witness a will, to support someone in court or to act as assessor.' All this seems important on the actual day, but quite pointless if you consider that you have done the same sort of thing every day, and still more pointless if you think about it when you are out of town. It is then that you realize how many days you have wasted in trivialities.

I always realize this when I am at Laurentum,[1] reading and writing and finding time to take the exercise which keeps my mind fit for work. There is nothing there for me to say or hear said which I would afterwards regret, no one disturbs me with malicious gossip, and I have no one to blame – but myself – when writing doesn't come easily. Hopes and fears do not worry me, and my time is not wasted in idle talk; I share my thoughts with no one but my books. It is a good life and a genuine one, a seclusion which is happy and honourable, more rewarding than any 'business' can be. The sea and shore are truly my private Helicon, an endless source of inspiration. You should take the first opportunity yourself to leave the din, the futile bustle and useless occupations of the city and devote yourself to literature or to leisure. For it was wise as well as witty of our friend Atilius to say that it is better to have no work to do than to work at nothing.

10. *To Attius Clemens*

If Rome has ever given a home to the liberal arts, they can be said to flourish there today; from amongst the many distinguished persons who are proof of this I need only name the philosopher Euphrates. When I was a young man doing my military service in Syria I came to know him well; I visited his home and took pains to win his affection, though that was hardly necessary as he has always been accessible and ready to make overtures, and is full of the courteous sympathy he teaches. I only wish I could have fulfilled the hopes he formed of me at that time in the same way that I feel he has increased his virtues: or perhaps it is my admiration which has increased now that I appreciate them better. I cannot claim to appreciate them fully even now, for if it takes an artist to judge painting, sculpture and modelling, only one philosopher can really understand another. But it is plain to my limited judgement that Euphrates has many remarkable gifts which make their appeal felt even by people of no more than average education. His arguments are subtle, his reasoning profound, and his words well-chosen, so that he often seems to have something of the sublimity and

1. In Latium, near Ostia (now Torre Paterno).

richness of Plato. He talks readily on many subjects with a special charm which can captivate and so convince the most reluctant listener. He is moreover tall and distinguished to look at, with long hair and a flowing white beard, and though these may sound like natural advantages of no real importance, they help to make him widely respected. His dress is always neat, and his serious manner makes no show of austerity, so that your first reaction on meeting him would be admiration rather than repulsion. He leads a wholly blameless life while remaining entirely human; he attacks vices, not individuals, and aims at reforming wrongdoers instead of punishing them. You would follow his teaching with rapt attention, eager for him to continue long after you are convinced.

He has moreover three children, two of them sons whom he has brought up with the greatest care; and his father-in-law, Pompeius Julianus, who has had a career of great distinction as a leading citizen of his province, has nothing more to his credit than the fact that from amongst many excellent offers he chose a son-in-law who was outstanding rather for his learning than for any official position.

I don't know why I say so much about a man whose company I am never free to enjoy, unless it is to chafe the more against my loss of freedom. My time is taken up with official duties,[1] important but none the less tiresome. I sit on the bench, sign petitions, make up accounts, and write innumerable – but unliterary – letters. Whenever I have the chance I complain about these duties to Euphrates, who consoles me by saying that anyone who holds public office, presides at trials and passes judgement, expounds and administers justice, and thereby puts into practice what the philosopher only teaches, has a part in the philosophic life and indeed the noblest part of all. But of one thing he can never convince me – that all this is better than spending whole days listening to his teaching and learning from him.

All the more then do I urge you to let him take you in hand and polish you up next time you are in town; you do have time for this, and the prospect should speed up your coming. For unlike many people, I don't grudge others the advantages which I cannot have myself: on the contrary, I feel a real sense of pleasure if I see my friends enjoying the plenty which is denied to me.

1. Either at the military Treasury or the Treasury of Saturn.

11. To Fabius Justus

I have not heard from you for a long time, and you can't say you have
nothing to write about because you can at least write that – or else
the phrase our elders used to start a letter with: 'If you are well, well
and good; I am well.' That will do for me – it is all that matters.
Don't think I am joking; I mean it. Let me know how you are; if I
don't know I can't help worrying.

12. To Calestrius Tiro

I have lost a very great man, if 'loss' is the right word for such a
bereavement. Corellius Rufus has died, and died by his own wish,
which makes me even sadder; for death is most tragic when it is not
due to fate or natural causes. When we see men die of disease, at least
we can find consolation in the knowledge that it is inevitable, but,
when their end is self-sought, our grief is inconsolable because we feel
that their lives could have been long. Corellius, it is true, was led to
make his decision by the supremacy of reason, which takes the place
of inevitability for the philosophers; but he had many reasons for
living, a good conscience and reputation, and wide influence, besides
a wife and sisters living and a daughter and grandchild: and, as well
as so many close relatives, he had many true friends. But he suffered
so long from such a painful affliction that his reasons for dying outweighed everything that life could give him.

At the age of thirty-two, I have heard him say, he developed trouble
in the feet, just as his father had done; for like other characteristics,
most diseases are hereditary. As long as he was young and active he
could keep it under control by temperate living and strict continence,
and latterly when he grew worse with advancing age, he bore up
through sheer strength of mind, even when cruelly tortured by unbelievable agony; for the disease was now no longer confined to his
feet as before, but was spreading through all his limbs. I went to see
him in Domitian's time as he lay ill in his house outside Rome. His
servants left the room, as they always did when one of his more
intimate friends came in, and even his wife went out, though she was
well able to keep any secret. He looked all round the room before
speaking, and then: 'Why do you suppose I endure pain like this so
long?' he said. 'So that I can outlive that robber if only by a single

day.' Had his body been equal to his spirit he would have made sure that he had his desire.

However, the gods heard his prayer; and knowing it was granted he relaxed and felt free to die. He broke off all his links with life, now unable to hold him, for his disease had progressed although he tried to check it by his strict regimen; and, as it grew steadily worse, he made up his mind to escape. Two days passed, then three, then four, but he refused all food. His wife, Hispulla, sent our friend Gaius Geminius to me with the sad news that Corellius was determined to die, and nothing she or her daughter could say would dissuade him; I was the only person left who might be able to recall him to life. I hurried to him, and was nearly there when Julius Atticus brought me another message from Hispulla that even I could do nothing now as he had become more and more fixed in his resolve. Indeed, when the doctor offered him food he had only said 'I have made up my mind'; and these words bring home to me how much I admired him and how I shall miss him now. I keep thinking that I have lost a great friend and a great man. I know he had lived to the end of his sixty-seventh year, a good age even for a really sound constitution: I know that he escaped from perpetual illness: I know too that he left a family to outlive him, and his country (which was still dearer to him) in a prosperous state: and yet I mourn his death as if he were a young man in full health. I mourn, too, on my own account, though you may think this a sign of weakness, for I have lost the guardian and mentor who watched over my life. In short, as I said to my friend Calvisius in my first outburst of grief, I am afraid I shall be less careful how I live now.

Send me some words of comfort, but do not say that he was an old man and ill; I know this. What I need is something new and effective which I have never heard nor read about before, for everything I know comes naturally to my aid, but is powerless against grief like this.

13. To Sosius Senecio

This year has raised a fine crop of poets; there was scarcely a day throughout the month of April when someone was not giving a public reading. I am glad to see that literature flourishes and there is a show of budding talent, in spite of the fact that people are slow to form an audience. Most of them sit about in public places, gossiping and wasting their time when they could be giving their attention, and give orders that they are to be told at intervals whether the reader has come in and has read the preface, or is coming to the end of the book. It is not till that moment – and even then very reluctantly – that they come dawdling in. Nor do they stay very long, but leave before the end some of them trying to slip out unobserved and others marching boldly out. And yet people tell how in our fathers' time the Emperor Claudius was walking on the Palatine when he heard voices and asked what was happening; on learning that Nonianus was giving a reading he surprised the audience by joining it unannounced. Today the man with any amount of leisure, invited well in advance and given many a reminder, either never comes at all, or, if he does, complains that he has wasted a day – just because he has not wasted it. The more praise and honour then is due to those whose interest in writing and reading aloud is not damped by the idleness and conceit of their listeners.

Personally I have failed scarcely anyone, though I admit that most of the invitations came from my friends; for there are very few people who care for literature without caring for me too. That is why I stayed in town longer than I intended, but now I can return to my country retreat and write something myself. I shall not read it to my friends, for I don't want it to seem that I went to hear them with the intention of putting them in my debt. Here as elsewhere a duty performed deserves no gratitude if a return is expected.

14. *To Junius Mauricus*

You ask me to look out for a husband for your brother's daughter, a responsibility which I feel is very rightly mine; for you know how I have always loved and admired him as the finest of men, and how he influenced my early years by his advice and encouraged me to become worthy of his praise. You could not entrust me with anything which I value or welcome so much, nor could there be any more befitting duty for me than to select a young man worthy to be the father of Arulenus Rusticus's grandchildren.

I should have had a long search if Minicius Acilianus were not at hand, as if he were made for us. He loves me as warmly as one young man does another (he is a little younger than I am), but respects me as his elder, for he aspires to be influenced and guided by me, as I was by you and your brother. His native place is Brixia,[1] one of the towns in our part of Italy which still retains intact much of its honest simplicity along with the rustic virtues of the past. His father is Minicius Macrinus, who chose to remain a leading member of the order of knights because he desired nothing higher; the deified Emperor Vespasian would have raised him to praetorian rank, but he has always steadfastly preferred a life of honest obscurity to our status – or our struggles to gain it. His maternal grandmother, Serrana Procula, comes from the town of Patavium,[2] whose reputation you know; but Serrana is a model of propriety even to the Patavians. His uncle, Publius Acilius, is a man of exceptional character, wisdom and integrity. You will in fact find nothing to criticize in the whole household, any more than in your own.

Acilianus himself has abundant energy and application, but no lack of modesty. He has held the offices of quaestor, tribune and praetor with great distinction, thus sparing you the necessity of canvassing on his behalf. He has a frank expression, and his complexion is fresh and high-coloured; his general good looks have a natural nobility and the dignified bearing of a senator. (I think these points should be mentioned, as a sort of just return for a bride's virginity.) I am wondering whether to add that his father has ample means; for if I picture you and your brother for whom we are seeking a son-in-law, I feel no more need be said; but in view of the prevailing habits of the day and the laws of the country which judge a man's income to be of primary importance, perhaps after all it is something which should not be omitted. Certainly if one thinks of the children of the marriage, and subsequent generations, the question of money must be taken into account as a factor influencing our choice.

It may seem to you that I have been indulging my affection, and going further than the facts allow, but I assure you on my honour that you will find the reality far better than my description. I do indeed love the young man dearly, as he deserves, but, just because I love him, I would not overload him with praise.

15. To Septicius Clarus

Who are you, to accept my invitation to dinner and never come? Here's your sentence and you shall pay my costs in full, no small sum

1. In Cisalpine Gaul (now Brescia).   2. In Cisalpine Gaul (now Padua).

either. It was all laid out, one lettuce each, three snails, two eggs, barley-cake, and wine with honey chilled with snow (you will reckon this too please, and as an expensive item, seeing that it disappears in the dish), besides olives, beetroots, gherkins, onions, and any number of similar delicacies. You would have heard a comic play, a reader or singer, or all three if I felt generous. Instead you chose to go where you could have oysters, sow's innards, sea-urchins, and Spanish dancing-girls. You will suffer for this – I won't say how. It was a cruel trick done to spite one of us – yourself or most likely me, and possibly both of us, if you think what a feast of fun, laughter and learning we were going to have. You can eat richer food at many houses, but no-where with such free and easy enjoyment. All I can say is, try me; and then, if you don't prefer to decline invitations elsewhere, you can always make excuses to me.

16. To Erucius Clarus

I was always much attached to our friend Pompeius Saturninus, and admired his talents long before I knew how versatile, sensitive and comprehensive they were. Now I am truly his, to have and to hold.

I have heard him plead in court with subtlety and fervour, and his speeches have the same finish and distinction when impromptu as when they are prepared. His aphorisms are apt and ready, his periods rounded with a formal dignity, his vocabulary impressive and classical. All of this I find peculiarly satisfying when it is carried along on the full stream of his oratory, and no less so when examined in detail. You will feel the same when you have a chance to handle his speeches and compare them with any one of the older orators to whose standards he aspires. His histories will please you even more by their conciseness and clarity, the charm and brilliance of their style and their power of exposition, for the words he puts into the mouths of his characters are as vivid as his own public speeches, though condensed into a simpler and terser style.

He also writes verses in the style of Catullus and Calvus which might indeed be theirs, for these are full of wit and charm, bitterness and passion; and, though he sometimes strikes a harsher note in the even flow of his measures, it is done deliberately and in imitation of his models. He has recently read me some letters which he said were written by his wife, but sounded to me like Plautus or Terence being read in prose. Whether they are really his wife's as he says, or his own (which he denies), one can only admire him either for what he has written or for the way he has cultivated and refined the taste of the girl he married.

So all my time is spent with him. If I have something of my own to write I read him first, and again afterwards; I read him for recreation and he never seems the same. I do urge you to read him too. The fact that he is still alive should not detract from his work. If he had been one of the writers before our own time we should be collecting his portraits as well as his books: are we then to let him languish without honour or popularity, as if we saw too much of him, just because he is living today? It is surely perverse and ungenerous to refuse recognition to one so deserving because we have the good fortune to enjoy his company and conversation, and can demonstrate our affection for the man as well as our appreciation of his work.

17. To Cornelius Titianus

There is still a sense of loyalty and duty alive in the world, and men whose affection does not die with their friends. Titinius Capito has obtained permission from the Emperor to set up a statue in the forum to Lucius Silanus.[1] To make use of one's friendly relations with the Emperor for such a purpose, and to test the extent of one's influence by paying tribute to others is a graceful gesture which deserves nothing but praise. It is indeed Capito's practice to show respect to famous men, and one must admire the reverence with which he cares for the family busts of Brutus, Cassius, and Cato which he has set up in his own home, not being able to do so elsewhere. He also celebrates the lives of his greatest heroes in excellent verse, and you may be sure that his love of the virtues of others means he has no lack of them himself. In his recognition of what is due to Lucius Silanus, Capito has won immortality for himself as well, for to erect a statue in the forum of Rome is as great an honour as having one's own statue there.

18. To Suetonius Tranquillus[2]

So you have had an alarming dream which makes you fear that the

---

1. Lucius Junius Silanus Torquatus, Nero's victim in 65 (see Tacitus, *Annals*, XVI: 9).
2. The author of *The Twelve Caesars*.

case which is coming on may go against you; and you want me to apply for an adjournment to get you off for a few days, or one day at least. It isn't easy but I will try, 'for a dream comes from Zeus'.[1] But it makes a difference whether your dreams usually come true or not, for to judge by a dream of my own, the one which has frightened you might well foretell that you will be successful. I had undertaken to act on behalf of Junius Pastor when I dreamed that my mother-in-law came and begged me on her knees to give up the case. I was very young at the time and I was about to plead in the Centumviral Court against men of great political influence, some of them also friends of the Emperor; any one of these considerations could have shaken my resolve after such a depressing dream, but I carried on, believing that 'The best and only omen is to fight for your country'[2] – or in my case for my pledge to Pastor, if anything can come before one's country. I won my case, and it was that speech which drew attention to me and set me on the threshold of a successful career.

See then if you can follow my example, and give a happy interpretation to your dream; but if you still think there is more safety in the warning given by all cautious folk, 'when in doubt do nothing', you can write and tell me. I will find some way out and deal with the case so that you can take it up when you wish. I admit that your position is different from mine; adjournments are never granted in the Centumviral Court, but in your case it is possible though not easy.

19. To Romatius Firmus

You and I both come from the same town, went to the same school, and have been friends since we were children. Your father was a close friend of my mother's and uncle's, and a friend to me too, as far as our difference in age allowed; so there are sound and serious reasons why I ought to try to improve your position. You are a town-councillor of Comum, which shows that your present capital is 100,000 sesterces, so I want to give you another 300,000 to make up your qualification for the order of knights. I can then have the pleasure of seeing you in that position as well as in your present one. The length of our friendship is sufficient guarantee that you will not forget this gift, and I shall not even remind you to enjoy your new status with becoming discretion, because it was received through me; as I ought to, did I not

1. *Iliad*, I: 63. 2. ibid., XII: 243.

know that you will do so unprompted. An honourable position has to be maintained with special care if it is to keep alive the memory of a friend's generous gift.

20. To Cornelius Tacitus

I am always having arguments with a man of considerable learning and experience, who admires nothing in forensic oratory so much as brevity. I admit that this is desirable if the case permits, but if it means that points which should be made are omitted, or hurried over when they should be impressed and driven home by repetition, one can only end by betraying one's client. Most points gain weight and emphasis by a fuller treatment, and make their mark on the mind by alternate thrust and pause, as a fencer uses his foil.

At this point he produces his authorities, and quotes me the Greek Lysias and our own Romans, the brothers Gracchus and Cato. It is true that most of their speeches are short and concise, but I counter Lysias with Demosthenes, Aeschines, Hyperides, and many others, and the Gracchi and Cato with Pollio, Caesar, Caelius, and above all Cicero, whose longest speech is generally considered his best.[1] Like all good things, a good book is all the better if it is a long one; and statues, busts, pictures and drawings of human beings, many animals and also trees can be seen to gain by being on a large scale as long as they are well-proportioned. The same applies to speeches; and when published they look better and more impressive in a good-sized volume.

He parries this and the other examples I usually cite to support my opinion, for he is too nimble in argument for me to come to grips with him. Then he insists that the speeches I instance were shorter when delivered than they are in their published form. This I deny. Several speeches by various authors confirm my opinion, notably two of Cicero's in defence of Murena and Varenus, where some sections are no more than a bare summary of certain charges which are indicated merely by headings. It is obvious from this that the published speech leaves out a great deal of what Cicero said in court. He also makes it clear that in accordance with the custom of his day he conducted the entire defence of Cluentius by himself, and actually took four days

1. *Pro Cluentio.*

over his defence of Gaius Cornelius. There can be no doubt then that if he took several days to deliver his speeches in full he must have subsequently pruned and revised them in order to compress them into a single volume, though admittedly a large one.

Then it is argued that there is a great difference between a speech as delivered and the written version. This is a popular view I know, but I feel convinced (if I am not mistaken) that, though some speeches may sound better than they read, if the written speech is good it must also be good when delivered, for it is the model and prototype for the spoken version. That is why we find so many rhetorical figures, apparently spontaneous, in any good written speech, even in those which we know were published without being delivered; for example, in Cicero's speech against Verres: 'An artist – now who was he? thank you for telling me; people said it was Polyclitus.'[1] It follows then that the perfect speech when delivered is that which keeps most closely to the written version, so long as the speaker is allowed the full time due to him; if he is cut short it is no fault of his, but a serious error on the part of the judge. The law supports my view, for it allows speakers any amount of time and recommends not brevity but the full exposition and precision which brevity cannot permit, except in very restricted cases. Let me add what I have learned from the best of all teachers, experience. On the many occasions when I have been counsel, judge, or assessor, I have found that people are influenced in different ways, and that small points often have important consequences. Men's powers of judgement vary with their temperaments; thus they can listen to the same case but reach different conclusions, or perhaps the same one by a different emotional reaction. Moreover, everyone is prejudiced in favour of his own powers of discernment, and will always find an argument most convincing if it leads to the conclusion he has reached for himself; everyone must then be given something he can grasp and recognize as his own idea.

Regulus once said to me when we were appearing in the same case: 'You think you should follow up every point, but I make straight for the throat and hang on to that.' (He certainly hangs on to whatever he seizes, but he often misses the right place.) I pointed out that it might be the knee or the heel he seized when he thought he had the throat. 'I can't see the throat,' I said, 'so my method is to feel my way

1. Cicero, *In Verrem*, II, 4, 3.

and try everything – in fact I "leave no stone unturned".' On my farms I cultivate my fruit trees and fields as carefully as my vineyards, and in the fields I sow barley, beans and other legumes as well as corn and wheat; so when I am making a speech I scatter various arguments around like seeds in order to reap whatever crop comes up. There are as many unforeseen hazards and uncertainties to surmount in working on the minds of judges as in dealing with the problems of weather and soil. Nor have I forgotten the words of the comic poet Eupolis in praise of the great orator Pericles: 'Speed marked his words, and persuasion sat upon his lips. Thus he could charm, yet alone among orators left his sting behind in his hearers.' But 'speed' alone (whether by that is meant brevity or rapidity or both, for they are different things) could not have given Pericles his power to persuade and charm had he not also possessed a supreme gift of eloquence. Charm and persuasion require fulness of treatment and time for delivery, and a speaker who leaves his sting in the minds of his hearers does not stop at pricking them, but drives his point in. And again, another comic poet[1] said of Pericles that 'he flashed lightning, thundered and confounded Greece'. It is no curtailed and restricted style but a grand oratory, spacious and sublime, which can thunder, lighten, and throw a world into tumult and confusion.

'All the same, the mean is best.' No one denies it, but to fall short through over-compression is to miss the mean just as much as to be diffuse and go beyond it. The criticism 'spiritless and feeble' is heard as often as 'excessive and redundant', when one speaker does not cover his ground and another goes outside it. Both fail, through weakness or vitality, but the latter is at least the fault of a more powerful talent, if a crude one. In saying this I do not mean to praise Homer's Thersites, 'unbridled of tongue',[2] but Odysseus with his 'words like flakes of winter snow'; and I can also very much admire Menelaus who spoke 'at no great length but very clearly'.[3] But, if I were given my choice, I prefer the speech like the winter snows, one which is fluent and vigorous, but also expansive, which is in fact divinely inspired.

'But a lot of people like a short speech.' So they do, if they are lazy, but it is absurd to take their idle whim as a serious opinion; if you

1. Aristophanes, *Acharnians*, 531. 2. *Iliad*, III : 212.
3. ibid., III : 222 and 224.

followed their advice you would do best not in a short speech but saying nothing at all.

This is the view I have held up to now, though I can modify it if you disagree; only please give me your reasons if you do. I know I should bow to your authority, but on an important question like this I would rather yield to a reasoned argument than to authority alone. So if you think I am right, you need only tell me so in as short a letter as you like, as long as you will write to corroborate my opinion. If you think me wrong, make it a long one, and I only hope this does not look like bribery – to demand a short letter if you agree with me, and a very long one if you don't.

21. To Plinius Paternus

I have the highest possible opinion of your judgement and critical eye, not because your taste is so *very* good (don't flatter yourself) but because it is as good as mine. Joking apart, I think the slaves you advised me to buy look all right, but it remains to be seen if they are honest; and here one can't go by a slave's looks, but rather by what one hears of him.

22. To Catilius Severus

I have been kept in town for a long time in an appalling state of mind. I am exceedingly worried about Titius Aristo, a man I particularly love and admire, who has been seriously ill for some time. He has no equal in moral influence and wisdom, so that I feel that it is no mere individual in danger, but that literature itself and all the liberal arts are endangered in his person. His experience of civil and constitutional law, his knowledge of human affairs and the lessons of history are such that there is nothing you might wish to learn which he could not teach. I certainly find him a mine of information whenever I have an obscure point to consider. He is genuine and authoritative in conversation, and his deliberate manner is firm and dignified; there can be few questions to which he cannot provide a ready answer, and yet he often pauses to weigh up the many alternative arguments which his keen and powerful intellect derives from their fundamental source and then selects with fine discrimination.

Moreover, his habits are simple and his dress is plain, and his bedroom and its furniture always seem to me to give a picture of bygone simplicity. It has its adornment in his greatness of mind, which cares nothing for show but refers everything to conscience, seeking reward for a good deed in its performance and not in popular opinion. In fact none of those people who parade their pursuit of knowledge by their personal appearance can be compared with a man like Aristo. He does not haunt the gymnasia and public places, nor does he entertain himself and his friends in their leisure hours with long dissertations, but he plays an active part in the business of civil life, helping many people professionally and still more by his personal advice. Yet none of those who rank high as philosophers can attain his high standard of virtue, duty, justice and courage.

His patience throughout this illness, if you could only see it, would fill you with admiration; he fights against pain, resists thirst, and endures the unbelievable heat of his fever without moving or throwing off his coverings. A few days ago, he sent for me and some of his intimate friends, and told us to ask the doctors what the outcome of his illness would be, so that if it was to be fatal he could deliberately put an end to his life, though he would carry on with the struggle if it was only to be long and painful; he owed it to his wife's prayers and his daughter's tears, and to us, his friends, not to betray our hopes by a self-inflicted death so long as these hopes were not vain. This I think was a particularly difficult decision to make, which merits the highest praise. Many people have his impulse and urge to forestall death, but the ability to examine critically the arguments for dying, and to accept or reject the idea of living or not, is the mark of a truly great mind. The doctors are in fact reassuring in their promises; it only remains for the gods to confirm these and free me at long last from my anxiety. If they do, I can then return to Laurentum, to my books and notes and freedom for work. At present I am always sitting by Aristo's bedside or worrying about him, so that I have neither time nor inclination for reading or writing anything.

There you have my fears, hopes, and plans for the future; in return, give me your news, past, present and to come, but please make your letter more cheerful than mine. It will be a great comfort in my trouble if you have no complaints.

23. To Pompeius Falco

You want to know what I think about your continuing to practise in the law courts while you hold the office of tribune. It depends entirely on the view you take of the tribunate – an 'empty form' and a 'mere title', or an inviolable authority which should not be called in question by anyone, not even the holder. When I was tribune myself, I acted on the assumption (which may have been a wrong one) that my office really meant something. I therefore gave up all my court work, for I thought it unsuitable for a tribune to stand while others were seated, when it was really every man's duty to rise and give place to him; to be cut short by the water-clock though he had the power to command anyone's silence; and, although it was sacrilege to interrupt him, to be exposed to insults which he could not pass over without an appearance of weakness, nor counter without seeming to abuse his power. I had also to face the difficulty of how to react if my client or my opponent were to appeal to me as tribune, whether to lend my aid by interposing my veto, or to keep silent as if I had laid down my office and resumed my status of private citizen. For these reasons I chose to be tribune to all rather than give my professional services to a few; but your own decision, as I said before, can only depend on your idea of the tribunate and the part you intend to play: a wise man will choose one within his capacity to play to the end.

24. To Baebius Hispanus

My friend Suetonius Tranquillus wishes to buy a small property which I hear a friend of yours is trying to sell. Please see that he has it at a fair price, so that he will be pleased with his purchase. A bad bargain is always annoying, and especially because it seems to reproach the owner for his folly. There is indeed much about this property to whet Tranquillus's appetite if only the price suits him: easy access to Rome, good communications, a modest house, and sufficient land for him to enjoy without taking up too much of his time. Scholars turned land-owners, like himself, need no more land than will suffice to clear their heads and refresh their eyes, as they stroll around their grounds and tread their single path, getting to know each one of their precious vines and counting every fruit tree.

I am writing this to show you how much he will be in my debt and I in yours if he is able to buy this small estate with all its advantages at a reasonable price which will leave him no room for regrets.

BOOK TWO

1. To Voconius Romanus

It is some years since Rome has had such a splendid sight to remember as the public funeral of Verginius Rufus, one of our greatest and most distinguished citizens whom we can also count a fortunate one. For thirty years after his hour of glory[1] he lived on to read about himself in history and verse, so that he was a living witness of his fame to come. He was three times consul, and thus attained the highest distinction short of the imperial power itself; for this he had refused. His virtues had been suspected and resented by certain of the Emperors, but he had escaped arrest and lived to see a truly good and friendly ruler safely established; so that he might have been spared for the honour of this public funeral we have just seen. He had reached the age of eighty-three, living in close retirement and deeply respected by us all, and his health was good, apart from a trembling of the hands, not enough to trouble him. Only death when it came was slow and painful, though we can only admire the way he faced it. He was rehearsing the delivery of his address of thanks to the Emperor for his election to his third consulship, when he had occasion to take up a heavy book, the weight of which made it fall out of his hands, as he was an old man and standing at the time. He bent down to pick it up, and lost his footing on the slippery polished floor, so that he fell and fractured his thigh. This was badly set, and because of his age it never mended properly.

Such was the man whose funeral does credit to the Emperor and our times, to the forum and its speakers. His funeral oration was

1. See VI:10. As commander of the army of Upper Germany, he had put down the revolt of Vindex in 68 and afterwards refused to allow his soldiers to make him Emperor in Nero's place.

delivered by the consul, Cornelius Tacitus, a most eloquent orator, and his tribute put the crowning touch to Verginius's good fortune. He died too when full of years and rich in honours, even those which he refused; and it is left to us to seek him and feel his loss as a figure from a past age. I shall feel it more than anyone, since my admiration for his public qualities was matched by personal affection. I had many reasons to love him; we came from the same district and neighbouring towns, and our lands and property adjoined each other; and then he was left by will as my guardian, and gave me a father's affection. So when I was a candidate for office, he gave me the support of his vote, and when I entered upon my duties, he left his retirement to hasten to my side although he had long since given up social functions of that kind; and on the day when the priests nominate those they judge suitable for a priesthood, he always nominated me. Even during his last illness, when he was anxious not to be selected for the Board of Five set up by senatorial decree to reduce public expenditure, in spite of my youth he chose me to make his official excuses (although many of his friends and contemporaries of consular rank were still living), and told me that he would have entrusted this to me even if he had had a son of his own.

Hence I must ask you to bear with my grief at his death as if he had died before his time; if indeed it is right to grieve or even to give the name of death to what has ended the mortal existence rather than the life of so great a man. For he lives and will live for ever, and in a wider sense in our memories and on our lips, now that he has left our sight.

I intended to write to you about many other things, but Verginius takes up all my thoughts. I see him in my mind's eye, and in these dreams, so vivid and so vain, I speak to him, he answers, and I feel his presence near. There may be some citizens with us now who can equal his merits, and there will be others, but none will win his fame.

2. *To Valerius Paulinus*

I am furious with you, rightly or not I don't know, but it makes no difference. You know very well that love is sometimes unfair, often violent, and always quick to take offence, but I have good reason, whether or not it is a just one, to be as furious as I would be in a just cause. It is so long since I have had a letter from you. The only way to placate me is to write me a lot of letters now, at long last – lengthy ones, too. That is how you can honestly win my forgiveness; I shall not hear of anything else. Don't say you were not in Rome or were too busy because I shan't listen, only for heaven's sake don't tell me you were ill. I am in the country, dividing my time between the two pleasures of a holiday – reading and relaxation.

3. *To Maecilius Nepos*

Isaeus's great reputation had reached Rome ahead of him, but we found him to be even greater than we had heard. He has a remarkably eloquent style, rich in variety, and though he always speaks extempore his speeches sound as though he had spent time on preparing them. He expresses himself in Greek, Attic to be precise; his introductory remarks have a neatness and polish which is very attractive, and can also be impressive in the grand style. His method is to ask his audience for a subject, leaving the choice and often the side he is to take with them; then he rises, wraps his cloak round him, and begins to speak. Whatever the subject he is ready at once, with every latent implication clear to him and expressed in words which are accurate and well-chosen; so that the extent of his reading and his practice in composition are immediately apparent. He comes straight to the point in his opening words, he is clear in exposition and penetrating in argument, he draws his conclusions boldly and expresses himself with dignity; it is in fact difficult to choose between his powers to instruct, to charm, or to move his hearers. He is ready with rhetorical figures and syllogisms, such as could not easily be worked out so concisely even in writing, and has an amazing memory, so that he can repeat his extempore speeches word for word without a single mistake, a technique he has developed by application and constant practice; for night and day every action and word of his are directed to this end alone.

He has reached the age of sixty, but has preferred to remain a teacher of rhetoric, keeping to a profession followed by some of the most genuinely sincere and honest of men. Those of us whose energies are wasted on the active litigation in the courts cannot help learning a good deal of sharp practice, but the imaginary cases in the schoolroom and lecture-hall do no harm with their blunted foils and are none the less enjoyable; especially to the old, who like nothing so much as to witness the joys of their youth. Consequently it seems to me that

Isaeus's gift of eloquence has also brought him very great happiness, and if you aren't eager to meet him, you can't have any human feeling at all. Nothing brings you to Rome, myself included, but do come to hear him. Have you never heard the story of the Spaniard from Gades?[1] He was so stirred by the famous name of Livy that he came from his far corner of the earth to have one look at him and then went back again. Only a boorish ignorance and a shocking degree of apathy could prevent you from thinking it worth an effort to gain an experience which will prove so enjoyable, civilized and rewarding. You may say that you have authors as eloquent whose works can be read at home; but the fact is that you can read them any time, and rarely have the opportunity to hear the real thing. Besides, we are always being told that the spoken word is much more effective; however well a piece of writing makes its point, anything which is driven into the mind by the delivery and expression, the appearance and gestures of a speaker remains deeply implanted there, unless there is no truth in the tale of Aeschines at Rhodes, who countered the general applause he won for his reading of one of Demosthenes' speeches with the words: 'Suppose you had heard the beast himself?' And yet, if we are to believe Demosthenes, Aeschines had a very good voice; all the same, he admitted that the speech had been much better when its author delivered it himself.

All this goes to show that you ought to hear Isaeus – indeed, the sole purpose of this letter is to make sure you do.

4. To Calvina

If your father had died in debt to more than one person, or to anyone other than myself, you might perhaps have hesitated to accept an inheritance which even a man would have found a burden. But I thought it my duty as your relative to pay off anyone who was rather pressing, though not actually offensive, so as to be left sole creditor; and during your father's lifetime I had contributed 100,000 sesterces towards your dowry on marriage in addition to what he had assigned you (which also came indirectly from me, as it could only be paid from his account with me). All this should be a firm guarantee of my generous feelings, and ought to give you confidence to defend your late father's honour and reputation; to provide you also with practical

1. Cadiz.

encouragement I shall give instructions for his debt to me to be entered as paid. You need not fear that such a gift will tax my finances. It is true that my resources as a whole are not very great and my position is expensive to keep up; being dependent on the way my property is farmed, my income is small or precarious, but its deficiencies can be made up by simple living. This is the spring from which my well of kindness is supplied, and though I must not draw upon it without restraint, lest it dry up after too lavish a flow, I can keep my restraint for others; I can easily make my accounts balance in your case even if they have passed their usual figure.

5. To Lupercus

I am sending you the speech[1] which you have often asked for and I have promised more than once, but not the whole of it yet, as part is still under revision. Meanwhile I thought that the more finished portions might suitably be handed over to you for your opinion. Please give them your close attention and write down your comments, for I have never handled any subject which demanded greater care. In my other speeches I have submitted to public opinion no more than my industry and good faith, but here my patriotic feelings were involved as well. Consequently the text has grown, for I was glad of the opportunity to pay a tribute of admiration to my native place, and at the same time not only to defend its interests but to bring it further fame. But these are the passages I want you to prune down as you think fit, for whenever I think of the whims and fancies of the reading public I realize that I can only win approval by keeping the text within bounds.

As well as this severity I am demanding from you I am compelled to ask for the exact opposite, that is, your indulgence for several passages. Some concessions must be made to a youthful audience, especially if the subject-matter permits; for example, descriptions of places (which are fairly frequent in this speech) may surely introduce a touch of poetry into plain prose. But, if anyone thinks that I have handled this subject too lightly for serious oratory, then his austerity, if I may call it so, will have to find appeasement in the rest of the speech. I have certainly tried to appeal to all the different types of reader by varying my style, and, though I am afraid that some people

1. On the opening of the library at Comum; see 1:8.

will disapprove of certain details because of their individual tastes, I still think I can be sure that the speech as a whole will be generally liked because of this variety. At a dinner party we may individually refuse several dishes, but we all praise the whole meal and the food which is not to our taste does not spoil our pleasure in what we do like.

I hope that you will understand by this not that I believe that I have achieved my aim, but that I have tried to so do; and perhaps my efforts will not have been in vain if you will only give your critical attention to what you have now, and afterwards to what follows. You may say that you need to have seen the whole speech if you are to do this accurately, and I realize this; but for the moment you can familiarize yourself with what I send, and there will be some passages which can be corrected apart from the whole. You could not judge whether the head or a limb of a statue is in proportion and harmonizes with the whole if you examine it detached from the trunk, but you could still decide if it was well formed in itself; and the only reason why books of selected extracts are circulated is because some passages are thought to be complete apart from their context.

It is a pleasure to talk to you, but I have run on too long; I must stop, or this letter will go beyond the bounds I think proper even for a speech.

6. To Junius Avitus

It would take too long to go into the details (which anyway don't matter) of how I happened to be dining with a man – though no particular friend of his – whose elegant economy, as he called it, seemed to me a sort of stingy extravagance. The best dishes were set in front of himself and a select few, and cheap scraps of food before the rest of the company. He had even put the wine into tiny little flasks, divided into three categories, not with the idea of giving his guests the opportunity of choosing, but to make it impossible for them to refuse what they were given. One lot was intended for himself and for us, another for his lesser friends (all his friends are graded) and the third for his and our freedmen. My neighbour at table noticed this and asked me if I approved. I said I did not. 'So what do you do?' he asked. 'I serve the same to everyone, for when I invite guests it is for a meal, not to make class distinctions; I have brought them as equals to the same table, so I give them the same treatment in everything.' 'Even the freedmen?' 'Of course, for then they are my fellow-diners, not freedmen.' 'That must cost you a lot.' 'On the contrary.' 'How is that?' 'Because my freedmen do not drink the sort of wine I do, but I drink theirs.' Believe me, if you restrain your greedy instincts it is no strain on your finances to share with several others the fare you have yourself. It is this greed which should be put down and 'reduced to the ranks' if you would cut down your expenses, and you can do this far better by self-restraint than by insults to others.

The point of this story is to prevent a promising young man like yourself from being taken in by this extravagance under guise of economy which is to be found at the table in certain homes. Whenever I meet with such a situation, my affection for you prompts me to quote it as a warning example of what to avoid. Remember then that nothing is more to be shunned than this novel association of extravagance and meanness; vices which are bad enough when single and separate, but worse when found together.

7. *To Caecilius Macrinus*

Yesterday on the Emperor's proposal the Senate decreed a triumphal statue to Vestricius Spurinna,[1] an honour granted to many who have never faced a battle, never seen a camp nor even heard the sound of a trumpet except at the theatre; but Spurinna was one of those heroes whose honours were won by the blood and sweat of action. It was Spurinna who established the chief of the Bructeri in his kingdom by force of arms, and by mere threat of war against a savage people he terrorized it into submission, so winning the finest type of victory. Now he has his reward of merit; and to bring him consolation in grief the honour of a statue was also granted to Cottius, the son who had died during his absence abroad. This is rarely granted to a young man, but in this case it was also due to the father whose grievous sorrow needed some special remedy to assuage it. Cottius himself had also given such marked indication of his promise that some sort of immortality was required to extend a life thus cut short. His high principles, his sense of duty and influence were such as to make him rival his elders in merit, and he is now raised to be their equal in honour. And indeed, in granting this honour the Senate would seem to me to have had in mind not only Cottius's memory and his father's

1. See also III: I.

grief, but also the effect on the public. The granting of such high rewards to the young, provided that they are worthy of them, will win our young men to virtue; and with the prospect of happiness if their sons survive, and such splendid consolation if they die, our leading citizens will be encouraged to undertake the responsibility of children.

For these public considerations, then, I am glad about the statue to Cottius, as I am for personal reasons. I loved this excellent young man dearly, so that I miss him now unbearably; it will therefore be a pleasure for me to contemplate his statue, turn back to look at it, stand at its foot, and walk past it. We seek consolation in sorrow in the busts of our dead we set up in our homes; still more then should we find it in the statues standing in public places, for these can recall men's fame and distinction as well as their forms and faces.

8. To Caninius Rufus

Are you reading, fishing, or hunting or doing all three? You can do all together on the shores of Como, for there is plenty of fish in the lake, game to hunt in the woods around, and every opportunity to study in the depths of your retreat. Whether it is everything or only one thing I can't say I begrudge you your pleasures; I am only vexed at being denied them myself, for I hanker after them as a sick man does for wine, baths, and cool springs. I wonder if I shall ever be able to shake off these constricting fetters if I am not allowed to undo them, and I doubt if I ever shall. New business piles up on the old before the old is finished, and, as more and more links are added to the chain, I see my work stretching out farther and farther every day.

9. To Domitius Apollinaris

My friend Sextus Erucius is standing for office, and this is worrying me very much; in fact I feel far more anxious and apprehensive for my 'second self' than I ever did on my own account. Besides, my own honour, my reputation, and my position are all at stake, for it was I who persuaded the Emperor to raise Sextus to senatorial rank by granting him a quaestorship, and it is on my nomination that he is now standing for the office of tribune. If he is not elected by the Senate, I am afraid it will look as though I have deceived the Emperor;

and so it is essential for me to see that everyone shares the high opinion which I led the Emperor to form.

Even if I had not this incentive I should still be anxious to support a young man of such outstanding merit, whose sense of duty is matched by his accomplishments and who is like all the rest of his family in deserving every form of praise. His father is Erucius Clarus, a model of ancient virtue and a skilled and practised advocate, who conducts all his cases with the utmost honesty and determination, equalled by his discretion. His uncle, Gaius Septicius, is the most genuinely reliable, frank and trustworthy man I know. The family is united in its affection for me, though each member tries to show it most, and now is my chance to show my gratitude to them all by helping one of them. Consequently I am approaching all my friends to beg their support, and going the round of private houses and public places, testing what influence and popularity I have by my entreaties; and I do beg you to think it worth while to relieve me of a part of my burden. I will do the same for you, asked or unasked. You are popular, admired, and much sought after; you have only to make your wishes plain, and there will be no lack of people positively anxious to think as you do.

10. *To Octavius Rufus*

Is it indifference, obstinacy, or a sort of cruelty which makes you withhold works of such distinction so long? How much longer will you deny us our pleasure and yourself your crowning glory? They should be on all our lips, to travel as widely as the speech of Rome. Our hopes have long been high, and you ought not still to cheat and defer them. Some of your verses have broken free in spite of you and have become more widely known; unless you recall them to be incorporated in the whole, like runaway slaves they will find someone else to claim them. Bear in mind that you are bound by man's mortality, but that this one memorial of yourself can set you free: everything else is fragile and fleeting like man himself, who dies and is no more. You will give your usual answer; that your friends can see to this. I only hope that you *have* friends who combine learning with loyalty and industry so that they are able as well as willing to undertake such a difficult and laborious task; but ask yourself whether it is not ill-advised to expect from others a service which you will not perform for yourself.

As for publication – do as you like for the present, as long as you give some readings. You may then feel more inclined to publish, and will at least have the pleasure which I have long been confidently anticipating for you. I picture to myself the crowds, the admiration and applause which await you, and the hushed stillness – for I personally like this as much as applause when I am speaking or reading, as long as it indicates a keen attentiveness and eagerness to hear what follows. A great reward awaits you, and you must stop denying your work its due by your interminable hesitation; for if this goes too far there is a danger that it will be given another name – idleness, indolence, or possibly timidity.

11. To Maturus Arrianus

You are always glad to hear of anything taking place in the Senate which is in keeping with its dignity, for though you have chosen to live in retirement in search of a quiet life you have kept your interest in the honour of the State. So here is the news of the last few days – a case which has attracted attention because of the celebrity of the defendant, has set an example of severity which will do a great deal of good, and is unlikely to be forgotten because of the importance of the issue involved.

A charge was brought by the province of Africa against their ex-governor, Marius Priscus.[1] He pleaded guilty and applied for a commission to assess compensation to be paid. Cornelius Tacitus and I were instructed to act for the provincials, and accordingly thought it our duty to inform the Senate that criminal offences of such monstrosity exceeded the powers of a commission, seeing that Priscus had taken bribes to sentence innocent persons to punishment and even to death. Catius Fronto replied in his defence with a plea for the charge to be limited to the question of restitution of money extorted, and, as he is practised in the art of drawing tears, he was able to fill all the sails of his speech with a breeze of pathos. There was a violent argument and an outcry all round, one side arguing that the Senate's judicial powers were limited by law, the other that they were free and unlimited and that the defendant should be punished to the full extent of his guilt. Finally Julius Ferox, the consul-elect, whose integrity

---

1. The second of the five big public trials in which Pliny appeared. Priscus was convicted in January 100, cf. VI:29, 8.

always commands respect, proposed that Priscus should be provisionally granted a commission, but that the persons named as having given bribes to procure the conviction of the innocent should be summoned as witnesses. Not only was this proposal carried but it was in fact the only one to gain much support after all the previous argument; experience shows that appeals for support and sympathy make an immediate strong impact, but gradually lose their fire and die down under the influence of a reasoned judgement. Hence the fact that in a general uproar many will support an opinion which no one is prepared to defend when silence is restored, for only when separated from the crowd is it possible to form a clear view of a situation which the crowd hitherto obscured.

The two witnesses, Vitellius Honoratus and Flavius Marcianus, were summoned to appear and duly arrived in Rome. Honoratus was charged with having procured the exile of a Roman knight and the death of seven of the latter's friends for a bribe of 300,000 sesterces, and Marcianus with having paid 700,000 for various punishments inflicted on a Roman knight, who had been flogged, condemned to the mines, and finally strangled in prison. However, Honoratus escaped justice at the hands of the Senate by his timely death, and Marcianus appeared in court in the absence of Priscus. Accordingly the ex-consul Tuccius Cerialis exercised the senatorial right to speak by demanding that Priscus be informed, thinking that either he would excite more sympathy or possibly more indignation by his presence, or, more probably to my mind, because it is common justice that a charge made against two persons should be defended by both of them, and both should be convicted if unable to clear themselves.

The hearing was adjourned until the next meeting of the Senate, and this was a most impressive sight. The Emperor presided (being consul), and this was the month of January when there are always large numbers of people and particularly senators in Rome. Then the gravity of the case, the rumours and expectations increased by the adjournment, and the natural curiosity of human nature for anything new and important had attracted members from all parts. You can imagine our nervous anxiety at having to speak on such a subject before the Emperor, and in an assembly of this kind. It is true that I have often addressed the Senate, and nowhere do I receive a more sympathetic hearing, but this time all the unusual features of the case made me unusually nervous. For, as well as the problems I have described, I was confronted with the special difficulties of the case. Before me stood a man who had up till recently been of consular rank and a member of one of the priestly colleges,[1] and was now degraded; as he was thus condemned, it was extremely difficult to make him the subject of a prosecuting speech, for in spite of the weight of the horrible charges against him he had in his favour a certain amount of sympathy aroused by his previous conviction.

However, I managed to pull myself and my thoughts together, and began to speak, meeting with a warm reception to make up for my fears. My speech lasted for nearly five hours, for I was allowed four water-clocks as well as my original twelve of the largest size; thus all those difficulties I had anticipated in my path were dispelled when I came to speak. The Emperor did indeed show such an attentive and kindly interest in me (I should not like to call it anxiety on my behalf) that more than once, when he fancied I was putting too much strain on my rather delicate constitution, he suggested to my freedman standing behind me that I should spare my voice and my lungs. Claudius Marcellinus replied on behalf of Marcianus, after which the court adjourned until the following day; any further speech would have had to be cut short at nightfall.

Next day Salvius Liberalis spoke in defence of Priscus. He is a precise and methodical speaker with a forceful command of words, and this case brought all his powers into full play. Cornelius Tacitus made an eloquent speech in reply, with all the majesty which characterizes his style of oratory. Catius Fronto resumed the defence and made an excellent speech, which at this stage he thought best to apply to pleas for mercy rather than defensive arguments. He finished speaking at the end of the day, but did not have to cut short his words. The summing-up was accordingly postponed until the third day, thereby following a good and long-established precedent in the Senate of interrupting proceedings at nightfall and resuming them next day in a continuous three-day session.

Cornutus Tertullus, the consul-elect, who always stands out for his strict adherence to the truth, then proposed that the bribe of 700,000

1. The *septemviri epulonum* responsible for arranging the sacrificial banquets for the gods. At this time a priesthood was a decoration conferred for distinguished public service.

sesterces which Priscus had taken should be paid by him into the Treasury, that Priscus should be exiled from Rome and Italy, and Marcianus from Rome, Italy, and Africa. He ended his speech by stating on behalf of the Senate that, by our conscientious and courageous handling of the prosecution entrusted to us, Tacitus and I were considered to have correctly carried out the duty assigned us. The consuls-elect supported him and so did all the consulars down to Pompeius Collega, who then proposed that the 700,000 sesterces should be paid into the Treasury and Marcianus banished for five years, but that Priscus should receive no sentence beyond the one already passed on him for extorting money. Both proposals found many supporters, especially the second one, being less severe, or if you prefer, more lenient; and there were some who seemed to be in agreement with Cornutus but went over to Collega after they heard him speak. But, when the division was taken, first the members standing by the consuls' chairs began to go over to Cornutus's side, then those who were letting themselves be counted with Collega crossed the floor, so that Collega was left with scarcely anyone. He complained bitterly afterwards about those who had led him on, especially Regulus, who had actually told him what to say and then deserted him. (Regulus's instability generally leads him into rash ventures which he afterwards regrets.)

So ended this important trial. There is still a minor matter, though not unimportant, concerning Priscus's deputy, Hostilius Firminus, who was implicated in the charge and, indeed, very heavily involved. It was proved from the accounts of Marcianus and from a speech made by Firminus in the town-council of Lepcis that he had helped Priscus in a particularly shocking piece of work, and had also bargained with Marcianus to receive 200,000 sesterces; and he had in fact been paid 10,000 under the disgraceful head of 'cosmetics' – an entry quite in keeping with his dandified elegance. The Senate adopted Cornutus's proposal to refer his case to the next session; for, either by chance or through knowledge of his guilt, Firminus was not present.

So much for the city. Now give me news of the country – how are your fruit trees and your vines, the harvest and your prize sheep? Unless you answer me in as long a letter as this, you can expect nothing in future but the shortest note.

12. To Maturus Arrianus

That 'minor matter' which I said in my last letter was left over from the case of Marius Priscus, is settled and done with, though it could have been better handled. Firminus was summoned before the Senate to answer the charge already known. Then the consuls-elect failed to agree on a sentence; Cornutus Tertullus proposed that he should be expelled from the Senate, but Acutius Nerva thought it sufficient if his claim were not considered when lots were drawn for provinces. This was the opinion which prevailed as being the more lenient, though in another sense it is more cruelly severe. Nothing could be worse than to be stripped of all the privileges of senatorial rank but not to be rid of its toils and troubles, and nothing more humiliating for anyone so disgraced than to remain in his conspicuous position exposed as a marked man to the public gaze instead of hiding himself in retirement. And besides, nothing could be more unsuitable or less conducive to the public interest than for a senator to retain his seat after he has been censured by the Senate, to remain equal in status to those who censured him, and though debarred from a governorship for his disgraceful conduct as governor's deputy to retain his power of passing judgement on other governors, to condemn or acquit them on charges on which he has himself been found guilty. But the majority gave their assent; for votes are counted, their value is not weighed, and no other method is possible in a public assembly. Yet this strict equality results in something very different from equity, so long as men have the same right to judge but not the same ability to judge wisely.

I have kept my word and the promise I made you in my previous letter, which I think must have reached you, judging by the date. I gave it to a fast and reliable courier – unless he has been delayed on the road. Now it is your turn to pay me for both these letters; there can be no lack of news from your part of the world.

13. To Javolenus (?) Priscus

You would gladly seize any opportunity to oblige me, and there is no one to whom I would rather be in debt than to you. So for two reasons I have singled you out to approach with a request which I am most anxious to be granted. Your command of a large army gives you a plentiful source of benefits to confer, and secondly, your tenure has been long enough for you to have provided for your own friends. Turn to mine – they are not many. You might wish them more, but modesty restricts me to one or two and the one I have most in mind is Voconius Romanus.

His father was distinguished in the order of knights; even more so was his stepfather, whom I should rather call his other father for his kindness to his stepson; his mother comes from a leading family. He himself recently held a priesthood in Hither Spain, a province well known to you for its high principles and good judgement. He was my close and intimate friend when we were students together, my companion in the city and out of it; with him I shared everything, work and play. No one could be a more faithful friend or more delightful companion. His conversation, voice, and whole expression have a special charm, and he is gifted besides with a powerful and penetrating intellect, trained by his profession at the bar to express itself with ease and grace. In addition, the letters he writes would make one believe that the Muses speak Latin. I love him dearly, as he does me. Ever since our youth together I have been anxious to do as much for him as my age permitted, and I recently obtained for him from our noble Emperor the privileges granted to parents of three children;[1] the Emperor used to grant this sparingly and after careful selection, but he granted my request as if the choice were his own. The best way for me to confirm my services is by adding to them, especially as Romanus's grateful appreciation in acceptance reveals him as worthy of more.

Now you know the man he is and how much I love and admire him, please provide for him as your generous nature and position permit. What is most important is that you should like him; for though you grant him the highest office in your power, you could give him nothing better than your friendship. It was to show you that he is worthy of it and even of your closest intimacy that I have thus briefly described his interests and character, in short his whole life. I would prolong my entreaties did you not dislike long begging letters, of which I am afraid this is one; for to be effective a request must give its reasons.

1. The *ius trium liberorum* allowed priority in holding public offices and permitted the holder to be below the statutory age.

14. To Novius (?) Maximus

You are quite right: cases at the Centumviral Court are taking up all
my time, and give me more work than pleasure. Most of them are
petty affairs and there is rarely one which stands out for the importance of the issue or the celebrity of the persons involved. There are
besides very few people with whom it is any pleasure to appear if you
consider the impudence of the rest – mostly unknown youngsters
who have arrived in our midst to practise rhetoric: which they do
with such effrontery and want of consideration that I think our friend
Atilius summed them up well when he said that boys begin their
career at the bar with Centumviral cases just as they start on Homer at
school. In both places they put the hardest first. But before my time
(as our elders always say), believe me, there was no place here for a
young man, however well-born, unless a consular senator introduced
him; so highly was a noble profession respected. Today the bars of
propriety and deference are down, everything is open to all and
sundry, and no introductions are needed for anyone to burst in.

Audiences follow who are no better than the speakers, being hired
and bought for the occasion. They parley with the contractor, take
the gifts offered on the floor of the court as openly as they would at a
dinner-party, and move on from case to case for the same sort of pay.
The Greek name for them means 'bravo-callers' and the Latin
'dinner-clappers'; witty enough, but both names expose a scandal
which increases daily. Yesterday two of my attendants (who would
only just have come of age if they were citizens) were induced to add
their applause for three denarii[1] each. That is all it costs you to have
your eloquence acclaimed. For this sum seats can be filled, any number of them, a huge crowd assembled, and endless cheering raised
whenever the chorus-master gives the signal. (A signal there must be
for people who neither understand nor even hear; most of them do
not listen but cheer as loud as anyone.) If you happen to be passing the
court and want to know about the speakers, there is no need to come
on to the bench or pay attention to the proceedings; it is easy to
guess – the man who raises most cheers is the worst speaker.

Larcius Licinus was the first to introduce this way of getting together an audience, but he went no further than sending invitations.

1. Twelve sesterces. See note, page 309.

At least that is what I remember hearing from my tutor Quintilian. He used to tell this story: 'I was working under Domitius Afer, who was addressing the Centumviri in his usual impressive and measured tones when he heard an extraordinary noise of loud shouting near by. He stopped speaking in amazement. Then silence was restored and he resumed his speech where he had broken off. Again the uproar, again he stopped, and when there was silence began again. The same thing happened a third time, and at last he asked who was speaking. "Licinus," was the answer. At that he abandoned his case: "Gentlemen," he said, "this means death to our profession."' In fact it was only dying when Afer believed it dead; now its ruin and destruction are almost complete. I am ashamed to describe the speeches of today, the mincing accents in which they are delivered, and the puerile applause they receive. That sort of sing-song needs only the clapping and cymbals and tambourines of Cybele to complete it, for of howling (no other word can express this applause which would be indecent even in the theatre) there is more than enough. However, I still stay on; but only through my wish to be of service to my friends and the thought that if I leave at my age it might look like an escape from work rather than a withdrawal from these disgraceful scenes. But my appearances are less frequent than they used to be, and this is the first step towards a gradual retirement.

15. To Julius Valerianus

How is your old Marsian[1] place? and the new purchase? Are you pleased with the new property now that it is yours? It rarely happens – nothing is quite so attractive in our possession as it was when coveted. My mother's property is treating me badly; still I love it for being my mother's, and, besides, long suffering has toughened me. Everlasting complaints come to an end through the shame of complaining further.

16. To Annius Severus (?)

It is like you to be punctilious about reminding me that the codicil left by Acilianus making me heir to part of his property must be held invalid because its existence is not confirmed in his will; but even I am aware of this point of law, which people generally know even if they

1. The region in Latium near Lake Fucinus.

know no other. I have in fact laid down a private law for myself whereby I treat the wishes of the deceased as formally expressed though they may not be legally binding. It is beyond doubt that this codicil of Acilianus is written in his own hand; therefore I intend to carry out its instructions as if it was confirmed in the will, though in fact it is not, especially as there is no longer any risk of prosecution. For, if I had any reason to fear that a gift I made from this bequest might be officially confiscated, I ought perhaps to pause and act with caution; but an heir is free now to give away what has come to him by inheritance. There is nothing then in the laws of the land in conflict with my private law, so nothing to prevent my acting on it.

17. *To Gallus*

You may wonder why my Laurentine place (or my Laurentian, if you like that better) is such a joy to me, but once you realize the attractions of the house itself, the amenities of its situation, and its extensive sea-front, you will have your answer. It is seventeen miles from Rome, so that it is possible to spend the night there after necessary business is done, without having cut short or hurried the day's work, and it can be approached by more than one route; the roads to Laurentum and Ostia both lead in that direction, but you must leave the one at the fourteenth milestone and the other at the eleventh. Whichever way you go, the side road you take is sandy for some distance and rather heavy and slow-going if you drive, but soft and easily covered on horseback. The view on either side is full of variety, for sometimes the road narrows as it passes through the woods, and then it broadens and opens out through wide meadows where there are many flocks of sheep and herds of horses and cattle driven down from the mountains in winter to grow sleek on the pastures in the springlike climate.

The house[1] is large enough for my needs but not expensive to keep up. It opens into a hall [A], unpretentious but not without dignity, and then there are two colonnades, rounded like the letter D, which enclose a small but pleasant courtyard [B]. This makes a splendid retreat in bad weather, being protected by windows and still more by the overhanging roof. Opposite the middle of it is a cheerful inner hall [C], and then a dining-room [D] which really is rather fine: it runs out towards the shore, and whenever the sea is driven inland by

1. See plan, page 305.

the south-west wind it is lightly washed by the spray of the spent breakers. It has folding doors or windows as large as the doors all round, so that at the front and sides it seems to look out on to three seas, and at the back has a view through the inner hall, the courtyard with the two colonnades, and the entrance-hall to the woods and mountains in the distance.

To the left of this and a little farther back from the sea is a large bed-room [E], and then another smaller one [F] which lets in the morning sunshine with one window and holds the last rays of the evening sun with the other; from this window too is a view of the sea beneath, this time at a safe distance. In the angle of this room and the dining-room is a corner which retains and intensifies the concentrated warmth of the sun, and this is the winter-quarters and gymnasium of my household [G] for no winds can be heard there except those which bring the rain clouds, and the place can still be used after the weather has broken. Round the corner is a room built round in an apse to let in the sun as it moves round and shines in each window in turn, and with one wall fitted with shelves like a library to hold the books which I read and read again [H]. Next comes a bedroom [I] on the other side of a passage which has a floor raised and fitted with pipes to receive hot steam and circulate it at a regulated temperature. The remaining rooms on this side of the house are kept for the use of my slaves and freedmen, but most of them are quite presentable enough to receive guests [J].

On the other side of the dining-room is an elegantly decorated bedroom [K], and then one which can either be a bedroom or a moderate-sized dining-room [L] and enjoys the bright light of the sun reflected from the sea; behind is another room with an ante-chamber, high enough to be cool in summer and a refuge in winter, for it is sheltered from every wind. A similar room and antechamber are divided off by a single wall [M]. Then comes the cooling-room of the bath, which is large and spacious and has two curved baths built out of opposite walls; these are quite large enough if you consider that the sea is so near. Next come the oiling-room, the furnace-room, and the antechamber to the bath, and then two rest-rooms, beautifully decorated in a simple style [N], leading to the heated swimming-bath [O] which is much admired and from which swimmers can see the sea. Close by is the ball-court [P] which receives the full warmth of the setting sun. Here there is a second storey, with two living-rooms below and two above, as well as a dining-room which commands the whole expanse of sea and stretch of shore with all its lovely houses [Q]. Elsewhere another upper storey contains a room which receives both the rising and setting sun, and a good-sized wine-store and granary behind, while below is a dining-room [R] where nothing is known of a high sea but the sound of the breakers, and even that as a dying murmur; it looks on to the garden and the encircling drive.

All round the drive runs a hedge of box, or rosemary to fill any gaps, for box will flourish extensively where it is sheltered by the buildings, but dries up if exposed in the open to the wind and salt spray even at a distance. Inside the inner ring of the drive is a young and shady vine pergola [S], where the soil is soft and yielding even to the bare foot. The garden itself is thickly planted with mulberries and figs, trees which the soil bears very well though it is less kind to others. On this side the dining-room away from the sea has a view as lovely as that of the sea itself, while from the windows of the two rooms behind [T] can be seen the entrance to the house and another well-stocked kitchen garden [U].

Here begins a covered arcade [V] nearly as large as a public building. It has windows on both sides, but more facing the sea, as there is one in each alternate bay on the garden side. These all stand open on a fine and windless day, and in stormy weather can safely be opened on the side away from the wind. In front is a terrace [W] scented with violets. As the sun beats down, the arcade increases its heat by reflection and not only retains the sun but keeps off the north-east wind so that it is as hot in front as it is cool behind. In the same way it checks the south-west wind, thus breaking the force of winds from wholly opposite quarters by one or the other of its sides; it is pleasant in winter but still more so in summer when the terrace is kept cool in the morning and the drive and nearer part of the garden in the afternoon, as its shadow falls shorter or longer on one side or the other while the day advances or declines. Inside the arcade, of course, there is least sunshine when the sun is blazing down on its roof, and as its open windows allow the western breezes to enter and circulate, the atmosphere is never heavy with stale air.

At the far end of the terrace, the arcade and the garden is a suite of rooms [x] which are really and truly my favourites, for I had them built myself. Here is a sun-parlour facing the terrace on one side, the sea on the other, and the sun on both. There is also a room which has folding doors opening on to the arcade and a window looking out on the sea. Opposite the intervening wall is a beautifully designed alcove which can be thrown into the room by folding back its glass doors and curtains, or cut off from it if they are closed: it is large enough to hold a couch and two arm-chairs, and has the sea at its foot, the neighbouring villas behind, and the woods beyond, views which can be seen separately from its many windows or blended into one. Next to it is a bedroom for use at night which neither the voices of my household, the sea's murmur, nor the noise of a storm can penetrate, any more than the lightning's flash and light of day unless the shutters are open. This profound peace and seclusion are due to the dividing passage which runs between the room and the garden so that any noise is lost in the intervening space. A tiny furnace-room is built on here, and by a narrow outlet retains or circulates the heat underneath as required. Then there is an ante-room and a second bed-room, built out to face the sun and catch its rays the moment it rises, and retain them until after midday, though by then at an angle. When I retire to this suite I feel as if I have left my house altogether and much enjoy the sensation: especially during the Saturnalia[1] when the rest of the roof resounds with festive cries in the holiday freedom, for I am not disturbing my household's merrymaking nor they my work.

Only one thing is needed to complete the amenities and beauty of the house – running water; but there are wells, or rather springs, for they are very near the surface. It is in fact a remarkable characteristic of this shore that wherever you dig you come upon water at once which is pure and not in the least brackish, although the sea is so near. The woods close by provide plenty of firewood, and the town of Ostia supplies us with everything else. There is also a village, just beyond the next house, which can satisfy anyone's modest needs, and here there are three baths for hire, a great convenience if a sudden arrival or too short a stay makes us reluctant to heat up the bath at home. The sea-front gains much from the pleasing variety of the houses built either in groups or far apart; from the sea or shore these

1. The week starting on 17 December.

look like a number of cities. The sand on the shore is sometimes too soft for walking after a long spell of fine weather, but more often it is hardened by the constant washing of the waves. The sea has admittedly few fish of any value, but it gives us excellent soles and prawns, and all inland produce is provided by the house, especially milk: for the herds collect there from the pastures whenever they seek water and shade.

And now do you think I have a good case for making this retreat my haunt and home where I love to be? You are too polite a townsman if you don't covet it! But I hope you will, for then the many attractions of my treasured house will have another strong recommendation in your company.

18. To Junius Mauricus

There is nothing you could ask me to do which I should like better than to look for a tutor for your brother's children. Thanks to you I have gone back to school and am reliving the happiest days of my life. I take my seat among the young men as I did in my youth; I am even finding how much consideration my own work has brought me from the younger generation. Only the other day, in a full lecture-room, they were joking amongst themselves in the presence of several senators. Then I came in and there was silence. I only mention this because it reflects more on their credit than on mine, and I want you to feel confident that there is no reason why your nephews should not be well-behaved students.

It remains for me to write and give you my opinion on each of the lecturers when I have heard them all, and, as far as a letter can, to make you feel you have heard them yourself. All my loyalty and devotion are yours to command in the service of your brother's memory, especially in a decision of such importance; for nothing could be of graver concern to you both than that these children (I should call them your children, did you not already love them more than your own) should be found worthy of the father he was and the uncle you are to them now. It is a duty I should have claimed myself, had you not entrusted it to me. I know very well the risk of giving offence in choosing a tutor, but that I must accept – and also the possibility of making enemies for myself – on behalf of your brother's children as cheerfully as parents do for their own.

19. To Tuccius (?) Cerialis

You urge me to give a reading of my speech to a group of friends. I will since you ask it, but with many misgivings. I know very well that speeches when read lose all their warmth and spirit, almost their entire character, since their fire is always fed from the atmosphere of court: the bench of magistrates and throng of advocates, the suspense of the awaited verdict, reputation of the different speakers, and the divided enthusiasm of the public; and they gain too from the gestures of the speaker as he strides to and fro, the movements of his body corresponding to his changing passions. (Hence the loss to anyone who delivers his speech sitting down – he is at a real disadvantage by the mere fact of being seated, though he may be as gifted generally as the speakers who stand.) Moreover, a man who is giving a reading has the two chief aids to his delivery (eyes and hands) taken up with his text, so it is not surprising if the attention of his audience wavers when there is no adventitious attraction to hold it nor stimulus to keep it aroused.

Furthermore, this is a fighting speech, disputatious if you like, and it is besides natural for us to think that what we found an effort to write will also demand an effort on the part of our hearers. There are certainly very few members of an audience sufficiently trained to prefer a stiff, close-knit argument to fine-sounding words. Such a disparity shocks, but it exists: for in general a bench of magistrates and an audience have very different demands, though a listener should really be influenced most by what would convince him if he were called on to pronounce judgement. However, it may be that in spite of these difficulties the speech you have in mind will gain from its novelty – at any rate in our own country, for the Greeks have a somewhat similar practice, though with the opposite intent. To demonstrate that a law was contrary to previous legislation their method of proof was by comparison with other laws; so to show that my accusation was covered by the law dealing with the extortion of money I had to base my argument on the analogy of other laws as well. This cannot have any appeal for the ordinary man, but its interest for the professional should be proportionately greater for the lack of it for the layman. It is certainly my intention, if I agree to this reading, to invite all the legal experts.

But now think carefully whether I ought to give one at all. Set out on both sides all the arguments I have put forward, and make your decision with good reason. You are the one who will have to produce the reason: I have an excuse by complying with your wishes.

20. To Calvisius Rufus

Have your copper ready and hear a first-rate story, or rather stories, for the new one has reminded me of others and it doesn't matter which I tell first. Piso's widow Verania was lying seriously ill – I mean the Piso Galba adopted. Along comes Regulus. What impudence – to intrude on her sickness when he had been her husband's deadly enemy and she hated the sight of him! The visit alone is bad enough, but he sits down by her bed and asks her the day and hour of her birth; after which he puts on a grave look and a fixed stare, moves his lips, works his fingers, and does sums. Then silence. After keeping the poor woman in suspense for a long time, he speaks: 'You are going through a danger period, out of which you will pass. However, to rid you of any doubts, I will consult a soothsayer with whom I have often had dealings.' Without delay he then performs a sacrifice and declares that the entrails accord with the planetary signs. Feeling her life in danger, Verania is ready to believe him; she asks for a codicil to be added to her will and puts Regulus down for a legacy. Subsequently she grows worse and dies, calling aloud on the wickedness and treachery, the worse than perjury of the man who swore her a false oath on the life of his son. This is the kind of scandalous thing Regulus is always doing, calling down the wrath of the gods (which he always manages to escape himself) on to the head of his unfortunate boy.

Velleius Blaesus is well known as an ex-consul and a rich man. He wished to alter his will on his death-bed, and Regulus was hoping for something from the new one as he had just begun courting Blaesus. He therefore begs and implores the doctors to prolong the man's life in some way. Once the will is signed there is a change of front, and the same doctors are attacked to know how long they intend to torture the poor man and why they grudge him an easy death when they cannot give him life. Blaesus dies; he might have heard the whole story, for he leaves Regulus nothing.

Are two stories enough, or do you want another according to the rule of three? There are more to come. The noble lady Aurelia had dressed in her best for the ceremony of signing her will. When Regulus arrived to witness her signature, he asked her to leave these clothes to him. Aurelia thought he was joking, but he pressed the point in all seriousness, and to cut a long story short, he forced her to open the will and leave him what she was wearing; he watched her writing and looked to see if she had done so. Aurelia is in fact alive today, but he forced this on her as if she were on the point of death. And this is the man who accepts estates and legacies as if they were his due.

'But why do I rouse myself'[1] over this, when I live in a country which has long offered the same (or even greater) rewards to dishonesty and wickedness as it does to honour and merit? Look at Regulus, who has risen by his evil ways from poverty and obscurity to such great wealth that he told me himself when he was trying to divine how soon he would be worth sixty million sesterces he had found a double set of entrails which were a sign that he would have twice that sum. So he will, too, if he goes on in the way he has begun, dictating wills which are not their own to the very people who are wanting to make them: the most immoral kind of fraud there is.

---

1. Demosthenes, *De Corona*, 142.

BOOK THREE

1. To Calvisius Rufus

I can't remember ever passing the time so pleasantly as I did on my recent visit to Spurinna; and, indeed, there is no one whom I would rather take for an example in my old age, if I am spared to live so long, for no way of living is better planned than his. A well-ordered life, especially where the old are concerned, gives me the same pleasure as the fixed course of the planets. A certain amount of irregularity and excitement is not unsuitable for the young, but their elders should lead a quiet and orderly existence; their time of public activity is over, and ambition only brings them into disrepute.

This is the rule strictly observed by Spurinna, and he even maintains a due order and succession in matters which would be trivial were they not part of a daily routine. Every morning he stays in bed for an hour after dawn, then calls for his shoes and takes a three-mile walk to exercise mind and body. If he has friends with him he carries on a serious conversation, if he is alone a book is read aloud, and this is sometimes done when there are friends present, so long as they do not object. Then he sits down, the book is continued, or preferably the conversation; after which he goes out in his carriage accompanied by his wife (a model to her sex) or one of his friends, a pleasure recently mine. There is a special sort of pleasure in being thus singled out and given the entry into a bygone age as he talks of great men and their deeds to give you inspiration, though modesty restrains him from any appearance of laying down the law. After a drive of seven miles he will walk another mile, then sit again or retire to his room and his writing, for he composes lyric verses in both Greek and Latin with considerable success; they are remarkable for their wit, grace, and delicacy, and their charm is enhanced by the propriety of their author. When summoned to his bath (in mid-afternoon in winter and an hour earlier in summer) he first removes his clothes and takes a walk in the sunshine if there is no wind, and then throws a ball briskly for some time, this being another form of exercise whereby he keeps old age at bay. After his bath he lies down for a short rest before dinner, and listens while something light and soothing is read aloud. Meanwhile his friends are quite free to do the same as he does or not, as they prefer. Dinner is brought on in dishes of antique solid silver, a simple meal but well served; he also has Corinthian bronze for general use, which he admires though not with a collector's passion. Between the courses there is often a performance of comedy, so that the pleasures of the table have a seasoning of letters, and the meal is prolonged into the night, even in summer, without anyone finding it too long amid such pleasant company.

The result is that Spurinna has passed his seventy-seventh year, but his sight and hearing are unimpaired, and he is physically agile and energetic; old age has brought him nothing but wisdom. This is the sort of life I hope and pray will be mine, and I shall eagerly enter on it as soon as the thought of my years permits me to sound a retreat. Meanwhile innumerable tasks fill my time, though here again Spurinna sets me a reassuring example, for he also accepted public offices, held magistracies, and governed provinces as long as it was his duty, and thus his present retirement was earned by hard work. I have set myself the same race and goal, and I bind myself to it now with you as my witness: so, if you see me fail to stop, you can call me to account with this letter of mine and bid me retire when I can do so without being accused of laziness.

2. *To Vibius Maximus*

I hope I am justified in asking you to do the sort of favour to one of my friends which I should certainly have done for yours had I the same opportunity. Maturus Arrianus is the leading citizen of Altinum,[1] and when I say this I am not referring to his wealth, which is considerable, but to his virtue and justice, his sense of responsibility and wisdom. His is the advice I follow in business, and his the opinion I seek on literary topics, for he is a man of exceptional sincerity,

1. On the coast of Venetia (now Altino).

integrity and understanding. He loves me as dearly as you do – I can
say no more.

He is incapable of pushing himself forward, and for this reason has
remained a member of the order of knights, though he could easily
have risen to the highest rank. However, I feel it is my duty to obtain
him promotion and advancement, and so I am anxious to improve
his position in some way, though he neither expects nor knows of
this, and may perhaps not wish it; but it must be a distinction which
he will not find a burden. Please grant him something of this kind
at your earliest opportunity. I shall be exceedingly grateful to you,
and so will he, for, though he would not approach you for this himself, he will receive it as gratefully as if he had set his heart on it.

3. To Corellia Hispulla

My love and admiration (I can't say which comes first) for your
father's noble sense of duty and high principles are matched by my
special affection for yourself on your own account as well as for his
sake; and so I must desire your son to take after his grandfather,[1]
and will make every effort I can to ensure this. I should prefer him to
resemble your own father, although on his father's side, too, fortune
has granted him a grandfather who is admired and respected, and a
father and uncle whose distinguished reputations are well known. He
will grow up to be like them only if he has been educated from the
start on the proper lines, and thus it is most important for him to have
the right teacher. Up to the present he has been too young to leave
your side, and has had teachers at home where there is little or no
opportunity for going astray. Now his studies must be carried farther
afield, and we must look for a tutor in Latin rhetoric whose school
shall combine a strict training along with good manners and, above
all, moral standards; for, as our boy happens to be endowed with
striking physical beauty amongst his natural gifts, at this dangerous
time of life he needs more than a teacher. A guardian and mentor
must be found.

I think then that I cannot do better than to draw your attention to
Julius Genitor. The affection I have for him has not blinded my
judgement, as it is in fact based on it. He is a man of serious character,
quite free from faults: indeed a little too blunt and austere for the

1. Corellius Rufus; for his death see I : 12.

licence of our times. On the subject of his eloquence you have many witnesses you may trust, for ability in speaking is obvious and readily recognized whenever it is displayed; whereas there are many deep secrets and hidden places in a man's personal life. You may rest assured that I answer for these on Genitor's behalf. Your son will hear nothing from him but what will benefit him, will learn nothing that would have been better left unknown. Genitor will remind him as often as we do of his obligations to his forbears and the great names he must carry on. So with the gods' good will you may entrust him to a teacher from whom he will learn right principles of conduct before he studies eloquence – for without principles this cannot be properly learned at all.

4: To Caecilius Macrinus

Public opinion and the friends who were with me at the time have apparently approved of my conduct, but even so I very much want to know what you think, for the opinion of someone whose advice I should have liked to ask before making my decision is still of great importance to me now that the matter is settled.

I had obtained leave of absence from my post in the Treasury and hurried out to my place in Tuscany[1] in order to lay the foundation stone of a temple which was to be built at my expense; at that moment the representatives of the province of Baetica (who had come to lodge a complaint against the conduct of their late governor, Caecilius Classicus) applied to the Senate for my services as their counsel. My Treasury colleagues, the best of men and most loyal of friends, tried to beg me off and excuse me by pleading the official duties we share. The Senate then passed the resolution – highly complimentary to me – that my services should be granted the province provided that I expressed my willingness in person. The representatives were brought in again, this time in my presence, and made their request a second time, appealing to my professional honour which they had experienced in the case against Baebius Massa,[2] and pleading that they had a claim on my patronage. There followed the open acclamation which usually indicates that a resolution is going to be passed; after which

1. Tifernum on Tiber (now Città di Castello), twenty miles east of Arretium (now Arezzo) and 150 miles from Rome; see also x: 8.
2. In 93; see VII: 33.

I begged leave to withdraw my opinion that I had given just reason for excusing myself. This was received with general approval, both for the meaning of my words and the modesty which prompted them.

I was in fact impelled to take this course not only by the unanimous feeling in the Senate, much though that influenced me, but by certain lesser considerations which could not be ignored. I recalled how our fathers needed no official direction to instigate prosecutions to avenge the wrongs of individual foreigners; which made it all the more disgraceful to neglect the rights of a whole people with whom I had ties of hospitality. Besides, when I remembered the dangers I had faced when acting for the Baetici on an earlier occasion, I felt that I ought to maintain my credit with them for my former service by adding a new one. It is generally agreed that past benefits cease to count unless confirmed by later ones; for, if a single thing is denied people who have every reason to be grateful, the denial is all they remember.

An additional influence was the fact that Classicus was now dead, which removed the most painful feature in this type of case – the downfall of a senator. I saw then that I should win the same gratitude for taking on the case as if he were alive, but without incurring ill-will. Finally I calculated that, if I discharged this duty for the third time, it would be easier for me to excuse myself if later faced by a defendant whom I felt I ought not to prosecute. All duties have their limits, and permission to be freed from them is best gained by previous compliance. These then are the reasons for my decision; it remains for you to give your opinion one way or the other, bearing in mind that you will please me just as much by frankness if you disapprove as by your encouragement if I have your support.

5. To Baebius Macer

I am delighted to hear that your close study of my uncle's books has made you wish to possess them all. Since you ask me for a complete list, I will provide a bibliography, and arrange it in chronological order, for this is the sort of information also likely to please scholars.

Throwing the Javelin from Horseback – one volume; a work of industry and talent, written when he was a junior officer in the cavalry.

The Life of Pomponius Secundus[1] – two volumes. My uncle was

1. Poet and tragedian, and distinguished as a commander in Germany during the reign of Claudius.

greatly loved by him and felt he owed this homage to his friend's memory.

The German Wars – twenty volumes, covering all the wars we have ever had with the Germans. He began this during his military service in Germany, as the result of a dream; in his sleep he saw standing over him the ghost of Drusus Nero, who had triumphed far and wide in Germany and died there. He committed his memory to my uncle's care, begging him to save him from the injustice of oblivion.

The Scholar – three volumes divided into six sections on account of their length, in which he trains the orator from his cradle and brings him to perfection.

Problems in Grammar – eight volumes; this he wrote during Nero's last years when the slavery of the times made it dangerous to write anything at all independent or inspired.

A Continuation of the History of Aufidius Bassus – thirty-one volumes.

A Natural History – thirty-seven volumes, a learned and comprehensive work as full of variety as nature itself.

You may wonder how such a busy man was able to complete so many volumes, many of them involving detailed study; and wonder still more when you learn that up to a certain age he practised at the bar, that he died at the age of fifty-five, and throughout the intervening years his time was much taken up with the important offices he held and his friendship with the Emperors. But he combined a penetrating intellect with amazing powers of concentration and the capacity to manage with the minimum of sleep.

From the feast of Vulcan[1] onwards he began to work by lamplight, not with any idea of making a propitious start but to give himself more time for study, and would rise half-way through the night; in winter it would often be at midnight or an hour later, and two at the latest. Admittedly he fell asleep very easily, and would often doze and wake up again during his work. Before daybreak he would visit the Emperor Vespasian (who also made use of his nights) and then go to attend his official duties. On returning home, he devoted any spare time to his work. After something to eat (his meals during the day were light and simple in the old-fashioned way), in summer when he was not too busy he would often lie in the sun, and a book was read aloud while he made notes and extracts. He made extracts of

1. 23 August.

everything he read, and always said that there was no book so bad that some good could not be got out of it. After his rest in the sun he generally took a cold bath, and then ate something and had a short sleep; after which he worked till dinner time as if he had started on a new day. A book was read aloud during the meal and he took rapid notes. I remember that one of his friends told a reader to go back and repeat a word he had mispronounced. 'Couldn't you understand him?' said my uncle. His friend admitted that he could. 'Then why make him go back? Your interruption has lost us at least ten lines.' To such lengths did he carry his passion for saving time. In summer he rose from dinner while it was still light, in winter as soon as darkness fell, as if some law compelled him.

This was his routine in the midst of his public duties and the bustle of the city. In the country, the only time he took from his work was for his bath, and by bath I mean his actual immersion, for while he was being rubbed down and dried he had a book read to him or dictated notes. When travelling he felt free from other responsibilities to give every minute to work; he kept a secretary at his side with book and notebook, and in winter saw that his hands were protected by long sleeves, so that even bitter weather should not rob him of a working hour. For the same reason, too, he used to be carried about Rome in a chair. I can remember how he scolded me for walking; according to him I need not have wasted those hours, for he thought any time wasted which was not devoted to work. It was this application which enabled him to finish all those volumes, and to leave me 160 notebooks of selected passages, written in a minute hand on both sides of the page, so that their number is really doubled. He used to say that when he was serving as procurator in Spain he could have sold these notebooks to Larcius Licinus for 400,000 sesterces, and there were far fewer of them then.

When you consider the extent of his reading and writing I wonder if you feel that he could never have been a public official nor a friend of the Emperor, but on the other hand, now that you know of his application, that he should have achieved more? In fact his official duties put every possible obstacle in his path; and yet there was nothing which his energy could not surmount. So I cannot help smiling when anyone calls me studious, for compared with him I am the idlest of men. And yet perhaps I am not, seeing that so much of my time is taken up with official work and service to my friends. Any one of your life-long devotees of literature, if put alongside my uncle, would blush to feel themselves thus enslaved to sleep and idleness.

I have let my letter run on, though I intended only to answer your question about the books left by my uncle. However, I feel sure that reading these details will give you as much pleasure as the actual books, and may even spur you on to the ambition of doing more than read them, if you can produce something similar yourself.

6. To Annius Severus

Out of a sum of money I have inherited I have just bought a Corinthian bronze statue, only a small one, but an attractive and finished piece of work as far as I can judge – though in general my judgement is limited, and certainly very much so here. But this is a status that I feel even I can appreciate, for being nude it does not hide any defects it may have nor fail to reveal its merits. It represents a standing figure of an old man; the bones, muscles, sinews, and veins and even the wrinkles are clear and lifelike, the hair is sparse and receding from a broad brow, its face is lined and neck thin, and it has drooping shoulders, a flat chest and hollow stomach. The back view, within its limits, gives the same impression of age. The bronze appears to have the true colour of a genuine antique; in fact every detail is such as to hold the attention of an artist as well as delight the amateur, and that is what persuaded me to buy it, novice though I am.

However, my intention was not to keep it in my house (I have not any Corinthian bronzes there yet) but to place it in some public position in my native town, preferably in the temple of Jupiter; it is clearly a gift well worthy of a temple and a god. Will you then carry out a commission for me as you always do, and give immediate orders for a pedestal to be made? Choose what marble you like, and have it inscribed with my name and official titles if you think they should appear too. I will send you the statue as soon as I can find someone who will not find it a trouble, or I will bring it myself, which you will like better, for I have it in mind to pay you a visit if my official duties permit. Your smile at this promise to come will change to a frown when I add that it will only be for a few days; the work which is still keeping me here will not let me be away for longer.

7. To Caninius Rufus

The news has just come that Silius Italicus has starved himself to death in his house near Naples. Ill-health was the reason, for he had developed an incurable tumour which wore him down until he formed the fixed resolve to escape by dying; though he had been fortunate in life and enjoyed happiness up to the end of his days, apart from the loss of the younger of his two sons. The elder and more gifted he left well established in his career and already of consular rank. Italicus had damaged his reputation under Nero – it was believed that he had offered his services as an informer – but he had maintained his friendship with Vitellius with tact and wisdom, won fame for his conduct as governor of Asia, and removed the stigma of his former activities by his honourable retirement. He ranked as one of our leading citizens without exercising influence or incurring ill-will; he was waited on and sought after, and spent many hours on his couch in a room thronged with callers who had come with no thought of his rank; and so passed his days in cultured conversation whenever he could spare time from his writing. He took great pains over his verses,[1] though they cannot be called inspired, and frequently submitted them to public criticism by the readings he gave. Latterly his increasing age led to his retirement from Rome; he made his home in Campania and never left it again, not even on the arrival of the new Emperor: an incident which reflects great credit on the Emperor for permitting this liberty, and on Italicus for venturing to avail himself of it. He was a great connoisseur; indeed he was criticized for buying too much. He owned several houses in the same district, but lost interest in the older ones in his enthusiasm for the later. In each of them he had quantities of books, statues, and portrait busts, and these were more to him than possessions – they became objects of his devotion, particularly in the case of Virgil, whose birthday he celebrated with more solemnity than his own, and at Naples especially, where he would visit Virgil's tomb as if it were a temple. In this peaceful atmosphere he completed his seventy-fifth year, surrounded by attentions though not really an invalid. He was the last consul to be appointed by Nero, and the last to die of all the consuls Nero appointed; and also remarkable is the fact that not only did the last of

1. His longest extant epic on the second Punic war runs to 12,200 verses.

Nero's consuls die in him but it was during his consulship that Nero perished.

The thought of this fills me with pity for human frailty; nothing is so short and fleeting as the longest of human lives. It must seem to you only the other day that Nero died, yet not one of those who held consulships in his time is alive today. I suppose I should not find this remarkable when only recently Lucius Piso, father of the Piso who was so criminally put to death in Africa by Valerius Festus, used to say that none of those he had called on to speak when he was consul could still be seen in the Senate. So narrow are the limits set to life, even in a large community, that it seems to me that the Persian king should be forgiven, or even admired for his famous tears; for it is said that after Xerxes had reviewed his vast army, he wept to think of the end awaiting so many thousands in so short a time.[1]

All the more reason then why we should prolong all our passing moments, uncertain though they are, not perhaps by action, since here the opportunity no longer rests with us, but at any rate by literary work. Since we are denied a long life, let us leave something to bear witness that at least we have lived. I know you need no incentive, but my affection prompts me to spur on a willing horse, as you do for me in return. 'Rivalry is good'[2] when friends stimulate each other by mutual encouragement to desire immortal fame.

8. To Suetonius Tranquillus

You give proof of your high regard for me by the delicacy with which you frame your request that I should transfer to your relative Caesennius Silvanus the military tribunate which I obtained for you from the distinguished senator Neratius Marcellus. For myself, I should have been delighted to see you as tribune, but I shall be equally pleased if Silvanus owes his office to you. If one has thought a man worthy of promotion it is, I think, illogical to begrudge him the right to show his family feeling, seeing that this does him more honour than any official title. I see too that as the performance of services is as laudable as the deserving of them, you will win praise on both accounts if you give up to someone else what you merited yourself, and I realize that some credit will be reflected on me, too, if as a result of your action it is known that my friends are free either to hold the

1. Herodotus, VII: 45.   2. Hesiod, Works and Days, 24.

office of tribune themselves or to give it away. Your wish is thus excellent in every way and shall be granted. Your name is not yet entered on the lists, so it is easy for me to substitute that of Silvanus; and I hope that your service will please him as much as mine pleases you.

9. To Cornelius Minicianus

At last I can give you a full account of all the trouble I have had over the public action brought by the province of Baetica, a most complicated case which after several hearings ended in a variety of sentences: the reason for which you shall hear.

Caecilius Classicus had been governor of Baetica in the same year that Marius Priscus was in Africa. His rapacity during this time was matched by his brutality, for he was a scoundrel who made no secret of his evil ways. It so happened that Priscus came from Baetica and Classicus from Africa; hence the joke current among the Baetici (for exasperation often breaks out into wit) – 'I got as bad as I gave'. However, Priscus was brought to trial by a single city along with several private individuals, whereas Classicus was attacked by the entire province. He forestalled the trial by his death, which might have been accidental or self-inflicted; there was much general suspicion but no definite proof, for, though it seemed likely that he intended to die since he could not defend himself, it is surprising that he should have died to escape the shame of condemnation for deeds which he was not ashamed to do. Nevertheless, the Baetici continued with their action after his death. (This was legally permissible, but the practice had lapsed, and was revived on this occasion after a long interval.) In addition to Classicus, they extended their charges to his friends and accomplices, demanding an individual investigation in each case.

I appeared for the Baetici, supported by Lucceius Albinus, a fluent and elegant orator whom I have long admired; since our association on this occasion I have come to feel a warm affection for him. The will to succeed implies some reluctance to share success, and especially where forensic oratory is concerned; but in our case there was no rivalry nor competition. We both put the needs of the case before personal considerations in a combined effort, for we felt that the importance of the issue and its outcome demanded that we did not assume such responsibility in a single speech from each of us. It looked as though we should run short of time and lose our breath and voice if we dealt with so many accusations and defendants collectively, and then the large number of names and charges might exhaust the attention of the magistrates and possibly leave them in confusion. Moreover, the combined influence of the individuals concerned might procure for each the effect of the whole, and, finally, the influential might make scapegoats of the humble, and so escape at their expense. (Privilege and self-interest are most likely to triumph when they can be concealed behind a mask of severity.) We also had in mind the well-known example of Sertorius,[1] when he set the strongest and the weakest of his soldiers to pull off the horse's tail – you know the rest of the story – and concluded that we too could deal with the large number of defendants if we took them one by one.

We decided that the first essential was to prove Classicus guilty; this would give us the best approach to his allies and accomplices, who could not be convicted unless he was. We coupled two of them with Classicus from the start, Baebius Probus and Fabius Hispanus, both formidable opponents through their influence, and Hispanus also for his fluent tongue. It was easy to make short work of Classicus. He had left accounts in his own hand of his receipts for every business deal and court case, and he had even sent a bragging letter to his mistress in Rome (these are his actual words): 'Hurrah, hurrah, I'm coming to you a free man – I've sold up half the Baetici and raised four million!'

Over Hispanus and Probus we had to sweat. Before I dealt with the charges against them I believed it was essential to establish the fact that the carrying out of orders was a chargeable offence; otherwise it would have been useless to prove they had done so. Their defence was in fact not to deny the charge, but to plead compulsion, saying that as provincials they were terrorized into carrying out any order of the governor. Claudius Restitutus, who replied for the defence, is a practised speaker who is alert and ready for anything unexpected, but he now says that he never felt so dumbfounded and bewildered as when he saw all the points he was most relying on for his defence anticipated and torn out of his grasp. The result of our policy was that the Senate decreed that all possessions owned by Classicus before his provincial appointment should be set aside and given to his daughter, that the remainder be handed over to the people he had robbed, and, further, that the money he had paid to his creditors should be recalled.

1. Horace, *Epistles*, II, 1, 45.

Hispanus and Probus were banished for five years, so serious did their conduct now seem, though at first it had been doubtful whether it was indictable at all.

A few days later we charged Claudius Fuscus, the son-in-law of Classicus, and Stilonius Priscus who had served under him as tribune of a cohort, with varying success: Priscus was banished from Italy for two years, and Fuscus was acquitted.

At the third hearing we thought it best to group several defendants together, fearing that if the trial were prolonged too far the presiding magistrates would be bored and tired and consequently their strict administration of justice would begin to flag. Moreover, there remained only people of less importance whom we had deliberately kept back until then, apart from Classicus's wife who was strongly suspected, though it did not look as though there was proof enough to convict her. Classicus's daughter, who had also been included in the charge, emerged quite free from suspicion. So when I reached her name at the end of my speech, as there was no longer the same danger of weakening the whole case as there was at the beginning, I felt that the only just course was to refrain from pressing a charge against an innocent person: and I said so openly in many ways. I first asked the representatives of the province if they had instructed me to make any special charge which they were confident could be substantiated, and then I appealed to the Senate for guidance whether I ought to direct all my powers of oratory against an innocent woman, like a knife at her throat. Finally, I brought the whole subject to this conclusion. 'If I am asked whether I am judging this case, my answer is No, but I cannot forget that I should have been amongst the judges, had I not been chosen to conduct the prosecution.'

So ended these complicated proceedings; of the persons involved, some were acquitted, but the majority were convicted and banished, either for a fixed period or for life. In its decree passing sentence, the Senate gave the fullest expression to its appreciation of Albinus and myself, for our thorough and scrupulous handling of the case and for our perseverance, the only just and adequate reward for our labours. You can imagine how tired we are after so much continuous speaking, debating and cross-examining of all the witnesses and supporting or refuting their replies; and how difficult and unpleasant it has been to have to say no to the confidential questions of the friends of the many defendants, and then to have to face their open attacks in court. I will quote one of the answers I gave when some of the magistrates were protesting on behalf of a highly influential defendant: 'His innocence will not be affected if I am allowed to finish my speech.' From this you can guess at the opposition and hostility we incurred, though admittedly not for long. Honesty offends those it thwarts for a time, but afterwards these are the people from whom it wins respect.

I can't do more to bring you to the scene of action. You may say that this is too much and that you never expected such a long letter – then don't ask again for news of what is happening in Rome, and remember that a letter cannot really be called long when it deals with so many days and inquiries, and all the defendants involved in so many cases. I think myself that I have kept my account short and accurate – no, that was rash: I have just remembered too late something I left out, and you must have it although out of place. (This is one of Homer's devices, and many writers imitate him; it can be very effective, though that was not my own intention.)

A witness who was either annoyed at being compelled to appear to give evidence, or had been suborned by one of the defendants to damage the case, charged Norbanus Licinianus (one of the representatives of Baetica who had been commissioned to collect evidence) with collusion in the case against Casta, the wife of Classicus. It is laid down by law that the trial of an accused shall be concluded before a charge of collusion with his accuser is investigated, doubtless because the honesty of the latter can best be judged from his handling of the case. However, Norbanus gained no protection from this legal provision, and none from his position as delegate nor his commission to prepare the case; he was swept away by the general indignation against his other misdemeanours and the fact that like many others he had profited by the reign of Domitian, and had in fact been chosen by his province to collect evidence on this occasion not for his honesty and reliability but for his hatred of Classicus (who had previously banished him). He asked for time and a statement of the charges against him, but both his requests were refused. He was obliged to defend himself on the spot, and did so with considerable promptitude, though the man's thoroughly bad and worthless character makes me wonder whether his reply showed courage or merely impudence. There were many other charges against him more damaging than that of collusion: indeed, two senators (the consulars Pomponius Rufus and Libo Frugi) produced the damning evidence that he had appeared in court in Domitian's time in support of the prosecution of Salvius Liberalis. He was found guilty and sentenced to banishment on an island. In charging Casta, therefore, I particularly emphasized the collusion for which her accuser had been convicted, but without success. On the contrary, the result was quite without precedent – the defendant was acquitted although her accuser was convicted of collusion with her.

You may be wondering what we were doing meanwhile. We explained to the Senate that, as it was from Norbanus that we had received our instructions on behalf of the province, if he was found guilty of collusion we must begin again with fresh ones; so while his trial was on, we remained seated. Afterwards Norbanus attended every day of the trial and kept up his courage – or impudence – to the end.

I am trying to think whether I have left anything out this time, and again I nearly did. On the last day Salvius Liberalis made a violent attack on the remaining delegates for not having brought to trial all the persons about whom their province had given them instructions, and, being a forceful and eloquent speaker, he put them in a perilous position. I undertook their defence, and found them honest men and most grateful to me; in fact they say they owe their escape from disaster entirely to me.

This is the end of this letter, really the end – I won't add another syllable even if I think of something else I have forgotten.

10. *To Vestricius Spurinna and Cottia*

I didn't mention when I was last with you that I had written something about your son, because, in the first place, I had not written it with the idea of telling you, but to give expression to my own feelings of love and grief, and then because I knew from what you had told me yourself that you, Spurinna, had heard that I had given a public reading, and I assumed that you had also heard what its subject was. I was anxious too not to upset you during a national holiday by reviving the memory of your tragic loss.

Even now I am still in some doubt whether to send you only the passages I read, as you ask, or to add what I was intending to keep back to present on another occasion. A single composition is quite inadequate for my sentiments, if I am to do justice to the memory of one I loved and revered so much, and his fame will be more widespread if it is published abroad by degrees. But while debating whether to show you all I have written so far, or to withhold something until later, I have come to see that honesty and friendship alike constrain me to send everything; especially as you assure me that nothing shall leave your hands until I have made up my mind about publication.

One thing remains: please be equally honest about telling me if you think there are any additions, alterations, or omissions to be made. It is difficult for you to concentrate on this at a time of sorrow, I know; but, nevertheless, if a sculptor or painter were working on a portrait of your son, you would indicate to him what features to bring out or correct; and so you must give me guidance and direction as I, too, am trying to create a likeness which shall not be short-lived and ephemeral, but one you think will last for ever. It is more likely to be long-lived the more I can attain to truth and beauty and accuracy in detail.

11. *To Julius Genitor*

The natural generosity of our friend Artemidorus always makes him enlarge on his friends' services, and so he is spreading an account of my merits which is not untrue, but more than I deserve. It is true that, when the philosophers were expelled from Rome,[1] I went to see him in his house outside the city, and as I was praetor at that time the visit involved some risk for the attention it attracted. He was also in need of a considerable sum at the time to pay off his debts contracted in honourable causes; I raised the money and lent it to him without interest, when certain of his rich and influential friends hesitated to do so. I did this at a time when seven of my friends had been put to death or banished – Senecio, Rusticus, and Helvidius were dead, and Mauricus, Gratilla, Arria, and Fannia were in exile – so that I stood amidst the flames of thunderbolts dropping all round me, and there were certain clear indications to make me suppose a like end was awaiting me.

However, I do not believe I deserve the exaggerated reputation in these matters which Artemidorus gives me: I have not disgraced myself, but that is all. For I greatly admired his father-in-law Gaius

Musonius, and loved him as much as our difference in age permitted; and when I was serving as military tribune in Syria I was on terms of close intimacy with Artemidorus himself. In fact the first sign I showed of having any judgement was that apparently I appreciated a man who was a true sage, or the nearest approach to one. Of all those who call themselves philosophers today, you will scarcely find one with his sincerity and integrity. I am saying nothing about his physical endurance in winter and summer, how he shrinks from no hardship and permits himself no indulgence in food and drink, nor licence in look or thought. All this may be important in another person, but for him it means little in comparison with his other virtues; which won him the honour of being chosen by Gaius Musonius from suitors of every rank to be his son-in-law.

As I recall these events I am indeed happy to think of the high tribute he pays me generally, and especially in your hearing, but at the same time I fear he may go too far; for (to return to the point I started from) his generosity puts no check on him. This is his only fault, albeit a good fault, in one otherwise so wise: he has too high an opinion of his friends.

12. To Catilius Severus

I will come to dinner, but only on condition that it is simple and informal, rich only in Socratic conversation, though this too must be kept within bounds; for there will be early-morning callers to think of. Cato himself could not escape reproach on meeting them, though Caesar's adverse comment is tinged with admiration. The passers-by whom Cato met when drunk, blushed when they discovered who he was, and (says Caesar) 'You would have thought they had been found out by Cato, not Cato by them'. What better tribute to Cato's prestige than to show him still awe-inspiring when drunk! But our dinner must have a limit, in time as well as in preparations and expense; for we are not the sort of people whom even our enemies cannot blame without a word of praise.

13. To Voconius Romanus

I am sending at your request the text of the speech in which I recently expressed my thanks to our noble Emperor for my consulship;[1] I

1. On 1 September 100; later published as the *Panegyricus*.

intended to do so in any case. I should like you to bear in mind that the nobility of the theme brings its own difficulties. In other speeches there is novelty, if nothing else, to hold the attention of the reader, but here everything is common knowledge and has been said before; consequently the reader has time and freedom to concentrate on the delivery without distractions, and if he forms his opinion by this alone he is not easily satisfied. I would prefer him to give equal attention to the arrangement, the transitions and figures of speech, for, although a powerful imagination and the gift of forceful expression are sometimes to be found in the uneducated, no one can display skill in arrangement and variety of figures except the trained expert. Nor should one always be searching for the elevated and the sublime, for a speech needs to lower as well as to raise its tone: just as in a picture, light is best shown up by shadow. But there is no need for me to say this to anyone of your attainments. I ought rather to ask you to mark any alterations you think should be made, for, if I have your criticisms of some points, I shall be more ready to believe that you like the rest of the speech.

14. *To Publius (?) Acilius*

This horrible affair demands more publicity than a letter – Larcius Macedo, a senator and ex-praetor, has fallen a victim to his own slaves. Admittedly he was a cruel and overbearing master, too ready to forget that his father had been a slave, or perhaps too keenly conscious of it. He was taking a bath in his house at Formiae[1] when suddenly he found himself surrounded; one slave seized him by the throat while the others struck his face and hit him in the chest and stomach and – shocking to say – in his private parts. When they thought he was dead they threw him on to the hot pavement, to make sure he was not still alive. Whether unconscious or feigning to be so, he lay there motionless, thus making them believe that he was quite dead. Only then was he carried out, as if he had fainted with the heat, and received by his slaves who had remained faithful, while his concubines ran up, screaming frantically. Roused by their cries and revived by the cooler air he opened his eyes and made some movement to show that he was alive, it being now safe to do so. The guilty slaves fled, but most of them have been arrested and a search is being made for the

1. In Latium (now Mola di Gaeta).

others. Macedo was brought back to life with difficulty, but only for a few days; at least he died with the satisfaction of having revenged himself, for he lived to see the same punishment meted out as for murder. There you see the dangers, outrages, and insults to which we are exposed. No master can feel safe because he is kind and considerate; for it is their brutality, not their reasoning capacity, which leads slaves to murder masters.

But let us change the subject. What news is there? None, or I would give you it, for I still have space, and today's holiday gives me time to continue. I will only put in a detail in connexion with Macedo which I have fortunately just remembered. He was in one of the public baths in Rome when a remarkable incident occurred which events have proved to be an omen. One of Macedo's slaves lightly touched a Roman knight to ask him to let them pass; the man turned round and struck not the slave who had touched him, but Macedo himself such a violent blow that he nearly knocked him down. So the baths have been the scene successively of insult to Macedo and then of his death.

15. To Silius Proculus

You want me to read through some of your poems while I am away on holiday, to see if they are worth publishing, and, in begging me to spend on your work any odd moments I can spare from my own, you can cite a precedent to support your plea; Cicero, you say, was wonderfully generous about encouraging the talent of poets.

But there was no need of prayers and entreaties – I have a profound regard for poetry and the warmest affection for yourself, and so I will gladly apply myself to doing what you ask. However, I see no reason why I should not say here and now that it is a splendid work and ought not to remain unpublished, to judge from the passages I have heard you read; unless I was carried away by your style of reading, which has very great charm and skill. But I feel sure that I am not seduced by the pleasures of the ear to the extent of losing all my critical powers; my sting may perhaps be dulled and lack a little of its sharpness, but it cannot be entirely pulled out. This then is my considered opinion on the work as a whole, and I will judge the parts after I have read them.

16. *To Maecilius Nepos*

I think I have remarked that the more famous words and deeds of men and women are not necessarily their greatest. I was strengthened in this opinion by a conversation I had yesterday with Fannia,[1] granddaughter of the famous Arria who sustained and encouraged her husband by her example at the time of his death. She told me several things about her grandmother which were quite as heroic though less well known, and I think they will make the same impression on you as you read them as they did on me during their telling.

Arria's husband, Caecina Paetus, was ill, so was their son, and it was thought that neither could recover. The son died, a most beautiful boy with an unassuming manner no less remarkable, and dear to his parents for reasons beyond the fact that he was their son. Arria made all the preparations for his funeral and took her place at the ceremony without her husband knowing; in fact whenever she entered his room she pretended that their son was still alive and even rather better, and, when Paetus kept asking how the boy was, she would answer that he had had a good sleep and was willing to take some food. Then when the tears she had held back for so long could no longer be kept from breaking out, she left the room; not till then did she give way to her grief. Her weeping over, she dried her eyes, composed her face, and returned as if she had left the loss of her child outside the room. It was a glorious deed, I know, to draw a dagger, plunge it into her breast, pull it out, and hand it to her husband with the immortal, almost divine words: 'It does not hurt, Paetus.' But on that well-known occasion she had fame and immortality before her eyes. It was surely even more heroic when she had no hope of any such reward, to stifle her tears, hide her grief, and continue to act the mother after she had lost her son.

At the time of the revolt against Claudius raised by Scribonianus in Illyricum,[2] Paetus had joined his party, and after Scribonianus's death was being brought as a prisoner to Rome. He was about to board ship when Arria begged the soldiers to take her with him. 'This is a senator of consular rank,' she insisted, 'and of course you will allow him a few slaves to serve his meals, dress him and put on his shoes;

1. See Introduction, page 22.
2. On the east coast of the Adriatic Sea (now a part of Jugoslavia).

all of which I can do for him myself.' Her request was refused. She then hired a small fishing smack, and the great ship sailed with her following in her tiny boat.

Again, when she came before Claudius and found the wife of Scribonianus volunteering to give evidence of the revolt, 'Am *I* to listen to *you*,' she cried, 'who could go on living after Scribonianus died in your arms?' This proves that her determination to die a glorious death was not a sudden impulse. Indeed, when her son-in-law Thrasea was trying to persuade her not to carry out her resolve, in the course of his argument he asked her whether if he ever had to die she would wish her daughter to die with him. 'If she lives as long and happily with you,' she said, 'as I have with Paetus – yes.' This answer increased the anxiety felt for her by her family and she was watched even more carefully. Perceiving this, 'It is no good,' she said. 'You can make me choose a painful death, but you cannot make it impossible.' With these words she leaped out of her chair and dashed her head against the wall opposite, so that she fell senseless from the violent blow. When she came round, 'I told you,' she said, 'that I should find a hard way to die if you denied me an easy one.'

Surely you think these words greater than the well-known 'It does not hurt, Paetus' which was their culmination? And yet this is widely famous, while the earlier sayings are not known at all. Hence the inference with which I began this letter, that the words and deeds which win fame are not always the greatest.

17. *To Julius Servianus*[1]

I have had no letter from you for such a long time – is it because all goes well? Or is the reason that all is well but you are too busy: or, if not actually busy, have you little or no opportunity to dispatch a letter? Please end my anxiety – I can't bear it. Do so even if you have to send a special messenger. I will pay his expenses and give him something for himself, as long as he brings me the news I want. I am well myself, if 'well' is the right word for living in such a state of worry and suspense, expecting and fearing to hear any moment that a dear friend has met with one of the accidents which can befall mankind.

1. He was probably serving with Trajan in the Dacian war of 101–2.

18. To Vibius Severus

My acceptance of the consulship brought with it the official duty of addressing a vote of thanks to the Emperor in the name of the State. After doing so in the Senate in the usual manner befitting the place and occasion, I thought it my proper duty as a loyal citizen to give the same subject a fuller and more elaborate treatment in a written version. I hoped in the first place to encourage our Emperor in his virtues by a sincere tribute, and, secondly, to show his successors what path to follow to win the same renown, not by offering instruction but by setting his example before them. To proffer advice on an Emperor's duties might be a noble enterprise, but it would be a heavy responsibility verging on insolence, whereas to praise an excellent ruler and thereby shine a beacon on the path posterity should follow would be equally effective without appearing presumptuous.

One thing has given me a great deal of pleasure. When I had decided to give a reading of the speech to my friends, I did not invite them by note or programme, but simply asked them to come 'if convenient' or if they 'really had time' (though as a matter of fact no one in Rome ever finds it convenient or really has time to attend public readings); the weather too was particularly bad, but nevertheless they attended two days running, and, when discretion would have put an end to the reading, they made me continue for a third day. Am I to look upon this as a tribute to myself or to the art of oratory? I hope the latter, as it is now enjoying a revival after almost dying out. And what was the subject which held their interest? A speech of thanks, which even in the Senate we used not to be able to endure without being bored after the first minute, can now find a reader and an audience willing to listen for three days on end, not through any improvement in our standard of eloquence, but because greater freedom of speech makes writing more of a pleasure. This is yet another tribute to our Emperor: a type of speech which used to be hated for its insincerity has become genuine and consequently popular today. But I much admired the critical sense as well as the enthusiasm of my audience, noticing that the least elaborate passages pleased them most. I have not forgotten that only a few friends have heard me read what I have written for the general public; but even so, my delight in their keen attentiveness makes me hopeful that popular opinion will coincide with theirs. I am also encouraged to hope that we may now have an audience in the theatre which will teach the players to perform properly, instead of encouraging the bad performances of the past. Every author who writes to please his public models his work on what he sees has given pleasure, and I personally am convinced that for this type of subject I did right to employ a livelier style, for a concise and terser manner is more likely to appear strained and artificial than the passages I wrote in a happier and more buoyant mood. Nevertheless, I still pray that some day the time will come – and I wish it had already – when these winning phrases, even where they are securely established, will withdraw their charms to make way for strict simplicity.

These then are my doings during the last three days. I wanted you to know them so that you could enjoy from afar the same pleasure as you would have had here, both on my account and for the cause of oratory.

19. To Calvisius Rufus

As usual, I am calling upon your expert advice on a matter of property. The estate adjoining my own[1] is for sale; the land runs in and out of mine, and, though there are many attractions tempting me to buy, there are some no less important reasons why I should not. The primary attraction is the obvious amenity if the properties were joined, and after that the practical advantage as well as the pleasure of being able to visit the two together without making more than one journey. Both could be put under the same steward and practically the same foremen, and it would only be necessary to maintain and furnish one house, so long as the other was kept in repair. In this account I include the cost of furniture, household staff, gardeners, workmen, and also hunting gear; for it makes a considerable difference whether one keeps all these in one place or distributes them between several. On the other hand I am afraid it may be rash to expose a property of such a size to the same uncertainties of weather and general risks, and it might be safer to meet the hazards of fortune by having estates in different localities; and then change of place and air is very enjoyable, and so is the actual travelling between one's possessions.

But the chief point for consideration is this. The land is fertile, the

1. As a native of Comum, Rufus would know about Pliny's estates in the district. This must be at Tifernum.

soil rich and well watered, and the whole made up of fields, vineyards, and woods which produce enough to yield a steady income if not a very large one. But this natural fertility is being exhausted by poor cultivation. The last owner on more than one occasion sold up the tenants' possessions, so that he temporarily reduced their arrears but weakened their resources for the future, and consequently their debts mounted up again. They will have to be set up and given a good type of slave, which will increase the expense; for nowhere do I employ chained slaves myself, and no one uses them there.

It remains for you to know the purchase price: three million sesterces. It used at one time to be five million, but this scarcity of tenants and the general bad times have reduced the income from the land and brought down its value. You will want to know if I can easily raise this three million. It is true that nearly all my capital is in land, but I have some investments and it will not be difficult to borrow. I can always have money from my mother-in-law, whose capital I am able to use as freely as my own. Don't let this worry you if you can dispose of the other points. I hope you will give them your full attention, for as regards the administration of large sums of money, as in everything else, you have abundant experience and wisdom.

20. *To Maesius Maximus*

You must have often read about the fierce controversy roused by the Ballot Act,[1] and the mixed praise and blame it brought its proposer; yet today the merits of the act have won the unanimous approval of the Senate. On the day of the recent elections everyone demanded voting-papers, for on the last occasions when we had publicly recorded our votes aloud we had certainly exceeded the disorders of the people's assemblies. No regard was paid to a time-limit in speaking, to the courtesy of not interrupting, nor even the propriety of remaining seated. On all sides rose the din of opposing cries: everyone rushed forward with his candidate and crowds mingled with small groups of people in the centre of the floor in disgraceful confusion. So far had we departed from our parents' procedure, where everything was calmly conducted in a restrained and orderly manner so as to maintain the honour and dignity of the House.

There are still some of the older generation living who have often

1. *Lex Gabinia* 139 B.C. and *lex Papiria* 131 B.C.

told me about their election procedure: the name of the candidate was read out and received in complete silence, after which he spoke on his own behalf, gave an account of his career and produced references to his character, either the commanding officer under whom he had served in the army or the governor whose quaestor he had been, and both if he could. He then called upon some of the electors supporting his candidature, who said a few sober words in his favour which carried more weight than entreaties. Sometimes the candidate would raise objections to his opponent's origin, age or character, and the Senate would hear him with strict attention. The result was that merit prevailed more often than mere popularity. But now that these practices have broken down through excessive personal influence, recourse was had to the secret ballot as a remedy, and, being a new and unaccustomed measure, for the time being it has proved successful. Yet I am afraid that as time goes on the remedy will breed its own abuses, with the risk of wanton irresponsibility finding a way in. Very few people are as scrupulously honest in secret as in public, and many are influenced by public opinion but scarcely anyone by conscience. It is too soon, though, to speak of the future; for the moment, thanks to the written vote, we are going to elect our public officials from the candidates who best deserve the honour. We have been called upon to pronounce an opinion in our elections with no more warning than is given at a summary trial, and have shown ourselves uncorrupted.

I have told you this primarily to give you some genuine news, and then to be able to talk a little about political matters; a subject which gives us fewer opportunities than in the old days, so none must be missed. Besides, hasn't the time come to give up the commonplace 'How are you? I hope you are well'? Our letters ought to contain something which rises above the trivialities and limitations of personal interests. Everything today, it is true, depends on the will of one man who has taken upon himself for the general good all our cares and responsibilities; yet mindful of our needs he sees that streams flow down to us from his fount of generosity so that we can draw on them ourselves and dispense them by letter to our absent friends.

21. *To Cornelius Priscus*

I am distressed to hear that Valerius Martial is dead. He was a man of great gifts, with a mind both subtle and penetrating, and his writings are remarkable for their combination of sincerity with pungency and wit. I had made him a present of his travelling expenses when he retired from Rome, in recognition of our friendship and the verses he wrote about me. It was the custom in the past to reward poets who had sung the praises of cities or individuals with gifts of office or money, but in our day this was one of the first things to fall out of fashion along with many other fine and honourable practices; for, now that we do nothing to merit a poet's tribute, it seems foolish to receive one.

You will want to know the verses which won my gratitude, and I would give you the reference had I not some of them by heart. If you like these, you can look up the others in his published works. The poet is addressing the Muse, telling her to seek my house on the Esquiline and approach it with respect:[1]

Muse, do not knock at his learned door drunk, and at time ill-chosen;
All the hours of his working day he devotes to crabbed Minerva,
While he prepares for the Hundred Court the speeches which after ages
Judge to be worthy of taking place by those of the son of Arpinum.
Wait till the lamps burn late and low, when Bacchus is ruling the revels,
Safer the night, when the brow is crowned with the rose and the hair
    drips perfume;
This is your hour, when the puritans' frown can relax with a smile for my
    verses.

Was I right then to part on such friendly terms from the author of these verses about me? Am I right to mourn his death now as one of my dearest friends? He gave me of his best, and would have given me more had he been able, though surely nothing more can be given to man than a tribute which will bring him fame and immortality. You may object that his verses will not be immortal; perhaps not, but he wrote them with that intention.

BOOK FOUR

1. To Calpurnius Fabatus, his wife's grandfather

Your granddaughter and I are touched to hear that you are anxious to see us both after so long an interval, and we share your feelings. I can't tell you how much we are looking forward to paying you both a visit, and it shall not be put off any longer – indeed, we are already packing so that we can travel as fast as the route we must follow permits. One thing will delay us, but not for long; we shall have to turn off to my place in Tuscany, not to look over the land and the house I have there – this can be put off to another time – but to perform what we feel is a necessary duty. Close to my property is the town of Tifernum on Tiber which adopted me as its patron when I was scarcely more than a child – its enthusiasm outrunning its discretion. The people always celebrate my arrivals, regret my departures, and rejoice in my official titles, and so to express my gratitude (one always feels disgraced at being outdone in friendly feeling) I defrayed the cost of building a temple in the town. As this is now completed, it would be sacrilegious to postpone its dedication any longer. So we shall be there for the day of the dedication, which I have decided to celebrate with a public feast, and we may have to stay on for the day following, but if so we will hurry over the journey the faster.

I only hope that we shall have the pleasure of finding you and your daughter well. It will certainly be a pleasure to see your happiness if we arrive safely.

2. To Attius Clemens

Regulus has lost his son, the one misfortune he did not deserve, but doubtless no real misfortune in his eyes. The boy was sharp-witted but unreliable; still he might have proved honest if he did not take after his father. Regulus released him from parental authority so that the boy could inherit his mother's estate, but having 'sold' him (so it was generally spoken of by those who knew the man's habits), he began to work on him with a disgusting show of indulgence, quite unnatural in a parent. It sounds incredible, but remember it was Regulus. Now that his son is dead he mourns with wild extravagance. The boy used to possess a number of Gallic ponies for riding and driving, also dogs of all sizes, and nightingales, parrots, and blackbirds; Regulus had them all slaughtered round his pyre. That was not grief, but parade of grief. It is amazing how he is now besieged by people who all loathe and detest him and yet flock round him in crowds as if they really loved and admired him. To put it briefly, they court Regulus by his own methods. He will not stir from his gardens beyond the Tiber, where he has covered a vast area with immense colonnades and littered the bank with his precious statues; for he is extravagant for all his avarice, and vainglorious in spite of his notoriety. Thus he upsets the whole city at the worst season of the year, and finds consolation in the nuisance he makes of himself.

He says he wants to marry again, and is as perverse on this point as he is in everything else. You will soon hear that the mourner is married, the old man is wed – the one too early and the other too late. How can I predict this? Not from anything Regulus has said, for nothing is less likely to be true, but because it is certain that Regulus will do whatever he should not.

3. To Arrius Antoninus

You have twice held the consulship with the dignity of a bygone age, and very few who have been governors of Asia before or after your term of office have proved your equal (your modesty forbids me to say there has been no one). In virtue, prestige and years you are our foremost citizen. So fine a record cannot fail to command respect, yet for your recreations I personally admire you even more. To temper a gravity like yours with a pleasantry no less remarkable, to combine such wit with your profound wisdom is an achievement as difficult as it is splendid; but you have been successful in the exceptional charm of your conversation, and even more so by your pen. When you speak the honey of Homer's Nestor seems to flow from your lips,[1]

1. *Iliad* 1 : 249.

while the bees fill your writings with sweetness culled from flowers. Such were certainly my impressions when I recently read your Greek epigrams and iambic mimes. Their sensitivity and grace, their charm and warmth of feeling, their wit which never wants propriety, made me imagine I held Callimachus or Herodas in my hands, or even some greater poet; though neither of them excelled in both types of verse nor even attempted them. Is such Greek possible for a Roman? Athens herself, believe me, could not be so Attic. In fact I envy the Greeks because you have preferred to write in their language; for it is easy to guess how you could express yourself in your native idiom when you can produce such masterpieces in a foreign and acquired tongue.

4. To Sosius Senecio

I am exceedingly fond of Varisidius Nepos; he is hard-working, honest, and trained in eloquence, a quality whereby I set great store. He is a near relative of my close friend Gaius Calvisius, who is also a friend of yours, and is in fact his sister's son. Please procure him the honour of a six-months' tribunate, both for his own and his uncle's sake. You will oblige me and our mutual friend Calvisius, and you will oblige Nepos himself, who is as worthy of being under obligation to you as you believe us to be. You have conferred many benefits on several people, but I venture to say that you have bestowed none more justly, and only one or two where they have been so well deserved.

5. To Julius Sparsus

There is a story that when the citizens of Rhodes asked Aeschines to read them a speech, he read first one of his own and then one of Demosthenes', and both were received with loud applause. It is no surprise to me that these great men won such a success with their orations, seeing that a recent speech of my own was given a two-days' hearing by a distinguished audience and was received with the same sort of enthusiasm and attentive concentration. And yet there was no comparison to be made between two speeches, nor any rivalry to rouse interest; for the Rhodians had both the respective merits of the speeches and the incentive of comparison to stimulate them, whereas my own won approval without gaining anything from competition. You will know if it was justly approved when you have read the published version – its length prevents me from introducing it to you in a longer letter. I must at least be brief where I can, in the hope of being excused for the length of the speech itself; though I don't think it is too long for the importance of the subject.

6. To Julius Naso

I hear that the hail has done a lot of damage to my property in Tuscany, and from beyond the Po comes the news that crops are very good but prices correspondingly low, so I have only Laurentum to bring me in anything. There I possess nothing but the house and garden and the adjoining sea-shore, but still it is the only place bringing something in. For there I do most of my writing, and, instead of the land I lack, I work to cultivate myself; so that I have a harvest in my desk to show you in place of full granaries elsewhere.

If then like me you want a property where you can be sure of a return, you should buy one on this coast.

7. To Catius Lepidus

I have often told you about Regulus's force of character. It is amazing how he carries out whatever he sets his heart on. He made up his mind to mourn his son, so he mourns as nobody ever did; he decided to commission as many statues and portraits of the boy as he possibly could, so he sets all the workshops busy portraying him in colour, in wax, bronze, silver, gold, ivory and marble. He even collected a vast audience the other day to hear him read a memoir of his son – the life of a mere boy, but nevertheless he read it, and has had countless copies made to distribute throughout Italy and the provinces. He has written an open letter to the town councils asking them to choose one of their number with the best voice to give a public reading of the work; and this has been done.

If he had applied to better ends this force (or whatever we are to call this determination to get one's own way), think how much good he could have done! And yet good men are less forceful than bad: 'Ignorance breeds confidence, reflection leads to hesitation'[1] as the saying goes, and so diffidence is the weakness of right-thinking minds, while depravity gains strength from reckless abandon. Regulus is

1. Thucydides, II, 40, 3.

proof of this. He has weak lungs, indistinct articulation, and a stammer, he is slow at finding the right word and has no memory, nothing in fact but a perverted ingenuity, and yet his crazy effrontery has won him the popular reputation of being an orator. So Herennius Senecio has cleverly adapted Cato's well-known definition of an orator to fit him: 'This orator is a bad man untrained in speaking.' Cato certainly did not define the real orator so neatly as Senecio has summed up Regulus!

Can you make me a proper return for a letter like this? You can if you will write and tell me whether any of my friends in your town – perhaps yourself – has had to read out this miserable effort of Regulus's, shouting in public like a cheap-jack, or, to quote Demosthenes, 'bawling in a loud and jubilant strain'.[1] For it is so absurd that it is more likely to meet with laughter than tears; you would think it was written *by* a boy rather than about one.

8. To Maturus Arrianus

Thank you for your very proper congratulations on my appointment to the office of augur: proper because in the first place it is an honour to accept the decisions of so wise a ruler as ours even in matters less important than this, and secondly because the priesthood is an old-established religious office and has a particular sanctity in that it is held for life. There are other positions no less honourable, but they can be bestowed and taken away, whereas in this the element of chance is limited to the bestowal. I can also think of a further reason for congratulation; I have taken the place of Julius Frontinus,[2] one of our greatest citizens, who in recent years never failed to put up my name for the priesthood on nomination day, with the apparent intention of making me his successor; so that now when events have approved of his choice, my election seems more than merely fortuitous. And you, as you say in your letter, are particularly pleased to see me an augur because Cicero held the same priesthood, and are glad that I am stepping into his offices as I am so anxious to make him my model in my literary work. As I have reached the same priesthood and consulship at a much earlier age than he did, I hope I may attain to something of

1. *De Corona*, 291.
2. The author of many technical works on military strategy, land surveying, and aqueducts.

his genius at least in later life. But whereas everything which man can bestow has fallen to my lot as it has to many another, such genius is difficult to achieve and almost too much to hope for; it can only be granted by the gods.

9. *To Cornelius Ursus*

The last few days have seen the trial of Julius Bassus, a much-harassed man who is notorious for his misfortunes. During Vespasian's reign a case was brought against him by two persons on their own account which was referred to the Senate. He was then left in suspense for a long time until finally found not guilty and acquitted. He was a friend of Domitian's, and consequently nervous of Titus; and then he was banished by Domitian. Recalled by Nerva, he drew the province of Bithynia and returned from there to stand trial, in the course of which he was violently attacked and loyally defended. The opinion of the court was divided on his sentence, but the majority took a more lenient view.

Pomponius Rufus, a ready and forceful speaker, opened the case against him and was followed by Theophanes, the representative of the province mainly responsible for sparking off the prosecution. I replied. Bassus had entrusted me with the task of laying the foundations of the whole defence, and my instructions were to refer to his official distinctions (and these because of his noble birth and hazardous career were not inconsiderable), then deal with the informers who were plotting to make a profit for themselves, and finally speak of the reasons for his unpopularity with every disturber of the peace, such as Theophanes himself. He had also declared it his wish that I should meet the principal charge against him; for on the other points, which sounded more serious, he really deserved congratulations as well as acquittal, whereas what weighed heavily against him was the fact that in all innocence he had thoughtlessly accepted certain gifts from the provincials as their friend (he had been quaestor in the same province). These his prosecutors called thefts and plunder, while he declared they were presents.

But the acceptance of presents is also forbidden by law.[1] How then was I to answer this, and what line of defence should I take? If I denied everything, I was afraid that an action which I dare not admit would

1. *Lex Julia Repetundarum*, 59 B.C.

be taken for an obvious theft. Besides, to deny a palpable fact was more likely to increase the gravity of the charge than to remove it, especially as the defendant had not given us a free hand at all; for he had told many people, including the Emperor himself, that he had accepted gifts, but only small ones, and only on his birthday and during the Saturnalia, and had usually sent something in return. Was I then to plead for mercy? It would be the death of my client to admit that his guilt made it impossible for anything short of mercy to save him. Should I attempt to justify his conduct? That would not help him, and would expose me to the charge of irresponsibility. Amidst these difficulties I decided to steer a middle course, and I believe I was successful.

Nightfall interrupted my speech, as it does a battle. I had spoken for three and a half hours, and still had an hour and a half, for, as the law allowed six hours to the prosecution and nine hours to the defence, Bassus had divided the time between me and the speaker to follow so that I should have five hours and he the remaining four. The success of my speech made me feel that I should stop and say no more, for it is risky not to rest content when things are going well. I was also afraid that my strength would fail with a renewed effort, for it is harder to make a new start than to go straight on. There was, too, the danger that the rest of my speech would meet with a cold reception after the interruption, or seem tedious when it was resumed. A torch will stay lit if it is kept moving, but, if once the spark is lost, it is difficult to revive it again; similarly, continuity keeps up a speaker's fire and an audience's attention, but both weaken once the tension is relaxed and broken. But Bassus begged and besought me almost in tears to take my full time, and I yielded, putting his interests before my own. All went well, and I found the attention of the Senate as keen and fresh as if it had been stimulated rather than sated by my first speech.

I was followed by Lucceius Albinus, whose apt choice of phrase made it appear that we combined the variety of our separate speeches with the continuity of a single one. Herennius Pollio made a forceful and well-reasoned reply, and then Theophanes spoke again. Here, too, he showed his lack of discretion, not only in claiming time to address the court after two accomplished speakers of consular rank, but also in continuing at length; for darkness fell while he was still speaking and he went on after dark when lamps were brought in. The following day Homullus and Fronto made an excellent defence of Bassus, and the fourth day was spent on examination of witnesses.

Then the consul-elect, Baebius Macer, proposed that Bassus should be dealt with under the law dealing with restitution of monies extorted, and Caepio Hispo that his penalty should be assessed by commission without loss of status. Both were correct, though you may wonder how this is possible when their proposals differed so widely. Macer looked to the letter of the law, and so quite rightly condemned a man who had accepted gifts illegally; whereas Caepio, taking the view that the Senate has the power (as indeed it has) to reduce or increase the severity of the law, had reason to excuse an action which was illegal, strictly speaking, but not without precedent. Caepio's proposal was carried; in fact on rising to speak he was greeted with the applause which is usually given when a speaker resumes his seat. You can judge then how his actual speech was received, when it was thus welcomed in anticipation. However, public opinion is no more unanimous than that of the Senate; those who approve of Caepio's proposal criticize Macer's for being too strict and severe, while others support Macer and call Caepio's suggestion lax and even illogical, saying that it is inconsistent for a man who has had a penalty assessed against him to retain his place in the Senate.

There was also a third opinion. Valerius Paulinus agreed with Caepio, but made the further proposal that the Senate should deal with Theophanes as soon as he had made his report on his commission; for it was clear that during his work for the prosecution he had committed a number of offences which came under the same law as that under which he had accused Bassus. But the consuls did not follow up this proposal, although it found great favour with the majority of the Senate. Paulinus at any rate won credit for making a firm stand for justice. When the court rose, Bassus was met by crowds of people clamouring to demonstrate their delight.[1] He had won public sympathy by the revival of the old story of his hazardous career, by his name, famous for his troubles in the past, and by the spectacle of his tall figure, bent with the afflictions and poverty of his old age.

This letter comes to you as a forerunner of the whole speech, which follows burdened with its details; you will have a long wait for it, as

1. But his acts in Bithynia were rescinded; see x : 56.

more than a superficial and cursory handling is needed for a subject of such importance.

10. To Statius Sabinus

I understand from your letter that Sabina in making us her heirs left us no instructions that her slave Modestus was to be given his freedom, but even so left him a legacy in the words: 'To Modestus whom I have ordered to be set free'; and you would like to hear my view. I have consulted the legal experts, and it was their unanimous opinion that Modestus should receive neither his freedom, as it was not expressly granted, nor his legacy, as it was bequeathed to him while his status was that of a slave. But it seems to me obvious that it was a mistake on Sabina's part, and I think we ought to act as if she had set out in writing what she believed she had written. I am sure you will agree with me, for you are always most scrupulous about carrying out the intention of the deceased. Once understood, it should be legally binding on an honest heir, as honour puts us under an obligation as binding as necessity is for other people. Let us then allow Modestus to have his liberty and enjoy his legacy as if Sabina had taken every proper precaution. She did in fact do so by her wise choice of heirs.

11. To Cornelius Minicianus

Have you heard that Valerius Licinianus is teaching rhetoric in Sicily? The news has only just come so I doubt if it will have reached you yet. It is not long since this senator of praetorian rank was considered one of the best advocates in Rome. Now he has sunk to his present position – the senator is an exile and the orator a teacher of rhetoric.

So in his introductory lecture these melancholy words made a great impression: 'O fortune, how you sport with us! You turn senators into teachers and teachers into senators.' (Such rancour and bitterness makes me wonder whether he turned teacher to be able to voice it.) Then, when he had made his entry clad in a Greek cloak (those who have been ritually banished are not allowed to wear the toga), he made himself ready, looked down at his dress, and announced that he would deliver his speech in Latin. All this, you may say, is pitiably sad but no more than the just fate of a man who disgraced his profession by the crime of violation of a Vestal Virgin.[1] But though Licinianus admitted this offence, it is not clear whether he did so because the charge was well founded or because he feared a worse one if he denied it. For at the time Domitian was beside himself with fury, raging at being left without witnesses when he had made up his mind to bury alive Cornelia, the chief priestess of the Vestal Virgins, with the idea of making his age famous by an example of this kind. Acting on his powers as Chief Pontiff, or rather displaying a tyrant's cruelty and a despot's licence, he summoned the other priests to meet at his Alban palace instead of in the Regia, and then condemned Cornelia in absence and unheard; thereby committing a crime as great as the one he made a show of punishing. He declared her guilty of violating her vows of chastity, although he had violated his own niece in an incestuous relationship and ended by causing her death, for she died as the result of an abortion during her widowhood. The priests were dispatched at once to carry out the burial and execution. Meanwhile Cornelia invoked the aid now of Vesta, now of the other gods, and amidst her many protestations was heard the frequent cry: 'How can the Emperor imagine I could have broken my vows when it was I who performed the sacred rites to bring him victories and triumphs!' It is not known whether she said this in mockery or to soften the Emperor's heart, through confidence in herself or out of contempt for him, but she continued to repeat it until she was led to her death. Whether she was innocent or not, she certainly appeared to be so. Moreover, when she was taken down into the famous underground chamber and her robe caught as she descended, as she turned to free it the assassin offered her his hand; but she drew away in disgust and thrust his loathsome touch from her pure and spotless person as if by a last act of chastity, and then, with due observance of the rules of modesty, like Polyxena she 'took great care to fall in decent fashion'.[2] Furthermore, when Celer, the Roman knight charged with being her accomplice, was publicly scourged, he never ceased to demand the reason and insist that he had done nothing.

Consequently Domitian was infuriated by the hatred he had incurred for his cruelty and injustice, and arrested Licinianus on the

1. The Vestal Virgins were the six priestesses in charge of the cult of the Roman hearth-goddess.
2. Euripides, *Hecuba*, 569.

grounds of having hidden one of Cornelia's freedwomen on his estate. Licinianus was advised by those interested in him that if he wished to escape a public scourging he should have recourse to confession and beg for mercy. This he did. Herennius Senecio spoke for him in his absence, rather after the style of the well-known 'Patroclus is dead';[1] for 'I come here as a messenger, not a defending counsel,' he said: 'Licinianus has withdrawn his defence.' This pleased Domitian so much that he betrayed himself by his delight. 'Licinianus has acquitted us!' he cried, and even went so far as to say there was no need to follow up his reasons for submission. Licinianus was accordingly granted permission to remove any of his possessions he could before they were confiscated, and was given easy conditions of exile as a reward. Later, however, he was allowed to move to Sicily through the generosity of the deified Emperor Nerva, and there he is teaching today (and avenging himself on Fortune in his introductions).

You see how readily I obey your orders, sending you news from abroad as well as writing about city affairs, and going into all the details; for I felt sure that as you were away at the time you would have heard nothing about Licinianus except his sentence of banishment for violating a Vestal. Gossip gives only the gist of events, not their sequence. I deserve to have a letter from you in return telling me what is happening in your town and neighbourhood – there is always something worth mentioning. In fact tell me whatever you like, only see that your letter is as long as mine. I shall count not only the pages but every line and syllable.

12. To Maturus Arrianus

I know you are very fond of Egnatius Marcellinus, when you are always recommending him to me, and you will love him all the more when you hear of something he did recently during his service abroad as quaestor. He had in his possession a sum of money intended for the salary of the secretary allotted to him who had died before the day his salary was due; and, feeling strongly that he ought not to retain this, he consulted the Emperor on his return, and with his permission the Senate, to know what was to be done with it. It was a small point, but a genuine one. The secretary's heirs claimed the money for themselves and the Treasury officials for the State. The

1. Quintilian, *Institutio Oratoria*, x, 1, 49, quoting *Iliad* xVIII : 20.

case was brought to court, where the representatives of the heirs and the State spoke in turn, both very much to the point; then Baebius Macer proposed that the money should be given to the heirs and Caecilius Strabo that it should be paid into the Treasury. This latter proposal was carried, but do give Marcellinus a word of praise, as I did on the spot; for, although he is amply rewarded by having won the approval of the Emperor and the Senate, he will still be glad to have your tribute. Everyone who is influenced by thoughts of honour and reputation takes an extraordinary pleasure in words of praise and appreciation even from a lesser man than himself, and in your case Marcellinus has such a high regard for you that he sets great store by your opinion. And, besides, if he knows that the news of his action has reached as far as your ears, he cannot help being delighted to think that his fame has spread so far and travelled so fast. For some reason it is widespread rather than outstanding fame which most men prefer.

13. *To Cornelius Tacitus*

I am glad to hear of your safe arrival in Rome: it is always the news I want most, and particularly so just now. I shall have to stay a few more days in Tusculum[1] to finish some work I am busy with, for I am afraid that if I let my present concentration slacken now that I am so near the end I shall find it difficult to start again. Meanwhile, to lose no time in my impatience, here is a begging letter as a sort of fore-runner to the request I intend to make in person; but you must first hear the reasons for this.

I was visiting my native town a short time ago when the young son of a fellow-citizen came to pay his respects to me. 'Do you go to school?' I asked. 'Yes,' he replied. 'Where?' 'In Mediolanum.'[2] 'Why not here?' To this the boy's father (who had brought him and was standing by) replied: 'Because we have no teachers here.' 'Why not? Surely it is a matter of great importance to you fathers (and luckily there were several fathers listening) that your children should study here on the spot? Where can they live more happily than in their native place? Where can they be brought up more strictly than under their parent's eye or with less expense than at home? If you put your money together, what would it cost you to engage teachers? And you could add to their salaries what you now spend on lodgings,

1. In Latium (near Frascati).   2. Milan.

travelling-expenses, and all the things which cost money away from home – and that means everything. Now, as I have not yet any children of my own, I am prepared to contribute a third of whatever sum you decide to collect, as a present for our town such as I might give to a daughter or my mother. I would promise the whole amount were I not afraid that someday my gift might be abused for someone's selfish purposes, as I see happen in many places where teachers' salaries are paid from public funds. There is only one remedy to meet this evil: if the appointment of teachers is left entirely to the parents, and they are conscientious about making a wise choice through their obligation to contribute to the cost. People who may be careless about another person's money are sure to be careful about their own, and they will see that only a suitable recipient shall be found for my money if he is also to have their own. So you should meet and come to some agreement; be encouraged by my generosity, for I want my own contribution to be as large as possible. You can do nothing better for your children, nothing more welcome for our town. The children born here should be brought up on their native soil, so that from their earliest years they may learn to love it and choose to stay at home. I hope that you will introduce teachers of repute, so that nearby towns will seek education here, and, instead of sending your children elsewhere as you do today, you will see other children flocking here to you.'

I thought I ought to give you a full account of this incident from the start so that you may be assured of my gratitude if you will carry out my request. I am prompted to make it by the genuine importance of the matter. From amongst the many students who gather round you in admiration for your abilities, will you please look for teachers for us to invite here, but on the understanding that I am not committed to anyone? I am leaving everything open for the parents: the decision and choice are to be theirs – all I want is to make the arrangements and pay my share. So if you find anyone who has confidence in his ability, send him to us, as long as he understands that his confidence is the only certainty he brings!

14. To Plinius (?) Paternus

Perhaps you want a speech of mine as usual and are expecting one, but I have some trifles to offer, something choice and exotic from my store. With this letter you will receive some hendecasyllables of mine with which I amuse myself when I have time to spare in my carriage, my bath, or at dinner. Here are my jokes and witticisms, my loves, sorrows, complaints and vexations; now my style is simple, now more elevated, and I try through variety to appeal to different tastes and produce a few things to please everyone. But if some of the passages strike you as rather indelicate, your reading ought to tell you how many distinguished and serious writers in dealing with such themes neither avoided lascivious subjects nor refrained from expressing them in plain language. If I have shrunk from this, it is not because my principles are stricter than theirs (why should they be?) but because I am less courageous; and yet I know that the best rule for this kind of thing is the one in Catullus, when he says that 'the true poet should be chaste himself, though his poetry need not be, for it must be relaxed and free from restraint if it is to have wit and charm'.[1]

You can judge how much I value your opinion from the fact that I have preferred to submit the whole work to your criticism rather than pick out passages for you to admire, though admittedly these lose some of their excellence if they show signs of monotony. Moreover, an intelligent and discerning reader should not compare totally different passages, but should judge each one on its own merits, nor think one inferior to another if each is perfect of its own kind. Here I will stop, for to excuse or recommend my follies in a long preamble would be the height of folly. One thing I think I must tell you now: I intend to give these trifles of mine the title of 'hendecasyllables', which refers only to the metre in which they are written. You call them what you like – epigrams, idylls, eclogues, or simply 'short poems', which is the popular name, but I shall stick to my 'hendecasyllables'. Please be honest, and tell me now what you are likely to say about my book to someone else. It is not much to ask, for if this little work were my chief or sole effort it might possibly seem unkind to tell me to 'find something else to do'; but there is nothing unkind in the gentle reminder that I '*have* something else to do'.

15. To Minicius Fundanus

If anything is proof that I do not lack judgement, it must be my special affection for Asinius Rufus. He is an exceptional person, the devoted admirer of every good citizen, of whom I hope I may count myself

1. Catullus, XVI: 5.

one. He is also the close friend of Cornelius Tacitus, and you know the sort of man Tacitus is. So, if you think highly of us both, you should feel the same about Rufus, since there is no stronger bond in friendship than similarity of character. He has several children, for here too he has done his duty as a good citizen, and has chosen to enjoy the blessing of a fruitful marriage at a time when the advantages of remaining childless make most people feel a single child a burden. Such advantages he has scorned, and has in fact sought the title of grandfather: and a grandfather he is, thanks to his son-in-law Saturius Firmus, whom you will appreciate as much as I do when you know him as well.

All this is to show you what a large and numerous family you can oblige by a single service, which I am led to seek through my own desires and also by my feeling of good omen for the future. I am anxious for you to hold the consulship next year, and prophesy that you will do so, for both your own merits and the Emperor's discernment surely point that way. It happens that this will be the year when Asinius Bassus, Rufus's eldest son, will be quaestor, and this young man is even better than his father, though I hesitate to say what the father wants me to think and say but the son is too modest to allow. It is difficult for you to take my word (though you usually trust me) for the exceptional industry and honesty, learning and ability, application and memory of a man you have not met, but you will discover all when you know him. I only wish our times were rich enough in merit for there to be others you ought to prefer to Bassus. I should then be the first to advise you seriously to look round and take time to consider before making your choice. As things are – but I do not want to presume too far in speaking of my friend; I will only say that the young man is worthy to be treated as your son, as our forefathers did their quaestors. Wise officials like yourself should welcome these young men as children given by the State, to stand in the same position as the sons we hope nature will give us all. It will befit your status as consul for you to have a quaestor whose father was a praetor and whose relatives were consuls, and one who in their opinion already does them credit even at his early age.

So grant my prayers, take my advice, but first of all forgive me if I seem to be hurrying matters. Affection usually runs ahead with its demands, and, besides, in a country where opportunities have to be seized for anything to be done, if things wait for their due season they ripen not in time, but too late; and, finally, anticipation of the object desired brings its own pleasure. Give Bassus the opportunity to wait on you as his consul, and give him your affection as your quaestor; and let me enjoy a twofold happiness in my love for you both. My regard for you and Bassus is such that I should use all my resources, energy and influence to help Bassus to be elected quaestor to any consul, and to support your quaestor whoever he might be: so it will give me great pleasure if my interests can be centred in the same young man, thanks to my double friendship and your prospective consulship; if in fact it is you who will further my wishes by giving him your support, seeing that the Senate is so ready to accept your decisions and has the highest confidence in your recommendations.

16. To Valerius Paulinus

Rejoice, I tell you, on my account and your own, and no less for our country; for oratory is still held in honour. When I was on my way the other day to plead before the Centumviral Court, there was no room left for me to take my place except by way of the magistrates' bench, through their assembled ranks, as the rest of the floor was crowded. And then a young patrician who had had his clothing torn, as often happens in a crowd, stayed on clad in nothing but his toga to listen for seven hours – which was the length of the speech I made, one which cost me much effort but brought a greater reward. So we must work at our profession and not make anyone else's idleness an excuse for our own. There is no lack of readers and listeners; it is for us to produce something worth being written and heard.

17. To Clusinius Gallus

I have your reminder of the case Gaius Caecilius, the consul-elect, is bringing against Corellia, and your request that I take charge of the defence in her absence. Thank you for the reminder, but I must protest against the request. I know I need to be reminded for my own information, but I ought not to be asked to do what would be disgraceful for me to leave undone. How can I hesitate to defend a daughter of Corellius? It is true that I am on friendly though not on intimate terms with the man you ask me to oppose; there is, moreover, his position to consider and the office to which he has been elected, for which I feel a special respect as I have already held it myself, and it is natural for anyone to wish high honour to a position he has once occupied. But every other consideration fades into insignificance beside the thought that it is Corellius's daughter whom I am to defend.

I can see him now, the greatest influence, the purest character, and the most penetrating intellect of our age. I came to love him through my admiration, and, contrary to the general rule, when I knew him intimately I admired him even more. For I did know him intimately; he kept nothing hidden from me, whether grave or gay, joy or sorrow. I was only a young man at the time, and yet he showed me the regard and, I will venture to say, the respect he would have shown an equal. When I sought office he gave me his support as sponsor, I was introduced and attended by him when I entered upon my duties, and had him for guide and counsellor while I discharged them. Indeed, throughout my official career he displayed the vigour of youth, despite his failing health and advancing age. What a reputation he built up for me, personal and public, until it even reached the ears of the Emperor! For there was an occasion when a discussion arose before the Emperor Nerva about the promising young men of the day and several people were singing my praises; for a time Corellius kept the silence which used to give his next words such weight, and then, in the impressive tones you will remember, 'I must be moderate in my praise of Pliny,' he said, 'seeing that he has my advice for everything he does.' In these words he paid me a tribute far beyond what I could have presumed to hope for, in implying that I did nothing which fell short of the highest wisdom, since I did everything with the advice of the wisest of men. Moreover, when he was dying he told his daughter (it is she who tells the story) that he had made many friends for her in the course of a long life, but none like Pliny and Cornutus Tertullus.

I can never recall this without realizing that I must endeavour not to fail in any degree the trust placed in me by one so thoughtful for the future. So I am very ready to appear for Corellia, and will not shrink from giving offence by doing so; and yet I venture to hope for pardon and even praise from the very opponent who is bringing what you call this novel form of action (possibly because it is directed against a woman) if I have an opportunity in the course of my defence to give a fuller expression to these thoughts than is possible in the limited space of a letter, hoping thereby to win forgiveness or even approval for my conduct.

18. To Arrius Antoninus

I have been trying to make a successful Latin translation of some of your Greek epigrams; can I give you any better proof of my admiration? A change for the worse, I know, the main reason being the inadequacy of my own talent, and then the limitations, or rather what Lucretius calls 'the poverty of our native tongue'.[1] But if these translations – into Latin and by me – retain for you any of their charm, you can imagine the delight I take in the originals – written in Greek and by you!

19. To Calpurnia Hispulla

You are a model of family affection, and loved your excellent and devoted brother as dearly as he loved you; you love his daughter as if she were your own, and, by filling the place of the father she lost, you are more than an aunt to her. I know then how glad you will be to hear that she has proved herself worthy of her father, her grandfather and you. She is highly intelligent and a careful housewife, and her devotion to me is a sure indication of her virtue. In addition, this love has given her an interest in literature: she keeps copies of my works to read again and again and even learn by heart. She is so anxious when she knows that I am going to plead in court, and so happy when all is over! (She arranges to be kept informed of the sort of reception and applause I receive, and what verdict I win in the case.) If I am giving a reading she sits behind a curtain near by and greedily drinks in every word of appreciation. She has even set my verses to music and sings them, to the accompaniment of her lyre, with no musician to teach her but the best of masters, love.

All this gives me the highest reason to hope that our mutual happiness will last for ever and go on increasing day by day, for she does not love me for my present age nor my person, which will gradually grow old and decay, but for my aspirations to fame; nor would any other feelings be suitable for one brought up by your hands and trained in your precepts, who has seen only what was pure and moral in your company and learned to love me on your

1. *De Rerum Natura*, 1 : 832.

recommendation. For you respected my mother-like a daughter, and have given me guidance and encouragement since my boyhood; you always foretold that I should become the man I am now in the eyes of my wife. Please accept our united thanks for having given her to me and me to her as if chosen for each other.

20. To Novius Maximus

I gave you my views on each section of your book as I finished reading it; now you shall have my general opinion of the work as a whole. It is a noble achievement, powerful and penetrating: its language is dignified, varied and well chosen, the style pure and rich in metaphor, the comprehensive scale has a breadth which will win you recognition. You are swept on by the force of genius as well as of indignation, and these have reinforced each other; genius has added dignity and grandeur to your indignation, and this in its turn has given your genius power and fury.

21. To Velius Cerealis

This premature death of Helvidius's daughters is tragic – both sisters giving birth to girls and dying in labour. I am deeply distressed, and not unduly, for these were noble young women in the flower of their youth and I must mourn to see them the victims of their motherhood. I grieve too for the plight of their infants left motherless at birth, and for their excellent husbands, and I grieve no less on my own account; for my love for their father has remained constant since his death, as my defence of him and my published speeches bear witness. Now only one of his three children survives, left as the sole prop and stay of a family which not so long ago had many members to support it. But if Fortune will keep him at least safe and sound, and make him as fine a man as his father and his grandfather, I can take comfort in my sorrow. I am all the more anxious for his safety and character now that he is the last of his line. You know my nervous apprehensions for anyone I love, so you must not be surprised at my fears being worst where my hopes are highest.

22. To Sempronius Rufus

I have just answered a summons to act as assessor to our noble Emperor during an inquiry he is holding on the gymnastic games at

Vienna.[1] These used to be celebrated under the terms of some person's will until Trebonius Rufinus (a distinguished citizen and a friend of mine) became a local magistrate and took steps to have them suppressed and abolished. It was then claimed that he had no official power to do this. Rufinus spoke eloquently in his own defence and won his case; for his speech won favour by the promptitude and dignity, suitable to a true Roman and a good citizen, with which he dealt with a personal issue. When the magistrates were asked in turn for their verdict, that staunch champion of honesty, Junius Mauricus, declared that the games should not be restored at Vienna, and added that he wished they could also be abolished at Rome. This showed great courage and resolution on his part, you will say, but surely this is nothing new for Mauricus. He displayed the same courage in the hearing of the Emperor Nerva. Nerva was dining with a small party where Veiento was his neighbour at table, and was even leaning on his shoulder – I need do no more than name the creature. The conversation turned on the blind Catullus Messalinus whose loss of sight had increased his cruel disposition, so that he knew neither fear, shame nor pity, and consequently was often used by Domitian to aim at honest men like a weapon which flies blindly and unthinkingly to its mark. Everyone at table was talking freely about his villainy and murderous decisions when the Emperor said: 'I wonder what would have happened to him if he were alive today.' 'He would be dining with us', said Mauricus.

I have wandered rather far from the point, but not however unintentionally. It was decided to abolish the games at Vienna, for they had long been a corrupting influence in the town. In the same way our games at Rome spread a more general corruption, since the vices of Vienna go no farther than their town, but ours travel far and wide. The most serious diseases of the body, personal or politic, are those which spread from the head.

23. To Pomponius Bassus

I was delighted to hear from our mutual friends that you are showing your natural wisdom in planning and spending your retirement. You live in a lovely spot, you can take exercise on the shore and in the sea, and have no lack of conversation or books to read and have read to

1. In Gallia Narbonensis, on the Rhône (now Vienne).

you, so that every day you can add something to your store of knowledge. This is the right way to grow old for a man who has held the
highest civil offices, commanded armies, and devoted himself entirely
to the service of the State as long as it was proper for him to do so.
It is our duty to give up our youth and manhood to our country, but
our last years are our own; this the law itself suggests in permitting
the old to retire. I wonder when this will be permitted me – when
shall I reach the honourable age which will allow me to follow your
example of a graceful retirement, when my withdrawal will not be
termed laziness but rather a desire for peace?

24. To Fabius Valens

The other day, when I had just finished addressing a joint session of
the four panels of the Centumviral Court, I remembered a speech
which I had made as a young man in the same court. As usual my
thoughts travelled on, and I began to reckon up the people with
whom I had worked on the present occasion and the earlier one. I was
the only person present who had spoken in both cases; such are the
changes due to mortal frailty or the fickleness of fortune. Some of
those who had spoken then are dead, others are in exile: age and ill-
health has silenced one man, another has chosen to enjoy the blessings
of retirement, another holds a military command, and another has
given up his career to become the Emperor's personal friend. In my
own case I have known many changes. My profession brought me
advancement, then danger, then advancement again; I was helped by
my friendship with honest men, then injured, and now helped again.
If you add up the years it would not seem very long, but it would be
a lifetime if you count the changes of fortune. This should be a warning never to lose heart and to be sure of nothing, when we see so
many fluctuations of fortune following each other in rapid succession.

It is a habit of mine to share my thoughts with you and to set out
for your guidance the rules and examples which shape my own conduct. That was the purpose of this letter.

25. To Maesius Maximus

I told you in my last letter[1] that there was a risk of the secret ballot's
leading to abuses, and this has already happened. At the recent election

some of the voting papers were found to have jokes and obscenities scribbled on them, and on one the names of the candidates were replaced by those of their sponsors. This incensed the Senate and members clamoured for the wrath of the Emperor to be visited on the culprit; but he kept quiet and undetected – he may even have joined in the general indignation. If this man can play such ribald tricks in an important matter on a serious occasion, and thinks the Senate is the place where he can pass for a nimble wit and a fine fellow, what are we to suppose his personal conduct can be? This is the confidence unprincipled characters derive from the assurance that 'No one will know'. This man could ask for a voting-paper, take a pen, and bend his head to write, with neither fear of anyone nor any self-respect. The result was that ribaldry fit for nothing but the vulgar stage. Where is one to turn in search of a remedy? Everywhere the disease has gone too far to be checked. 'But this will concern the power above' whose daily task of vigilance is greatly increased by the futile impudence in our midst which we cannot control.

26. To Maecilius Nepos

You want me to re-read and correct the copies of my speeches which you have assembled with such care. Of course I will, for there is nothing which I ought to do so gladly, especially at your request. When a man of your judgement, scholarship and eloquence (and moreover as busy as yourself and the future governor of an important province) thinks my writings worth carrying around with him, I should surely do my utmost to see that this item of luggage is not a useless encumbrance. My first care then shall be to make your present travelling companions as congenial as possible; and my second to provide you with more which you may like to add to them on your return. The fact that you are one of my readers is no small encouragement to new work.

27. To Pompeius Falco

For the last three days I have been present at a reading given by Sentius Augurinus which gave me great pleasure and filled me with admiration for his works. He calls them 'short poems'. Many are simple, many in the grand style: many are full of delicate charm and express either tender feeling or indignation. It is many years, I think, since anything of this kind has attained such perfection, unless my judgement is affected by my feeling for Augurinus or the fact that he has paid me a tribute in taking my occasional attempts at versifying as a theme. You may be judge of my opinion if I can remember the second line of this: I have all the others clear in my mind.

> My verse is light and tender, as Catullus long ago,
> But what care I for poets past, when I my Pliny know?
> Outside the courts in mutual love and song he makes his name;
> You lovers and you statesmen, to Pliny yield your fame!

This will give you an idea of the wit and polished perfection of his style, and I can promise you that it is a true specimen of the whole book. As soon as it is published I will send it to you. Meanwhile, give the young poet your affection, and congratulate our age on having produced such talent allied to fine character. He spends much time with Spurinna and Antoninus, being related to one and the close friend of both, and from this you may estimate the merit of a young man who has thus won the affection of his elders and superiors in judgement. Nothing is more true than that 'you may know a man by the company he keeps'.

28. To Vibius Severus

The well-known scholar Herennius Severus is very anxious to hang in his library portraits of your fellow-townsmen, Cornelius Nepos and Titus Catius,[1] and asks me to have the originals copied in colour if, as seems likely, they are in your possession. I am passing on his request to you rather than anyone else for three reasons: your usual kindness in falling in with my wishes, your deep admiration for literature and warm feeling for its students, and your affectionate regard for your native place and for all who have made its name famous. All I ask is that you find as accurate a painter as you can, for it is hard enough to make a likeness from life, but a portrait from a portrait is by far the most difficult of all. Please do not let the artist you choose depart from the original even to improve on it.

1. Nepos, the historian, and Catius, an Epicurean philosopher, both from the Insubrian district of Cisalpine Gaul; the town may be Milan.

29. To Romatius Firmus[1]

Now then, you really must come along somehow to take your place on the bench next time the court is sitting – you can't rely on me to let you sleep soundly; if you default, you will suffer. Along comes our stern praetor Licinius Nepos: bold man, he has just fined a senator! The culprit made his defence before the Senate, but he had to plead for pardon. He was let off the fine, but he had a fright; he had need of mercy and had to beg for it. You may say that all praetors are not so strict, but you are wrong there. It may take a strict one to establish or revive such a precedent, but once that is done the mildest of men can act on it.

30. To Licinius Sura[2]

I have brought you a small present from my native place – a problem fully worthy of your great learning. There is a spring which has its source in a mountain and then runs down over the rocks to a small artificial grotto, where it is caught and held for a time; then it flows down into Lake Como. This is its remarkable feature: three times a day it fills and empties with a regular increase and decrease of water, and this can be seen quite clearly and is a great pleasure to watch. You settle yourself close by for a meal and also a drink from the ice-cold water of the spring; meanwhile it ebbs and flows at regular intervals. Put a ring or anything else on the margin where it is dry, and the waters gently creep over it until it is covered, then reveal it again as they gradually recede. If you watch long enough you can see the process repeated a second and third time.

Is there some hidden current of air which opens and closes the vent and outlet of the spring, possibly by blocking the way on entry and leaving it free when forced out? We see this happen in the case of bottles and similar vessels with narrow restricted necks, which, though tilted downwards, pour out their contents in jerks with a repeated gulping sound as if checked by the opposing inrush of air. Or is the spring substantially the same as the sea, so that its lesser volume of water is alternately driven back and forth by the same laws which govern the ebb and flow of the tide? Or is there something to drive back the outflow of the spring in the same way as rivers flowing into

1. Of Comum. 2. Trajan's friend and famous general.

the sea are turned back if they meet an opposing force of wind and tide? Or is there a fixed supply of water in a hidden channel, so that the stream diminishes and flows slowly while water accumulates after it has emptied, but flows faster and increases when the supply is sufficient? Or is there some force of water hidden out of sight which sets the spring in motion when it has drained away, but checks and cuts off the flow when it has filled up? It is for you to investigate the cause of this phenomenon, as you have the ability. I have done more than enough if I have managed to describe it clearly.

BOOK FIVE

1. *To Annius Severus*

I have just come in for a legacy: not a large one, but more welcome
than a substantial sum for reasons which I will explain. The donor,
Asudius Curianus, had previously been disinherited by his mother,
Pomponia Galla, who had then divided her estate between myself, the
senator and ex-praetor Sertorius Severus, and several distinguished
Roman knights. Curianus had begged me to present him with my
share and help him by setting a precedent, on the tacit understanding
that he should eventually restore the capital untouched. I replied that
it was not my nature to do one thing in public and another in private,
nor did I think it honest to make a present of money to a rich and
childless man; in short, that I could do him no good by giving him my
share, but he would benefit if I waived my claim to it. This I was
willing to do only if I was satisfied that he had been unfairly disinherited. He then asked me to hold an inquiry, and after some hesitation
I agreed, remarking that as he apparently thought me capable of doing
so I saw no reason not to share his opinion, but reminding him that
I should not hesitate to pronounce judgement in favour of his mother
if that was my honest opinion. He told me to act as I thought fit, as
that was sure to be fair. I then invited the support of the two most
respected citizens of the day, Corellius and Frontinus, and the three
of us took our seats in my room. Curianus put forward his best
arguments, and I made a brief reply myself, for there was no one else
present to defend the honour of the deceased. Then after withdrawing
for consultation I told him our joint decision: namely that we found
his mother had a just reason for her displeasure with him.

Subsequently he served a notice on the other heirs, though not on me, of a charge to be brought before the Centumviral Court. As the day fixed for the case approached, my co-heirs were anxious to compromise and settle out of court, not out of any lack of confidence in their cause, but through distrust of the times; they feared the fate they had seen overtake many another – that they might leave the Centumviral Court with a criminal case against them. Some of them, too, could be made to suffer for their friendship with Gratilla and Rusticus.[1] They therefore asked me to speak to Curianus, and I met him in the temple of Concord. There I put this question: 'Would you have any cause for complaint if your mother had left you the statutory fourth part of her estate,[2] or if you were made her sole heir, but with so many legacies to be paid out that your share was reduced to a fourth? Then you should be satisfied if you are given a fourth share by your mother's heirs, after being disinherited yourself. However, I will add something to it myself. You must realize that you have brought no action against me, and the two years have elapsed which establish my claim. But to make you more willing to negotiate with the others and prevent your losing anything by showing me special consideration, I am prepared to give you a sum equivalent to my share.'

I have had my reward in reputation as well as a good conscience, for it is this Curianus who has left me a legacy and paid this notable tribute to my conduct – conduct which (unless I flatter myself) was in the best tradition. I have told you this tale since I always talk about all my joys and sorrows as freely to you as I would to myself, and then because I thought it cruel to deny my best friend a pleasure which I was enjoying. Nor am I enough of a philosopher to remain quite indifferent whether what I believe to be a good deed of mine is to win some just reward.

2. To Calpurnius Flaccus

Thank you for the fine field-fares, but being at Laurentum I can't match them with anything from town, nor can I send you any fish as long as the weather is so bad. So all you will get is a letter which comes empty-handed, nothing but thanks without any of Diomedes'

1. See III : II.
2. By the *lex Falcidia* of 40 B.C. the heir-at-law was entitled to a minimum quarter of an estate.

ingenuity in exchanging gifts.[1] However, I know you are kind enough to be all the readier to excuse where an excuse is admittedly undeserved.

3. *To Titius Aristo*

I have many welcome acts of kindness to thank you for, but you do me a real service by thinking I ought to know that my verses have been the subject of much discussion at your house, a discussion which was prolonged because of difference of opinion. There were some people, you say, who had no criticism to make of the actual poems, but thought I deserved their censure – in a frank and friendly way – for composing and reading them in public. My answer to these critics will probably aggravate the offence. I admit that I do often write verse which is far from serious, for I also listen to comedy, watch farces, read lyric poetry, and appreciate Sotadic[2] verse; there are besides times when I laugh, make jokes, and enjoy my fun, in fact I can sum up all these innocent relaxations in a word: 'I am human.'[3] I am not complaining if my character is valued so highly that some people express surprise at my writing on such themes, if they are themselves unaware that the same thing has often been done by serious scholars of blameless reputation. But I am sure that those who realize what famous authors have set me an example can easily be persuaded to let me go astray, so long as I am in their company; for it is an honour to imitate their lighter as well as their more serious work. I am not citing a living author, lest I seem exaggerated in my praises, but surely I need not be afraid that this practice is unsuitable for me, when it was perfectly proper in the case of Cicero, C. Calvus, Asinius Pollio, M. Messala, Q. Hortensius, M. Brutus, L. Sulla, Q. Catulus, Q. Scaevola, Servius Sulpicius, Varro, Torquatus (in fact all the Torquati), C. Memmius, Lentulus Gaetulicus and Annaeus Seneca, and also Verginius Rufus in our own times. If these individuals are not enough, I can quote the deified Julius Caesar and the deified Emperors Augustus and Nerva and Tiberius Caesar. I except Nero, though I know that what is the occasional practice of the vicious is not corrupted

1. *Iliad*, VI:235.
2. This type of verse (called after the Alexandrian iambic poet) was notorious. See Quintilian, 1, 8, 6.
3. Terence, *Heauton Timorumenos*, 77.

thereby, but retains its integrity through being the usual practice of the virtuous. In the latter class Virgil, Cornelius Nepos, and, before their date, Accius and Ennius must rank high: it is true they are not senators, but moral integrity knows no class distinctions.

However, it can be said that I give readings of my work without knowing if these authors did. So I do; but they could rest content with their own judgement, whereas I am too diffident to feel confident that I have done everything I can to what has only my own approval. I have therefore two reasons for reading in public; the reader is made more keenly critical of his own work if he stands in some awe of his audience, and he has a kind of expert opinion to confirm his decision on any doubtful point. He receives suggestions from different members, and, failing this, he can infer their various opinions from their expressions, glances, nods, applause, murmurs and silence, signs which make clear the distinction between their critical judgement and polite assent. And then if any of the company is interested in reading what he has heard, he will realize that I shall have made certain alterations or omissions which may perhaps accord with his opinion, although this was never actually expressed. But now I am arguing this point as if I invited the general public to a lecture hall instead of having my friends in my own room – though if I have many friends to invite this has been a source of pride to many people and a reproach to none.

4. To Julius Valerianus

This is a small matter, but likely to go far. A praetorian senator named Sollers asked the Senate for permission to hold a weekly market on his property. This was opposed by representatives of the town of Vicetia,[1] with Tuscilius Nominatus acting on their behalf, and the case was adjourned until a subsequent meeting of the Senate. The Vicetians then appeared without anyone to plead for them and said they had been cheated – whether a verbal slip on their part or their genuine opinion I don't know. Asked by the praetor Nepos whom they had instructed to act for them, they replied, 'The same as before.' To the question whether he had taken on the case without a fee, they said that they had given him 6,000 sesterces. Had they paid him a second fee? Yes, another 4,000. Nepos then issued a summons to Nominatus to appear before the court. This was as far as the matter went that day,

1. In Venetia (Vicenza).

but in my opinion it will not end there, for often a mere touch is enough to set things moving with far-reaching consequences.

That has made you prick up your ears, but now you will have to beg me nicely for a long time before you hear the rest of the story – unless you come to Rome first to find it out, and see things for yourself as a change from reading about them.

5. To Novius Maximus

I have just heard that Gaius Fannius is dead, news which has upset me very much. Not only did I love and admire his good taste and learning, but I could always rely on his judgement; for his natural intelligence had been trained by experience and he was always ready with an accurate opinion. It distresses me, too, that he had the misfortune to die without making a new will, when the old one leaves out some of his dearest friends and benefits people who are now his enemies.

This is hard but not unbearable; much more serious is the fact that he has left his finest work unfinished. Although his career at the bar took up much of his time, he was bringing out a history of the various fates of the people put to death or banished by Nero. His accuracy in research and purity of style (which was midway between the discursive and historical) were evident in the three volumes he had already finished, and he was all the more anxious to complete the series when he saw how eagerly the first books were read by a large public. Death always seems to me cruel and untimely when it comes to those who are engaged on some immortal work, for when people abandon themselves to pleasure and live from day to day, their reasons for living are finished as each day comes to an end; but for those who think of posterity and seek to be remembered in their works, death is always sudden as it always cuts short some unfinished project. Fannius had in fact had a premonition long ago of what has now happened. He dreamed that he was lying on his couch at dead of night, dressed and ready for work, and with his desk in front of him, just as usual; then he fancied that Nero appeared, sat down on the couch, took up the first volume Fannius had published about his crimes, and read it through to the end; then he did the same to the second and third volumes, after which he departed. Fannius was horrified, and inferred that his writing would end at the point where Nero stopped reading; and so it did. When I remember this, I am filled with pity for all the wakeful hours he spent and the trouble he took, all in vain; and I think of my own mortality and what I have written. Doubtless the same thought makes you equally fearful for the work you have in hand, so while life lasts we must see there shall be as little as possible for death to destroy.

6. To Domitius Apollinaris

I am touched by your kind concern when you try to dissuade me from my intention of staying in Tuscany in summer. You think the place is unhealthy, but while it is perfectly true that the Tuscan strip of sea-coast is relaxing and dangerous to the health, my property is some distance away from the sea, and is in fact at the very foot of the Apennines, which are considered the healthiest of mountains. So to rid you of all your fears on my account, let me tell you about the climate, the countryside, and the lovely situation of my house, which will be a pleasure alike for me to tell and you to hear.

The climate in winter is cold and frosty, and so quite impossible for myrtles and olives and any other trees which will only flourish in a continuous mild temperature, but the laurel can grow and does very well; it is sometimes killed off by the cold, but not oftener than in the neighbourhood of Rome. The summer is wonderfully temperate, for there is always some movement of the air, more often a breeze than a real wind. Hence the number of elderly people living there – you can see the grandfathers and great-grandfathers of people who have reached their own manhood, and hear old stories and tales of the past, so that a visit here is like a return to another age.

The countryside is very beautiful. Picture to yourself a vast amphi-theatre such as could only be a work of nature; the great spreading plain is ringed round by mountains, their summits crowned by ancient woods of tall trees, where there is a good deal of mixed hunting to be had. Down the mountain slopes are timber woods interspersed with small hills of soil so rich that there is scarcely a rocky outcrop to be found; these hills are fully as fertile as the level plain and yield quite as rich a harvest, though it ripens rather later in the season. Below them the vineyards spreading down every slope weave their uniform pattern far and wide, their lower limit bordered by a belt of shrubs. Then come the meadows and cornfields, where the land can be broken up only by heavy oxen and the strongest ploughs, for the soil is so stiff that it is thrown up in great clods at the first ploughing and is not thoroughly broken until it has been gone over nine times. The meadows are bright with flowers, covered with trefoil and other delicate plants which always seem soft and fresh, for everything is fed by streams which never run dry; though the ground is not marshy where the water collects, because of its downward slope, so that any surplus water it cannot absorb is drained off into the river Tiber flowing through the fields. The river is navigable, so that all produce is conveyed to Rome by boat, but only in winter and spring – in summer its level falls and its dry bed has to give up its claim to the title of a great river until the following autumn. It is a great pleasure to look down on the countryside from the mountain, for the view seems to be a painted scene of unusual beauty rather than a real landscape, and the harmony to be found in this variety refreshes the eye wherever it turns.

My house is on the lower slopes of a hill but commands as good a view as if it were higher up, for the ground rises so gradually that the slope is imperceptible, and you find yourself at the top without noticing the climb. Behind it is the Apennine range, though some way off, so that even on a still and cloudless day there is a breeze from the mountains, but one which has had its force broken by the distance so that it is never cutting nor boisterous. It faces mainly south, and so from midday onwards in summer (a little earlier in winter) it seems to invite the sun into the colonnade. This is broad, and long in proportion, with several rooms opening out of it as well as the old-fashioned type of entrance hall.

In front of the colonnade is a terrace laid out with box hedges clipped into different shapes, from which a bank slopes down, also with figures of animals cut out of box facing each other on either side. On the level below there waves – or I might have said ripples – a bed of acanthus. All round is a path hedged by bushes which are trained and cut into different shapes, and then a drive, oval like a racecourse, inside which are various box figures and clipped dwarf shrubs. The whole garden is enclosed by a dry-stone wall which is hidden from sight by a box hedge planted in tiers; outside is a meadow, as well worth seeing for its natural beauty as the formal garden I have described; then fields and many more meadows and woods.

From the end of the colonnade projects a dining-room: through its folding doors it looks on to the end of the terrace, the adjacent meadow, and the stretch of open country beyond, while from its windows on one side can be seen part of the terrace and the projecting wing of the house, on the other the tree-tops in the enclosure of the adjoining riding-ground. Almost opposite the middle of the colonnade is a suite of rooms set slightly back and round a small court shaded by four plane trees. In the centre a fountain plays in a marble basin, watering the plane trees round it and the ground beneath them with its light spray. In this suite is a bedroom which no daylight, voice, nor sound can penetrate, and next to it an informal dining-room where I entertain my personal friends; it looks on to the small courtyard, the colonnade, and the view from the colonnade. There is also another room, green and shady from the nearest plane tree, which has walls decorated with marble up to the ceiling and a fresco (which is no less attractive) of birds perched on the branches of trees. Here is a small fountain with a bowl surrounded by tiny jets which together make a lovely murmuring sound. At the corner of the colonnade is a large bedroom facing the dining-room; some windows look out on to the terrace, others on to the meadow, while just below the windows in front is an ornamental pool, a pleasure both to see and to hear, with its water falling from a height and foaming white when it strikes the marble. This room is very warm in winter when it is bathed in sunshine, and on a cloudy day hot steam from the adjacent furnace-room serves instead. Then you pass through a large and cheerful dressing-room, belonging to the bath, to the cooling-room, which contains a good-sized shady swimming-bath. If you want more space to swim or warmer water, there is a pool in the courtyard and a well near it to tone you up with cold water when you have had enough of the warm. Next to the cooling-room is a temperate one which enjoys the sun's kindly warmth, though not as much as the hot room which is built out in a bay. This contains three plunging-baths, two full in the sun and one in the shade, though still in the light. Over the dressing-room is built the ball court, and this is large enough for several sets of players to take different kinds of exercise. Not far from the bath is a staircase leading to three rooms and then to a covered arcade. One room looks on to the small court with the four plane trees, another on to the meadow, and the third faces the vineyard and has an uninterrupted view across the sky. The head of the arcade is divided off as a room, from which can be seen the riding-ground, the vineyard, and the mountains. Next to it is another room which has plenty of sun, especially in winter, and then comes a suite which connects the riding-ground with the house.

That is the appearance and lay-out of the front of the house. Down the side is a covered arcade for summer use which is built on higher ground and seems not to look down on but be actually touching the vineyard below; half-way along is a dining-room which receives the fresh breezes blowing down the Apennine valleys. Its broad windows at the back look on to the vineyard, and so do its folding doors, but through the arcade between, and along the side where there are no windows, there is a private staircase which is used for serving at dinner parties. At the far end is a bedroom with a view of the arcade as pleasant as that of the vineyard. Underneath runs a semi-underground arcade which never loses its icy temperature in summer and is airy enough not to need to admit the outside air. Next to both these arcades begins an open one where the dining-room ends, which is cool before noon but hot during the later part of the day. It leads to two suites, one of four and the other of three rooms, which are alternately sunny or shady as the sun moves round.

The design and beauty of the buildings are greatly surpassed by the riding-ground. The centre is quite open so that the whole extent of the course can be seen as one enters. It is planted round with ivy-clad plane trees, green with their own leaves above, and below with the ivy which climbs over trunk and branch and links tree to tree as it spreads across them. Box shrubs grow between the plane trees, and outside there is a ring of laurel bushes which add their shade to that of the planes. Here the straight part of the course ends, curves round in a semicircle, and changes its appearance, becoming darker and more densely shaded by the cypress trees planted round to shelter it, whereas the inner circuits – for there are several – are in open sunshine; roses grow there and the cool shadow alternates with the pleasant warmth of the sun. At the end of the winding alleys of the rounded end of the course you return to the straight path, or rather paths, for there are several separated by intervening box hedges. Between the grass lawns here there are box shrubs clipped into innumerable shapes, some being letters which spell the gardener's name or his master's; small obelisks of box alternate with fruit trees, and then suddenly in the midst of this ornamental scene is what looks like a piece of rural country planted there. The open space in the middle is set off by low plane trees planted on each side; farther off are acanthuses with their flexible glossy leaves, then more box figures and names.

At the upper end of the course is a curved dining-seat of white marble, shaded by a vine trained over four slender pillars of Carystian marble. Water gushes out through pipes from under the seat as if pressed out by the weight of people sitting there, is caught in a stone cistern and then held in a polished marble basin which is regulated by a hidden device so as to remain full without overflowing. The preliminaries and main dishes for dinner are placed on the edge of the basin, while the lighter ones float about in vessels shaped like birds or little boats. A fountain opposite plays and catches its water, throwing it high into the air so that it falls back into the basin, where it is played again at once through a jet connected with the inlet. Facing the seat is a bedroom which contributes as much beauty to the scene as it gains from its position. It is built of shining white marble, extended by folding doors which open straight out among the trees; its upper and lower windows all look out into the greenery above and below. A small alcove which is part of the room but separated from it contains a bed, and although it has windows in all its walls, the light inside is dimmed by the dense shade of a flourishing vine which climbs over the whole building up to the roof. There you can lie and imagine you are in a wood, but without the risk of rain. Here too a fountain rises and disappears underground, while here and there are marble chairs which anyone tired with walking appreciates as much as the building itself. By every chair is a tiny fountain, and throughout the riding-ground can be heard the sound of the streams directed into it, the flow of which can be controlled by hand to water one part of the garden or another or sometimes the whole at once.

I should have been trying long ago not to say too much, had I not suggested that this letter should take you into every corner of the place. I don't imagine you will find it tiresome to read about a spot which could hardly tire you on a visit, especially as you have more opportunities if you want an occasional rest, and can take a seat, so to speak, by putting down the letter. Besides, I have been indulging the love I have for all the places I have largely laid out myself or where I have perfected an earlier design. In short (for why should I not state my opinion, right or wrong?) I think a writer's first duty is to read his title, to keep on asking himself what he set out to say, and to realize that he will not say too much if he sticks to his theme, though he certainly will if he brings in extraneous matter. You know the number of lines Homer and Virgil devote to their descriptions of the arms of Achilles and Aeneas: yet neither passage seems long because both poets are carrying out their original intention. You see too how Aratus traces and tabulates the smallest stars, but because this is his main subject and not a digression his work does not lack proportion. It is the same with me, if I may 'compare small things with great'. I am trying to set my entire house before your eyes, so, if I introduce nothing irrelevant, it is the house I describe which is extensive, not the letter describing it.

But to return to my starting-point – for I shall justly be censured under my own law if I pursue this digression further – these are my reasons for preferring my home in Tuscany to one in Tusculum, Tibur, or Praeneste.[1] And I can add another reason: I can enjoy a profounder peace there, more comfort, and fewer cares; I need never wear a formal toga and there are no neighbours to disturb me; everywhere there is peace and quiet, which adds as much to the healthiness of the place as the clear sky and pure air. There I enjoy the best of health, both mental and physical, for I keep my mind in training with work and my body with hunting. My servants too are healthier here than anywhere else; up to the present I have not lost a single one of those I brought here with me – may I be forgiven for saying so, and may the gods continue to make this the pride of the place and a joy to me.

7. To Calvisius Rufus

It is well known that a corporation cannot be made heir to an estate nor receive a preliminary legacy, but Saturninus, who has made me his heir, left a fourth part of his estate to our native town of Comum, and later changed this to a preliminary legacy of 400,000 sesterces. This is null and void from the legal point of view, but clearly valid if one looks to the intention of the deceased. I shudder to think how the legal experts will receive what I am going to say, but this intention

1. In Latium (Frascati, Tivoli, and Palestrina). These are popular places for a country seat; Pliny does not own property there himself.

carries more weight with me than the law, at any rate as regards the sum Saturninus intended to come to Comum. I have given 1,600,000 sesterces to the town out of my own money, so surely I ought not to grudge it this 400,000, little more than a third of my unexpected inheritance. I am sure you will share my opinion, for you love our birthplace as a loyal citizen should. So next time the town Council meets, I should be grateful if you would make a statement, quite simply and shortly, on the legal question; then add that I am making this offer of 400,000 sesterces in accordance with Saturninus's instructions. The gift and the generosity are his – I can only be said to comply with his wishes.

I have refrained from writing officially to the Council for two reasons: I remembered that our close friendship obliges you to act for me as you would for yourself, just as your wise judgement enables you to do so, and I was afraid that a letter might seem lacking in the restraint which you will have no difficulty in keeping in a speech. There the tone is set by the expression, gestures and voice of the speaker, whereas a letter lacks such recommendations and is liable to wilful misinterpretation.

8. To Titinius Capito

Your suggestion that I should write history has often been made, for a good many people have given me the same advice. I like the idea: not that I feel at all sure of being successful – it would be rash in an amateur – but because the saving of those who deserve immortality from sinking into oblivion, and spreading the fame of others along with one's own, seem to me a particularly splendid achievement. Nothing attracts me so much as that love and longing for a lasting name, man's worthiest aspiration, especially in one who is aware that there is nothing in him to blame and so has no fear if he is to be remembered by posterity. So day and night I wonder if 'I too may rise from earth'; that would answer my prayer, for 'to hover in triumph on the lips of man'[1] is too much to hope. 'Yet O if I could – '[2] but I must rest content with what history alone seems able to guarantee. Oratory and poetry win small favour unless they reach the highest standard of eloquence, but history cannot fail to give pleasure however it is presented. Humanity is naturally inquisitive, and so factual

1. Virgil, *Georgics*, III: 8–9.   2. *Aeneid*, v: 195.

information, plain and unadorned, has its attraction for anyone who can enjoy small talk and anecdote.

In my case family precedent is an additional incentive to work of this kind. My uncle, who was also my father by adoption, was a historian of scrupulous accuracy, and the philosophers say that it is an excellent thing to follow in the footsteps of one's forbears, provided that they trod an honest path. Why then do I delay? I have acted in certain important and complicated cases, and I intend to revise my speeches (without building too many hopes on them) so that all the work I put into them will not perish with me for want of this last attention. For, if one looks to posterity, anything left unfinished might as well not have been begun. You will tell me that I can rewrite my speeches and write history at the same time. I wish I could, but both are such great undertakings that it will be more than enough to carry out one. I was eighteen when I began my career at the bar, and it is only now, and still only dimly, that I begin to realize the true qualities of the orator. What would happen if I shouldered a new burden in addition to the old? It is true that oratory and history have much in common, but they differ in many of the points where they seem alike. Both employ narrative, but with a difference: oratory deals largely with the humble and trivial incidents of everyday life, history is concerned with profound truths and the glory of great deeds. The bare bones of narrative and a nervous energy distinguish the one, a fulness and a certain freedom of style the other. Oratory succeeds by its vigour and severity of attack, history by the ease and grace with which it develops its theme. Finally, they differ in vocabulary, rhythm and period-structure, for, as Thucydides says,[1] there is all the difference between a 'lasting possession' and a 'prize essay': the former is history, the latter oratory. For these reasons I am not inclined to mix two dissimilar subjects which are fundamentally opposed in the very quality to which each owes its prominence, lest I am swept away in the resultant confusion and treat one in the manner proper to the other. And so, to keep to my own language, for the time being I apply for an adjournment.

You can, however, be considering now what period of history I am to treat. Is it to be ancient history which has had its historians? The material is there, but it will be a great labour to assemble it. Or shall

1. Thucydides, 1 : 22.

it be recent times which no one has handled? I shall receive small thanks and give serious offence, for beside the fact that there is much more to censure than to praise in the serious vices of the present day, such praise as one gives, however generous, is considered grudging, and however restrained one's blame it is said to be excessive. But I have enough courage of my convictions not to be deterred by such considerations. All I ask of you is to prepare the way for what you want me to do and to choose me a subject; or another good reason for delay and hesitation may arise when I am ready to start at last.

9. *To Sempronius Rufus*

I had gone down to the Basilica Julia to listen to the speeches in a case where I had to appear for the defence at the next hearing. The court was seated, the presiding magistrates had arrived and counsel on both sides were coming and going; then there was a long silence, broken at last by a message from the praetor. The court adjourned and the case was suspended, much to my delight, for I am never so well prepared as not to be glad of a delay. The reason for this one was a short edict published by the praetor Nepos, who is dealing with the case, in which he warned both prosecution and defence that he would strictly enforce all the provisions of the senatorial decree appended: 'All persons bringing cases before the court are hereby required to state on oath before their case is heard that they have neither paid, promised, nor guaranteed any sum to any person for his legal assistance.' By these words, and a great many more, the buying and selling of counsels' services were expressly forbidden; but permission was given, after a case was settled, for clients to give their counsel a sum not exceeding 10,000 sesterces. This action of Nepos's had raised doubts in the mind of the president of the Centumviral Court, and, in order to consider whether to follow his example, he gave us our unexpected holiday.

Meanwhile the edict is the subject of praise or criticism throughout the city. Many people are saying that 'We have found someone to set the crooked straight, but were there no praetors before him? Who is he to correct public morals?' The other party says that Nepos has done well; he has learnt the law before taking up office, reads the Senate's decrees, puts a check on disgraceful bargaining, and will not allow a noble profession to sell its services in this scandalous way. So everyone talks, but events will have to show which view will prevail. Right and wrong intentions are praised and blamed only insofar as their results are good or bad – that is the generally accepted practice, though it is none the less unfair. Hence it generally happens that the self-same actions are variously ascribed to zeal, conceit, independence, or folly.

10. *To Suetonius Tranquillus*

Do please release my hendecasyllables from their promise – they were guarantors to our friends for the appearance of your work, and every day brings in some new request and demand; so they now run the risk of being served with a writ to produce it. I know I am very slow to publish my own work, but you outdo even my doubts and hesitations. So bestir yourself, or else beware lest I drag those books out of you by the fury of my iambics, since my hendecasyllables failed to entice them with honeyed words! The work is already finished and perfect; revision will not give it further polish but only dull its freshness. Please let me see your name published and hear that my friend's books are being copied, read and sold. In view of our warm friendship, it is only fair that you should let me have the same pleasure from you as you enjoy in me.

11. *To Calpurnius Fabatus, his wife's grandfather*

Thank you for your letter telling me about your dedication of a handsome public colonnade in your own name and that of your son, followed on the next day by your promise of a sum of money for the decoration of the doors, thus making your second act of generosity the consummation of the first. I am glad of this, primarily on account of your own reputation, from which I have some reflected glory through my connexion with you; I am glad too to see my father-in-law's memory perpetuated in such a fine monument, and, finally, the enrichment of our native place is a source of pleasure to me whoever it is who honours her, but especially so when that person is you.

It remains for me to pray that the gods will continue to grant you this generous spirit and as many years as possible in which to employ it, for I am sure that once you have carried out your recent undertaking you will begin on another: generosity cannot stand still when once set in motion, and its beauty shines out the more it is exercised.

12. To Terentius Scaurus

I invited some friends to hear me read a short speech which I am thinking of publishing, just enough of an audience to make me nervous,
but not a large one, as I wanted to hear the truth. I have in fact a
double motive for these readings, hoping to gain both a stimulus by
my anxiety to succeed and criticism where any faults have escaped my
notice through being my own. Here I succeeded, and found people
to give me the benefit of their advice; I also noticed for myself some
corrections to be made, and, now that these are done, I am sending
you the result. The title will tell you the subject and the text will
explain everything else, for it ought by now to be intelligible without
any introduction. I should be grateful for your opinion on the speech
as a whole and in detail, for I shall be the more careful to withhold it
or determined to publish, whichever way you pronounce judgement.

13. To Julius Valerianus

I have just had your request for the result of the summons issued by
Nepos to Tuscilius Nominatus,[1] which I promised I would let you
know if you asked for it.

Nominatus came before the court and made his own defence. No
one brought any charge, for the repres ntatives of Vicetia did not
press theirs – they were in fact now ready to defend him. His line of
defence was that it was his courage not his sense of duty which had
failed him when he came to make his speech. He had arrived with
good intentions and had even been seen in the Senate, but then he had
been alarmed by talking to his friends and had left the court. They had
advised him not to be too persistent in opposing the wishes of a senator
(and especially in the Senate) who was no longer fighting the case on
account of the proposed market, but because his influence, reputation
and position were at stake; otherwise Nominatus would make himself
more unpopular than on the last occasion. (He had in fact received
some applause as he went out, but not from many people.) He went
on to weep and beg for leniency, and indeed, throughout his speech,
he was careful to give the impression that he was not defending his
conduct but appealing for mercy; as a practised speaker he knew that
this was safer and more likely to win favour.

He was acquitted on a proposal of the consul-elect, Afranius Dexter,

1. See v : 4.

to the effect that though Nominatus would have done better to complete the case for the Vicetians in the same spirit as he had undertaken it, his negligence was without fraudulent intent and no punishable offence could be proved against him. He should then be discharged on condition that he returned his fee to the Vicetians. Everyone agreed except Fabius Aper, who proposed that Nominatus should be forbidden to conduct a case for five years, and he stuck stoutly to his opinion although he could not persuade anyone to support him. He even quoted the statute on senatorial procedure, and insisted that Dexter (who had been the first to put forward the contrary motion) should state on oath that his proposal was in the interests of the State. His demand was in order, but it met with a good deal of protest, as it appeared to be accusing Dexter of corrupt practice. But before a vote could be taken, Nigrinus, the tribune of the people, read out a well-phrased statement of great importance. In this he complained that counsel sold their services, faked lawsuits for money, settled them by collusion, and made a boast of the large regular incomes to be made by robbery of their fellow-citizens. He quoted the relevant paragraphs of the law, reminded the Senate of its decrees, and ended by saying that our noble Emperor should be asked to remedy these serious evils himself, since the law and the Senate's decrees were fallen into contempt. After a few days the Emperor issued a decree, which was firm but moderate in tone. It is published in the official records, so you can read it.

How glad I am that I have always kept clear of any contracts, presents, remunerations, or even small gifts for my conduct of cases! It is true that one ought to shun dishonesty as a shameful thing, not because it is illegal; but, even so, it is a pleasure to find an official ban on a practice one would never have permitted oneself. Perhaps I shall lose some of the credit and reputation I won from my resolve – in fact I am sure to do so, when everyone is compelled to behave as I did of my own free will – but meanwhile I am enjoying my friends' teasing, when they hail me as a prophet or pretend that this measure is directed against my own robberies and greed.

14. *To Pontius Allifanus*

I had left Rome for a visit to my native town when news reached me that Cornutus Tertullus had accepted the office of Curator of the

Aemilian Road. Words cannot express my delight, for both our sakes; for although he is known to be far removed from any feelings of ambition, the unsolicited offer of this post cannot fail to give him pleasure, and I am better pleased with the duties assigned to me[1] now that I see Cornutus in a similar position. To be in the same rank as a good citizen is as welcome as a promotion. And is there anyone who can equal Cornutus in merit and integrity, anyone who is a more perfect example of the ancient virtues in every way? His character is known to me not from the splendid reputation he so justly deserves, but from the close personal experience of many years. Together we have admired and still admire almost every man or woman who is an example to our generation, and this association has been a close bond of intimacy between us. Another link was forged in our public relations; as you know, Cornutus was my colleague as a Treasury official and as consul, as if in answer to my prayers. It was then that I knew him to the full for the great man he is; I followed him as my teacher and honoured him as a parent, for his was the ripe wisdom not of years but of experience. For these reasons I congratulate myself no less than him, for public as well as personal considerations. Now at last men's merits bring them official recognition instead of the dangers of the past.

I could let my letter run on indefinitely to give free expression to my joy, but I must turn to what I was doing when the news reached me. I was staying with my wife's grandfather and aunt, meeting friends I had long wished to see; I was going the round of my few acres, hearing the peasants' complaints and looking over the accounts – unwillingly and superficially I must admit, for I am devoted to literary documents of a very different order. I had also begun to make preparations for my return, for I am restricted by the shortness of my leave, especially now that the news of Cornutus's duties is a reminder of my own. I trust that your Campania will let you return about the same time, so that I shall not lose a day of your company once I am back in Rome.

15. To Arrius Antoninus

It is only when I try to imitate your verse that I fully realize its excellence, for my halting efforts fall short of the original just as an artist's copy can never be more than a poor version of a wholly beautiful

1. As curator of the bed and banks of the Tiber and the sewers of Rome.

model. That is why I urge you to produce as much as possible for all of us to try to emulate even though none or very few will be successful.

16. To Aefulanus Marcellinus

I am writing to you in great distress: our friend Fundanus has lost his younger daughter. I never saw a girl so gay and lovable, so deserving of a longer life or even a life to last for ever. She had not yet reached the age of fourteen, and yet she combined the wisdom of age and dignity of womanhood with the sweetness and modesty of youth and innocence. She would cling to her father's neck, and embrace us, his friends, with modest affection; she loved her nurses, her attendants and her teachers, each one for the service given her; she applied herself intelligently to her books and was moderate and restrained in her play. She bore her last illness with patient resignation and, indeed, with courage; she obeyed her doctors' orders, cheered her sister and father, and by sheer force of will carried on after her physical strength had failed her. This will power remained with her to the end, and neither the length of her illness nor fear of death could break it. So she has left us all the more sad reasons for lamenting our loss. Hers is a truly tragic and un-timely end – death itself was not so cruel as the moment of its coming. She was already engaged to marry a distinguished young man, the day for the wedding was fixed, and we had received our invitations. Such joy, and now such sorrow! No words can express my grief when I heard Fundanus giving his own orders (for one heart-rending detail leads to another) for the money he had intended for clothing, pearls and jewels to be spent on incense, ointment and spices. He is indeed a cultivated man and a philosopher who has devoted himself from youth to higher thought and the arts, but at the moment he rejects every-thing he has so often heard and professed himself: he has cast off all his other virtues and is wholly absorbed by his love for his child. You will forgive and even admire him if you think of what he has lost – a daughter who resembled him in character no less than in face and ex-pression, and was her father's living image in every way.

If then you write anything to him in his very natural sorrow, be careful not to offer any crude form of consolation which might suggest reproof; be gentle and sympathetic. Passage of time will make him readier to accept this; a raw wound shrinks from a healing hand but later permits and even seeks help, and so the mind rejects and repels any consolation in its first pangs of grief, then feels the need of comfort and is calmed if this is kindly offered.

17. To Vestricius Spurinna

I know your interest in the liberal arts and your pleasure when any of our young men of good family do anything worthy of their ancestry, so I am hastening to give you my news. Today I was among the audience to which Calpurnius Piso read his poem on the *Legends of the Stars*, a scholarly treatment of a splendid theme, written in flowing elegiac couplets whose delicate flexibility could rise to grandeur when required. He showed an appropriate versatility in raising or lowering his tone, and the same talent whether he descended from the heights to a lower level, rose to complexity from simplicity or moved between a lighter and more serious approach to his subject. His unusually pleasant voice was a further asset, and gained much itself from his modesty, his blushes, and anxious expression, which always add charm to a reading – for some reason shyness suits an author better than confidence. To cut short my story (though I should like to say more, as these qualities are so becoming in the young and rare in the upper classes), after the recital I gave him a warm and prolonged embrace, the most stimulating kind of encouragement, and urged him by my congratulations to complete the task he had begun and pass on to posterity the torch his ancestors had handed to him. I also congratulated his excellent mother and his brother who, as a member of the audience, won as much credit for his brotherly affection as Piso did for his eloquent reading, for the concern he showed during the recital and his delight afterwards were most striking.

I pray the gods to give me more news like this to send you; for I believe in this generation, and am anxious for it not to prove barren and outworn. Still less do I want our noble families to have no distinction in their homes other than family portraits; though these, I think, must now be silently congratulating and encouraging these two young men and doing them both the honour of acknowledging them as descendants.

18. To Calpurnius Macer

All is well with me since it is with you. You have your wife and son with you, and all the pleasures of the sea, streams, woods and fields are yours, along with your lovely house; which I know must be lovely, when it was the retreat of the man[1] who was so fortunate before he rose to the supreme good fortune. I am in my home in Tuscany, hunting and writing, either in turn or both at once, but I'm not yet ready to pronounce judgement on which I find harder to do.

19. To Valerius Paulinus

I have noticed your kindness to your household, so will frankly confess my indulgence to mine. I always have in mind the phrase of Homer's: 'he was gentle as a father',[2] and also our own 'father of the household'; but, even if I were harsh and unfeeling by nature, my heart would be softened by the illness of my freedman Zosimus, whose claim to sympathy is all the stronger now that he needs it so much. He is an honest fellow, obliging and educated, marked out by his talent for acting, where he has great success. His delivery is clear and intelligent, his acting correct and balanced, and he plays the lyre well, better than an actor need do. He also reads speeches, history, and poetry so well that it might be his sole accomplishment. I have told you all this in detail so that you may better realize all the pleasant services I receive from Zosimus which no one else can give me. I have moreover long felt for him an affection which has increased with the dangers he has come through; for it seems a law of nature for nothing to excite and intensify love so much as the fear of losing its object, and this has happened to me more than once in his case.

Some years ago he was exerting himself during a passionate performance when he began to spit blood. I then sent him to Egypt, and after a long stay there he recently returned with his health restored. Now after demanding too much of his voice for several days on end he has had a slight return of his cough as a reminder of the old trouble, and once again has brought up blood. I think the thing to do is to send him to your place at Forum Julii,[3] for I have often heard you say that the air is healthy there and the milk excellent for treating this kind of case. Please write to your people and ask them to receive him on the estate and in your home, and to meet the expenses of anything he may need. This will not be much, for he is abstemious and moderate

---

1. The Emperor Nerva; or possibly the dictator Sulla.
2. Homer, *Odyssey*, 11 : 47.
3. In Gallia Narbonensis (now Fréjus).

in his habits to the point of frugally denying himself not only delicacies but even essentials for his health. I will see that he has sufficient money for his journey to you when he sets out.

20. *To Cornelius Ursus*

The Bithynians again! It is no time since their case against Julius Bassus,[1] but they have brought another one against the governor Varenus Rufus – the Varenus they had previously demanded and accepted to conduct their case against Bassus. Summoned before the Senate, they applied for time to collect evidence. Then Varenus also requested the right himself to call witnesses from the province in his defence. The Bithynians objected, so the case was heard at once. I appeared for Varenus, not without success: whether my speech was good or bad will be seen when it is published. In a speech as delivered chance is the dominant factor either way, for much can be gained or lost by the speaker's memory, voice and gestures, the occasion and the good or bad impression made by the defendant; whereas the written speech is quite free from influence one way or the other, and owes nothing to chance, whether lucky or not. I was opposed by one of the Bithynians, Fonteius Magnus, whose words were many and arguments few, for, like most Greeks, he mistakes volubility for fulness of expression; they all pour out a torrent of long monotonous periods without taking breath. Hence Julius Candidus's frequent witticism that eloquence and loquacity are two different things. Scarcely anyone has the gift of eloquence – or no one if we are to believe Marcus Antonius – but what Candidus calls loquacity is common to many people and the special gift of every impudent rascal.

The following day Homullus defended Varenus with considerable subtlety, spirit and elegance, and Nigrinus made a concise, impressive and well-phrased speech in reply. The consul elect, Acilius Rufus, then moved that the Bithynians should be given permission to collect their evidence, but he passed over Varenus's application in silence, which was tantamount to a refusal. The consular Cornelius Priscus proposed to grant the petitions of both parties, and his motion was carried by a majority. So we won our point, not one mentioned in law or covered by precedent, but none the less just. Why it was I shall not say by letter, for I want you to ask for the speech. If Homer is right,

1. See IV: 9.

and 'Men praise most the song which rings newest in their ears'[1] I must be careful not to talk too much, or my letter will nip in the bud the bloom of novelty which is my speech's chief attraction.

21. To Pompeius Saturninus

I received your letter with mixed feelings, for it was a mixture of good and bad news. It is good news that you are kept in Rome (against your will, you will say, but it is not against mine) and that you intend to give a reading as soon as I arrive. Thank you for waiting for me. It was sad, however, to hear that Julius Valens is lying seriously ill – though perhaps not so sad if one considers what a blessing it would be for him to be released as quickly as possible from an incurable disease. But it is more than sad, it is tragic that Julius Avitus should have died, and died at sea on his way home from the province where he had been quaestor, far from his loving brother, his mother, and his sisters. All this cannot affect him now that he is dead, but must have done while he was dying; and it affects those he leaves behind, as does the thought that a young man of such promise has died in early youth when he might have attained the highest honours had his gifts been allowed to mature. Think of his ardent love of literature and all he read and wrote: all of which has died with him, leaving nothing for posterity. But I must not give way to my grief, for anything becomes disproportionate if unchecked. I will end this letter, and with it the tears it has brought to my eyes.

1. *Odyssey*, I: 351–2.

BOOK SIX

1. To Calestrius Tiro

As long as I was staying north of the Po and you were in Picenum[1] I did not notice your absence so much, but now that I am back in Rome again and you are still away, I feel it much more. Perhaps I think of you more in the places where we are usually together, or else it is that we never miss our absent friends so keenly as when they are not far away; the nearer you are to enjoying their company, the less you are able to be patient without it. Whatever the cause, do take me out of my misery and come, or I shall return to the place I foolishly left in a hurry, with no other purpose than to see if you will write me letters like this when you find yourself in Rome without me.

2. To Maturus Arrianus

I often find myself missing Marcus Regulus in court, though I don't mean I want him back again. But I miss him as a person who really valued oratory. He used to be pale with anxiety, would write out his speeches though he could never learn them by heart, paint round one of his eyes (the right if he was appearing for the plaintiff and the left for the defendant), change a white patch over from one eyebrow to the other, and never fail to consult the soothsayers on the result of his case. This may have been gross superstition on his part, but it did show respect for his profession. Besides, two of his habits were very pleasant for anyone acting with him; he used to gather an audience by invitation and apply for unlimited time to speak, and nothing could be more enjoyable than to find yourself addressing someone else's audience on his responsibility, and to go on at your ease for as long as you liked.

1. The coastal region north-east of the Apennines (now Ancona).

All the same, Regulus did well to die, and would have done better to die sooner; though today he could certainly have been alive without being a public nuisance, now that we have an Emperor who would prevent him from doing harm. So there is now no reason why we should not miss him, especially as since his death the custom of applying for and granting two water-clocks[1] or one (or even half of one) has gained ground and is generally accepted. Counsel would rather get their speeches over than go on speaking, and judges care more about finishing a case than passing judgement: such is the widespread neglect, indifference, and general disrespect for oratory and its attendant risks. Are we wiser than our forbears and juster than the very laws which assign us so many hours, days and adjournments? Perhaps our predecessors were stupid and unduly slow, and we are clearer speakers, quicker thinkers, and more scrupulous judges than they were, when we hurry through our cases in fewer hours than the days they spent on developing their case. To think that Regulus's self-interest won from every judge a concession which few today will grant to honest intentions!

Personally, whenever I am hearing a case (which I do more often than I conduct one) I allow all the time anyone asks for, thinking it rash to predict the length of anything still unheard and to set a time-limit to a trial before its extent is known, especially when one of the first duties of a magistrate under oath is patience – an important element in justice itself. You will protest that a good deal is said which is irrelevant. That may be, but it is better than leaving out essentials, and it is impossible to judge what is irrelevant without first hearing it.

But I can really discuss these and other public abuses better when we meet; you too have the general interest at heart and are anxious for reform even where it has become difficult to put things right. To turn to domestic affairs – is all well with you? I have no news, but I'm increasingly grateful for my blessings while they last, and I notice my troubles less now that I am used to them.

3. *To Verus*

Thank you for taking over the working of the small farm I gave my nurse. At the time I gave it to her it was worth 100,000 sesterces, but since then it has done badly and depreciated in value. It will recover

1. There were three water-clocks to the Roman hour.

now that it is in your hands, but do remember that I have entrusted to you more than vines and land, though these of course are included. I am thinking of my little gift, for it means as much to me, the donor, as it does to my nurse that the farm shall prove as profitable as you can make it.

4. To his wife Calpurnia

Never have I complained so much about my public duties as I do now. They would not let me come with you to Campania in search of better health, and they still prevent me from following hard on your heels. This is a time when I particularly want to be with you, to see with my own eyes whether you are gaining in strength and weight, and if the pleasures of your holiday and the luxuries of the district are doing you no harm. Indeed, I should worry when you are away even if you were well, for there are always anxious moments without news of anyone one loves dearly, and, as things are, I have the thought of your health as well as your absence to alarm me with fluctuating doubts and fears. I am full of forebodings of every imaginable disaster, and like all nervous people dwell most on what I pray fervently will not happen. So do please think of my anxiety and write to me once or even twice a day – I shall worry less while I am reading your letters, but my fears will return as soon as I have finished them.

5. To Cornelius Ursus

I told you in my last letter[1] that Varenus obtained permission to call witnesses in his defence from his province. The majority approved of this, but some people (notably Licinius Nepos) held that it was illegal, and clung stubbornly to their opinion. At the next meeting of the Senate, although there was other business under discussion, Nepos brought up the motion passed at the last meeting and reopened a case that had been settled. He went on to declare that the consuls should be asked to raise the whole question of the law of restitution of money extorted and to determine whether, following the procedure of the law of bribery, a clause should not henceforward be added to give the defendant the same powers to prepare his case and to compel the attendance of witnesses as the law allows the plaintiff. Some members found fault with this speech as being too late, ill-timed and misplaced.

1. V : 20.

Nepos, they said, had let the right moment go by for raising objections, and had withheld his censure until the affair was finally settled, though he could have opposed it before. In fact the praetor, Juventius Celsus, attacked him violently and at length for setting himself up as a reformer of the Senate. Nepos replied, and Celsus spoke again, neither of them refraining from abuse.

I have no wish to repeat words which I found distasteful to hear, and still less do I approve of certain of our senators who ran to and fro between Celsus and Nepos (according to which one was speaking) in their eagerness to hear every word. They seemed now to be spurring them on to fresh fury, then to be trying to appease them and restore order, as they called on the Emperor to favour one party or another or sometimes both. The whole scene might have been a public show. Another thing which disgusted me very much was the fact that each was informed of the other's intentions; Celsus addressed Nepos from a written speech and Nepos replied from his notes, for their friends had gossiped so much that they knew each other's arguments as if it had all been arranged beforehand.

6. To Minicius Fundanus

If ever I wished you were in Rome, it is now. Please come, for I need someone to share my prayers, efforts and anxiety. Julius Naso is a candidate for office, along with several other likely young men, so victory over his rivals will be difficult though it will be a real triumph if he succeeds. I am on tenterhooks, torn between hope and fear, and I can't realize that I have already been a consul – I feel as though I am putting up again for all the offices I have ever held.

I owe this to Naso in return for his long-standing regard for me, and am bound to him by ties of friendship; and, though difference in age made it impossible for me to be a friend of his father, when I was only a child his father was pointed out for me to admire. He was indeed a true lover of learning and its students, and would come every day to hear Quintilian[1] and Nicetes Sacerdos[2] whose lectures I was then attending. A man of his character and distinction should benefit his son by the reputation he leaves behind him, but there are many people in the Senate today who never knew him, many too who knew him but pay

1. The famous Quintilian, teacher and author of the *Institutio Oratoria*.
2. A teacher of rhetoric from Smyrna.

regard to none but the living. Consequently, Naso cannot rely on his father's fame – he may take great pride in it but it has little influential value – and must try to get on by his own efforts. This indeed he has always been careful to do, as if he foresaw this occasion; he has made friends and cultivated their friendship, and, in my own case, he singled me out for his friend and model as soon as he felt he could trust his own judgement. He is at my side, full of concern, when I plead in court or give a reading; he is there to take an interest the moment my trifling works see the light, and is there alone since he lost the brother who came with him and whose place I must now try to fill. I mourn the cruel death which has taken him from us so young, and I grieve, too, for Naso, who has lost such a brother's support and has no one left him but his friends.

This is what makes me insist that you come and add your vote to mine. It means so much to me to be able to show you off and take you canvassing with me; knowing your influence, I think I shall meet with a better response even from my friends if I have your support. Break off whatever is keeping you – my situation, honour, and official position all demand this. Everyone knows I have backed a candidate, and it is I who am canvassing and running the risks; in fact, if Naso wins his election the credit is his, but if he fails the defeat is mine.

7. *To his wife Calpurnia*

You say that you are feeling my absence very much, and your only comfort when I am not there is to hold my writings in your hand and often put them in my place by your side. I like to think that you miss me and find relief in this sort of consolation. I, too, am always reading your letters, and returning to them again and again as if they were new to me – but this only fans the fire of my longing for you. If your letters are so dear to me, you can imagine how I delight in your company; do write as often as you can, although you give me pleasure mingled with pain.

8. *To Neratius (?) Priscus*

You know and love Atilius Crescens – is there anyone at all distinguished who does not? But I am more than one of his many acquaintances, I am his close friend. Our home towns are only a day's journey apart, we became friends as boys when feelings are warmest, and later judgement has not cooled our affection but strengthened it, as anyone who knows either of us at all intimately is aware. Atilius boasts widely of his friendship with me, and I make no secret of my concern for his honour, security, and peace of mind. In fact when he told me he was nervous about the insolent attitude of one of the tribunes-elect, like Achilles I replied that no one should harm him 'while I live'.[1] All this goes to show that Atilius cannot be wronged without my being concerned, but you may still wonder what I am leading up to. Well, Valerius Varus has died owing him some money. Varus's heir is our mutual friend Maximus, and, as you are more intimate with him than I am, I beg, or rather insist, in the name of our friendship, that you will see that Atilius recovers not only his principal intact, but also the accumulated interest of several years. He is a man who never covets other people's possessions and is careful of his own, and he has no investments to support him, and no income but what he saves out of his frugal way of life; for though he makes such a success of his studies, he pursues them only for pleasure and the reputation they bring him. The slightest loss is serious for him, though it can be worse if one has to recover after a set-back. Do rid him and me of this worry, and let me still enjoy his charm and wit. I can't bear to see him in distress, when his natural gaiety never lets me be sad. You know his witticisms: please do not let injustice turn them to bitterness and gall. The warmth of his affection should convince you of his passion if offended, and his bold spirit of independence will not submit to loss coupled with insult. In any case, I should count the loss and insult my own, but be far angrier than I should for myself.

But this is no time for threats and intimidations – I will end as I began, and implore you to make every effort; then Atilius will not feel that I am doing nothing for him, as I very much fear he will, nor shall I feel the same about you. I am sure you will do this if you care as much for my feelings as I do for his.

9. To Cornelius Tacitus

So you recommend Julius Naso as a candidate for office. Naso to me? It might be me to myself! Never mind, I will forgive you. I should have done the same myself, had I been away and you still in Rome: anxiety has a way of thinking nothing superfluous. My advice is that

1. *Iliad*, 1 : 88.

you go away and canvass someone else, then I will support you and add my plea to yours.

10. *To Lucceius Albinus*

I have been visiting my mother-in-law at Alsium,[1] staying in the house which once belonged to Verginius Rufus.[2] The mere sight of the place revived all my grief and longing for that great and noble man. This was where he lived in retirement, calling it the nest of his old age, and wherever I went I realized how I missed the sight of him there. I had also an urge to see his tomb, but regretted it afterwards. It is still unfinished, not through any difficulty of construction (it is on a modest, even a humble scale) but because the man in charge of it takes no interest. I was filled with indignation and pity to think that nine years after Verginius's death his remaining ashes should still lie neglected without a name or inscription, although his glorious memory travels over the whole world. And yet he had made proper provision for recording in verse the immortal deed whereby his name lives for ever:

> Here lies Rufus, who once defeated Vindex and set free the imperial power
> Not for himself, but for his country.

Loyalty in friendship is so rare and the dead so easily forgotten that we ought to set up our own monuments and anticipate all the duties of our heirs. Which of us has no reason to fear the fate of Verginius? His fame only makes the wrong done to him all the more conspicuous for being undeserved.

11. *To Maximus*

This has been a happy day for me. I was called upon by the City Prefect to act as assessor, and heard two young men of outstanding ability and promise plead opposite each other. They were Fuscus Salinator and Ummidius Quadratus, a remarkable pair who are likely to prove an ornament not only to the present age but to literature itself. Both combined exceptional honesty with strength of character; their appearance was pleasant, their accent pure, and their voices fully developed, and they both had excellent memories and discretion to match their ability. All this delighted me, as did the fact that they looked to me

---

1. A coastal town of Etruria.   2. See 11 : 1.

as their guide and teacher, and gave their hearers the impression that they sought to follow in my footsteps. So it was a happy day, as I said before – a real red-letter day. What could be happier for our country than for two such distinguished young men to make their name and reputation in eloquence? What more could I desire than to be chosen to lead them on the right road? I pray the gods that I shall always be so happy, and you can bear me witness that I hope all who think me worth imitating may wish to be better men than I.

12. *To Calpurnius Fabatus, his wife's grandfather*

You are the last person who should hesitate to bring to my notice anyone you think needs assistance, for, if helping many is your proper concern, taking on any case you have at heart is mine. So I will do all I can for Bittius Priscus; especially in my own sphere of action, the Centumviral Court. You bid me forget the letters which you call outspoken, but there are none I like better to remember. They make me realize as never before how you love me, when you make the same demands on me as you used to on your own son. I admit my pleasure was increased by knowing that I had a good case: I had already done my best to carry out your request. I do beg you most earnestly to reprove me with the same frankness whenever I seem to fail in my duty (I say 'seem' because I shall never really fail). I shall understand that true love prompts your reproaches, and you may be glad to find that I did not deserve them.

13. *To Cornelius Ursus*

Have you ever seen anyone so tried and harassed as my friend Varenus? He won his concession[1] after a hard fight, and now he has had to defend it and practically apply for it all over again. The Bithynians have had the audacity to approach the consuls, impugn the Senate's decision, and try to have it reversed, and they have even dared to address a complaint to the Emperor, who is not in Rome. He has referred them back to the Senate, but their attacks have not ceased. Claudius Capito spoke on their behalf, not out of principle so much as with a certain irresponsibility which led him to attack a decree in front of the Senate which had passed it. Catius Fronto made an impressive and convincing reply. The Senate behaved admirably, for

1. See VI : 5.

even the members who had previously refused Varenus's application were in favour of granting it now that the proposal had been carried, on the grounds that though individuals were at liberty to dissent while a matter was still under discussion, once it had been settled the whole assembly should abide by the will of the majority. Only Acilius Rufus and seven or eight others (seven to be precise) held to their previous opinion; and several of this small minority raised a laugh for their temporary conscience, or rather their affectation of one. But you can guess what a struggle awaits us when the real battle begins, if this kind of preliminary skirmishing has made feeling run so high.

14. To Junius Mauricus

I accept your invitation to stay with you at Formiae[1] on the understanding that you don't put yourself out in any way – and I will keep to these terms myself. It is not the sea and shore which attract me, but the peace and freedom I shall enjoy in your company; otherwise I might just as well stay in town. Every man has to choose between pleasing others and pleasing himself, and I personally have no taste for half-measures.

15. To Voconius Romanus

You have missed an extraordinary scene, and so did I, though the tale has reached me almost at once. Passennus Paulus, a distinguished Roman knight and a scholar of repute, writes elegiac verse. This runs in his family, for he comes from the same town[2] as Propertius and considers him one of his ancestors. Paulus was giving a public reading and began by saying 'You bid me, Priscus – ' at which Javolenus Priscus,[3] who was present as a great friend of Paulus, exclaimed 'Indeed I don't!' You can imagine the laughter and witticisms which greeted this remark. It is true that Priscus is somewhat eccentric, but he takes part in public functions, acts as assessor, and is also one of the official experts on civil law; which makes his behaviour on this occasion all

1. On the coast of Latium (now Mola di Gaeta).
2. Asisium in Umbria (Assisi).
3. Javolenus Priscus was in fact a distinguished jurist, head of a school of jurisprudence, legate of Britain, Upper Germany, and Syria, and governor of Africa, and this outburst is more likely to have been an indication of boredom and impatience.

the more remarkable and absurd. Meanwhile Paulus has someone else's folly to blame for a chilly reception, and this shows how anyone giving a reading must beware of eccentricity either in himself or in the audience he invites.

16. To Cornelius Tacitus

Thank you for asking me to send you a description of my uncle's death so that you can leave an accurate account of it for posterity; I know that immortal fame awaits him if his death is recorded by you. It is true that he perished in a catastrophe which destroyed the loveliest regions of the earth, a fate shared by whole cities and their people, and one so memorable that it is likely to make his name live for ever: and he himself wrote a number of books of lasting value: but you write for all time and can still do much to perpetuate his memory. The fortunate man, in my opinion, is he to whom the gods have granted the power either to do something which is worth recording or to write what is worth reading, and most fortunate of all is the man who can do both. Such a man was my uncle, as his own books and yours will prove. So you set me a task I would choose for myself, and I am more than willing to start on it.

My uncle was stationed at Misenum,[1] in active command of the fleet. On 24 August, in the early afternoon, my mother drew his attention to a cloud of unusual size and appearance. He had been out in the sun, had taken a cold bath, and lunched while lying down, and was then working at his books. He called for his shoes and climbed up to a place which would give him the best view of the phenomenon. It was not clear at that distance from which mountain the cloud was rising (it was afterwards known to be Vesuvius); its general appearance can best be expressed as being like an umbrella pine, for it rose to a great height on a sort of trunk and then split off into branches, I imagine because it was thrust upwards by the first blast and then left unsupported as the pressure subsided, or else it was borne down by its own weight so that it spread out and gradually dispersed. Sometimes it looked white, sometimes blotched and dirty, according to the amount of soil and ashes it carried with it. My uncle's scholarly acumen saw at once that it was important enough for a closer inspection, and he ordered a boat to be made ready, telling me I could come with him

1. The northern arm of the bay of Naples (now Capo Miseno).

if I wished. I replied that I preferred to go on with my studies, and as it happened he had himself given me some writing to do.

As he was leaving the house he was handed a message from Rectina, wife of Tascius whose house was at the foot of the mountain, so that escape was impossible except by boat. She was terrified by the danger threatening her and implored him to rescue her from her fate. He changed his plans, and what he had begun in a spirit of inquiry he completed as a hero. He gave orders for the warships to be launched and went on board himself with the intention of bringing help to many more people besides Rectina, for this lovely stretch of coast was thickly populated. He hurried to the place which everyone else was hastily leaving, steering his course straight for the danger zone. He was entirely fearless, describing each new movement and phase of the portent to be noted down exactly as he observed them. Ashes were already falling, hotter and thicker as the ships drew near, followed by bits of pumice and blackened stones, charred and cracked by the flames: then suddenly they were in shallow water, and the shore was blocked by the debris from the mountain. For a moment my uncle wondered whether to turn back, but when the helmsman advised this he refused, telling him that Fortune stood by the courageous and they must make for Pomponianus at Stabiae.[1] He was cut off there by the breadth of the bay (for the shore gradually curves round a basin filled by the sea) so that he was not as yet in danger, though it was clear that this would come nearer as it spread. Pomponianus had therefore already put his belongings on board ship, intending to escape if the contrary wind fell. This wind was of course full in my uncle's favour, and he was able to bring his ship in. He embraced his terrified friend, cheered and encouraged him, and thinking he could calm his fears by showing his own composure, gave orders that he was to be carried to the bathroom. After his bath he lay down and dined; he was quite cheerful, or at any rate he pretended he was, which was no less courageous.

Meanwhile on Mount Vesuvius broad sheets of fire and leaping flames blazed at several points, their bright glare emphasized by the darkness of night. My uncle tried to allay the fears of his companions by repeatedly declaring that these were nothing but bonfires left by the peasants in their terror, or else empty houses on fire in the districts

1. Four miles south of Pompeii.

they had abandoned. Then he went to rest and certainly slept, for as he was a stout man his breathing was rather loud and heavy and could be heard by people coming and going outside his door. By this time the courtyard giving access to his room was full of ashes mixed with pumice-stones, so that its level had risen, and if he had stayed in the room any longer he would never have got out. He was wakened, came out and joined Pomponianus and the rest of the household who had sat up all night. They debated whether to stay indoors or take their chance in the open, for the buildings were now shaking with violent shocks, and seemed to be swaying to and fro as if they were torn from their foundations. Outside on the other hand, there was the danger of falling pumice-stones, even though these were light and porous; however, after comparing the risks they chose the latter. In my uncle's case one reason outweighed the other, but for the others it was a choice of fears. As a protection against falling objects they put pillows on their heads tied down with cloths.

Elsewhere there was daylight by this time, but they were still in darkness, blacker and denser than any ordinary night, which they relieved by lighting torches and various kinds of lamp. My uncle decided to go down to the shore and investigate on the spot the possibility of any escape by sea, but he found the waves still wild and dangerous. A sheet was spread on the ground for him to lie down, and he repeatedly asked for cold water to drink. Then the flames and smell of sulphur which gave warning of the approaching fire drove the others to take flight and roused him to stand up. He stood leaning on two slaves and then suddenly collapsed, I imagine because the dense fumes choked his breathing by blocking his windpipe which was constitutionally weak and narrow and often inflamed. When daylight returned on the 26th – two days after the last day he had seen – his body was found intact and uninjured, still fully clothed and looking more like sleep than death.

Meanwhile my mother and I were at Misenum, but this is not of any historic interest, and you only wanted to hear about my uncle's death. I will say no more, except to add that I have described in detail every incident which I either witnessed myself or heard about immediately after the event, when reports were most likely to be accurate. It is for you to select what best suits your purpose, for there is a great difference between a letter to a friend and history written for all to read.

17. To Claudius Restitutus

I have come away from a reading given by a friend of mine in such a sorry state of indignation that I simply must pour out the whole story to you by letter, seeing that there is no chance of doing so in person. The work being read was highly finished in every way, but two or three clever persons – or so they seemed to themselves and a few others – listened to it like deaf mutes. They never opened their lips, stirred a hand, nor even rose to their feet if only as a change from sitting still. What is the point of all this dignity and learning, or rather this laziness and conceit, this want of tact and good sense, which makes you spend a whole day giving offence and leaving an enemy in the man you came to hear as your dearest friend? Are you cleverer than he is? All the more reason not to grudge him his success, for jealousy is a sign of inferiority. In fact, whether your own performance is better or worse or on a par with his, you should show your appreciation; for if your superior does not meet with applause neither will you, and it is in your own interests that anyone you equal or surpass should be well received.

Personally I always respect and admire anyone who achieves something in literature, for she is an uncertain mistress, coy and hard to please, apt to despise those who despise her. Perhaps you think otherwise, though there is no more serious and appreciative critic of this subject than yourself. That is why I have chosen you rather than anyone else to hear about my indignation: you are most likely to share it.

18. To Statius Sabinus

I will do my best to take on the case for Firmum,[1] as you ask me, although I have a great deal of business on my hands; I am glad to oblige such a distinguished town by my professional services, and you too by a favour which will please you so much. You are always saying that you sought my friendship for the help and distinction I bring you, so there is nothing I should deny you, especially when your request is made on behalf of your native town. No petition is so honourable as a loyal citizen's, none so effective as a friend's. You can pledge my word then to your people of Firmum, or rather *our* people; their excellent reputation is a sufficient guarantee that they are worthy of

1. In Picenum (now Fermo).

my care and attention, added to the fact that there is likely to be nothing but good in the people who can claim a citizen like you.

19. *To Maecilius Nepos*

Have you heard that the price of land has gone up, particularly in the neighbourhood of Rome? The reason for the sudden increase in price has given rise to a good deal of discussion. At the last election, the Senate expressed the very proper opinion that 'Candidates should be prohibited from providing entertainments, distributing presents, and depositing money with agents'. The first two practices were employed without restraint or concealment, and the third was done secretly but was well known to all. When the debate reached our friend Homullus, he was quick to take advantage of the agreement in the Senate; he asked that the consuls should inform the Emperor of this unanimous feeling and petition him to take thought, as on previous occasions, to find means to remedy this evil. This he has done, by applying the law against bribery to force candidates to limit their scandalously gross expenditure; and he has also compelled them to invest a third of their capital in real estate, thinking it unseemly (as indeed it was) that candidates for office should treat Rome and Italy not as their native country, but as a mere inn or lodging-house for them on their visits. Consequently candidates are rushing about, struggling to buy up anything they hear is for sale, and thus bringing more into the market. So if you are tired of your Italian estates, now is the time, believe me, for selling out and buying in the provinces – the same candidates are selling there to be able to buy here.

20. *To Cornelius Tacitus*

So the letter which you asked me to write on my uncle's death has made you eager to hear about the terrors and hazards I had to face when left at Misenum, for I broke off at the beginning of this part of my story. 'Though my mind shrinks from remembering . . . I will begin.'[1]

After my uncle's departure I spent the rest of the day with my books, as this was my reason for staying behind. Then I took a bath, dined, and then dozed fitfully for a while. For several days past there had been earth tremors which were not particularly alarming because they are frequent in Campania: but that night the shocks were so violent that

1. *Aeneid*, 11:12.

everything felt as if it were not only shaken but overturned. My mother hurried into my room and found me already getting up to wake her if she were still asleep. We sat down in the forecourt of the house, between the buildings and the sea close by. I don't know whether I should call this courage or folly on my part (I was only seventeen at the time) but I called for a volume of Livy and went on reading as if I had nothing else to do. I even went on with the extracts I had been making. Up came a friend of my uncle's who had just come from Spain to join him. When he saw us sitting there and me actually reading, he scolded us both – me for my foolhardiness and my mother for allowing it. Nevertheless, I remained absorbed in my book.

By now it was dawn, but the light was still dim and faint. The buildings round us were already tottering, and the open space we were in was too small for us not to be in real and imminent danger if the house collapsed. This finally decided us to leave the town. We were followed by a panic-stricken mob of people wanting to act on someone else's decision in preference to their own (a point in which fear looks like prudence), who hurried us on our way by pressing hard behind in a dense crowd. Once beyond the buildings we stopped, and there we had some extraordinary experiences which thoroughly alarmed us. The carriages we had ordered to be brought out began to run in different directions though the ground was quite level, and would not remain stationary even when wedged with stones. We also saw the sea sucked away and apparently forced back by the earthquake: at any rate it receded from the shore so that quantities of sea creatures were left stranded on dry sand. On the landward side a fearful black cloud was rent by forked and quivering bursts of flame, and parted to reveal great tongues of fire, like flashes of lightning magnified in size.

At this point my uncle's friend from Spain spoke up still more urgently: 'If your brother, if your uncle is still alive, he will want you both to be saved; if he is dead, he would want you to survive him – why put off your escape?' We replied that we would not think of considering our own safety as long as we were uncertain of his. Without waiting any longer, our friend rushed off and hurried out of danger as fast as he could.

Soon afterwards the cloud sank down to earth and covered the sea; it had already blotted out Capri and hidden the promontory of

Misenum from sight. Then my mother implored, entreated and commanded me to escape as best I could – a young man might escape, whereas she was old and slow and could die in peace as long as she had not been the cause of my death too. I refused to save myself without her, and grasping her hand forced her to quicken her pace. She gave in reluctantly, blaming herself for delaying me. Ashes were already falling, not as yet very thickly. I looked round: a dense black cloud was coming up behind us, spreading over the earth like a flood. 'Let us leave the road while we can still see,' I said, 'or we shall be knocked down and trampled underfoot in the dark by the crowd behind.' We had scarcely sat down to rest when darkness fell, not the dark of a moonless or cloudy night, but as if the lamp had been put out in a closed room. You could hear the shrieks of women, the wailing of infants, and the shouting of men; some were calling their parents, others their children or their wives, trying to recognize them by their voices. People bewailed their own fate or that of their relatives, and there were some who prayed for death in their terror of dying. Many besought the aid of the gods, but still more imagined there were no gods left, and that the universe was plunged into eternal darkness for evermore. There were people, too, who added to the real perils by inventing fictitious dangers: some reported that part of Misenum had collapsed or another part was on fire, and though their tales were false they found others to believe them. A gleam of light returned, but we took this to be a warning of the approaching flames rather than daylight. However, the flames remained some distance off; then darkness came on once more and ashes began to fall again, this time in heavy showers. We rose from time to time and shook them off, otherwise we should have been buried and crushed beneath their weight. I could boast that not a groan or cry of fear escaped me in these perils, had I not derived some poor consolation in my mortal lot from the belief that the whole world was dying with me and I with it.

At last the darkness thinned and dispersed into smoke or cloud; then there was genuine daylight, and the sun actually shone out, but yellowish as it is during an eclipse. We were terrified to see everything changed, buried deep in ashes like snowdrifts. We returned to Misenum where we attended to our physical needs as best we could, and then spent an anxious night alternating between hope and fear. Fear predominated, for the earthquakes went on, and several hysterical

individuals made their own and other people's calamities seem
ludicrous in comparison with their frightful predictions. But even
then, in spite of the dangers we had been through and were still
expecting, my mother and I had still no intention of leaving until we
had news of my uncle.

Of course these details are not important enough for history, and
you will read them without any idea of recording them; if they seem
scarcely worth putting in a letter, you have only yourself to blame
for asking for them.

21. To Caninius Rufus

I am an admirer of the ancients, but, not like some people, so as to
despise the talent of our own times. It is not true that the world is too
tired and exhausted to be able to produce anything worth praising:
on the contrary, I have just heard Vergilius Romanus reading to a small
audience a comedy which was so skilfully modelled on the lines of the
Old Comedy that one day it may serve as a model itself. I don't know
whether you know the man, but you certainly ought to. He is remarkable for his moral integrity, his intellectual refinement, and his
versatility as an author. His iambic mimes are subtle, witty, and altogether delightful, in the best style for their type – for there is no type
which cannot command the best style if this achieves perfection. He
has also written comedies in imitation of Menander and his contemporaries which can be classed with those of Plautus and Terence.
This was his first appearance in Old Comedy, though it did not seem
like a first attempt. He lacked neither vigour, grandeur, nor subtlety
of style, pungency, charm, nor humour; he praised virtue and attacked
vice, introduced fictitious names when suitable and made appropriate
use of real ones. Only in my own case did his excess of kind feeling
lead him to exaggerate, but, after all, poets are not obliged to keep to
the truth.

I will get the book out of him and send it to you to read, or rather to
learn by heart, for I am quite sure that once you have laid hands on it
you will never be able to put it down.

22. To Calestrius Tiro

An important case has just been heard which is of interest to all future
provincial governors and to anyone who trusts his friends without

reserve. Lustricius Bruttianus had detected his colleague, Montanius Atticinus, in a number of criminal offences and had sent a report to the Emperor. Atticinus then added to his misdeeds by bringing a case against the friend he had deceived. The trial came on, and I acted as assessor. Each side conducted his own case, dealing with the main items one by one, which is the quickest way at arriving at the truth. Bruttianus produced his will, which he said was written in the hand of Atticinus, as a proof both of the confidence he had placed in their relationship and of the necessity which constrained him to complain about a man who had been so dear to him. He cited a number of shocking charges, all clearly proved; being unable to refute them, Atticinus retorted with counter-charges, but merely proved himself a rogue in his defence and a scoundrel by his accusations. He had bribed a slave belonging to Bruttianus's secretary, had intercepted certain papers and falsified some of them, and, worst of all, had directed a charge intended for himself against his friend.

The Emperor dealt with him admirably, asking for an immediate verdict not on Bruttianus but on Atticinus, who was found guilty and banished to an island. Bruttianus received a well-deserved tribute to his honesty, and has also won a reputation for determination, for he finished his defence as quickly as he could and then pressed his charges vigorously; thus proving his spirit as well as his honour and good faith.

I have described this case to you as a warning, now you have been allotted your province,[1] to rely chiefly on yourself and trust no one very far. I want you to know, too, that if by any chance any one does deceive you (though I pray that no one will) there is punishment awaiting him. But be always on your guard so that it shall not be necessary, for the satisfaction of obtaining redress is no compensation for the misery of being deceived.

23. To Triarius

As you are so anxious for me to appear in a case in which you are interested (a good cause, you say, which will add to my reputation), I will do so, but not for nothing. 'Impossible,' you will say, 'for *you* to want a fee!' But it *is* possible, and my fee does no more credit than offering my services for nothing. I have a request, or rather a stipulation

1. Baetica, in Spain.

to make: that Cremutius Ruso shall act with me. This is my usual way of treating young men of distinction, for I take a special pleasure in introducing promising young people to the courts and setting them on the path to fame. My friend Ruso should have my help before anyone, for he comes of a good family and has a marked regard for me, and I think it important for him to be seen and heard in the same case and acting on the same side as myself. Please do me this favour, and do it before you hear him speak; you will thank me for it afterwards. The case is important and you will be anxious, but I promise you he will come up to my expectations. He is a highly talented young man and will soon be bringing others forward if in the meantime he has his introduction from us. No one can make a start, however outstanding his abilities, if he lacks scope and opportunity and a patron to support him.

24. To Calpurnius Macer

How often we judge actions by the people who perform them! The self-same deeds are lauded to the skies or allowed to sink into oblivion simply because the persons concerned are well known or not.

I was sailing on our Lake Como with an elderly friend when he pointed out a house with a bedroom built out over the lake. 'From there,' he said, 'a woman of our town once threw herself with her husband.' I asked why. The husband had long been suffering from ulcers in the private parts, and his wife insisted on seeing them, promising that no one would give him a more candid opinion whether the disease was curable. She saw that there was no hope and urged him to take his life; she went with him, even led him to his death herself, and forced him to follow her example by roping herself to him and jumping into the lake. Yet even I, who come from the same town, never heard of this until the other day – not because it was less heroic than Arria's famous deed,[1] but because the woman was less well known.

25. To Baebius Hispanus

You say that the distinguished Roman knight Robustus travelled as far as Ocriculum[2] with my friend Atilius Scaurus, and then completely vanished, and you want Scaurus to come and see if he can put us on

1. See III:16. 2. In Umbria, on the Via Flaminia (now Otricoli).

the scent. He shall come, though I fear it may be no use. I suspect something has happened to Robustus of the same sort as once befell my fellow-townsman Metilius Crispus. I had obtained his promotion to the rank of centurion and had given him 40,000 sesterces for his outfit and equipment when he set out, but I never had a letter from him afterwards, nor any news of his death. Whether he was killed by his slaves or along with them, no one knows: at any rate, neither Crispus nor any of them were seen again, any more than the slaves of Robustus. But let us try, and send for Scaurus – this much we can do in answer to your request and the very proper entreaties of the worthy young man who is showing intelligence as well as devotion to his father in the way he is organizing the search. I pray that with the gods' help he will be as successful in finding his father as he was in discovering the man who travelled with him.

26. To Julius Servianus

I am glad to hear that your daughter is to marry Fuscus Salinator, and must congratulate you on your choice. He belongs to one of our noble families and his father and mother are both highly respected; while he himself is scholarly, well read, and something of an orator, and he combines a childlike frankness and youthful charm with mature judgement. Nor am I blinded by affection – I love him as dearly as his merits and regard for me deserve, but I have kept my critical powers: in fact they are sharpened by my love for him. I can assure you (knowing him as I do) that he will be a son-in-law who will prove better than your fondest hopes could wish. It only remains for him to give you grandchildren like himself as soon as possible. It will be a happy day for me when I can take his children, who are also your grandchildren, from your arms as if it were my right and they were my own.

27. To Vettenius Severus

You ask me to consider what tribute you should pay the Emperor in your speech as consul-elect. His virtues provide abundant material, so that it is easy enough to think of subjects but not so easy to choose between them. However, I will write and send you my opinion, or preferably give it you when we meet; but I must first explain my hesitation. I am wondering whether I ought to advise you to do as I did when I was consul-elect. I made a point of avoiding anything which looked like flattery, even if not intended as such, acting not on any principle of independence but on my knowledge of our Emperor. I realized that the highest praise I could offer him was to show that I said nothing because it was expected of me. I also had in mind the many tributes paid to the worst of his predecessors, and I felt that nothing could distinguish our noble Emperor from them so well as a different type of speech. I made no attempt to conceal my intention and did not pass over it without mention, for I did not want him to think it forgetfulness on my part rather than a deliberate decision.

This was the line I took on that occasion, but the same method does not appeal to everyone nor is it always suitable, and our reasons for doing or not doing anything depend on changes in human affairs as well as times and situations. In fact, the recent achievements[1] of our great ruler give you an opportunity to say something original which shall be genuinely worth saying. Hence my doubts, as I said above, whether I should advise you to act as I did in my time. One thing I don't doubt – I could not give you any advice without telling you what I did myself.

28. To Pontius Allifanus

I know what has kept you from being here to welcome my arrival in Campania, but though absent in person you might have been here with all you possess, to judge by the quantities of town and country delicacies I have been offered in your name. I must own I was shameless enough to accept everything. Your servants begged me to do so and I was afraid you would be angry with us all if I refused. In future I shall have to set bounds to your hospitality myself if you will not, and I have already warned your people that if they bring so much another time they will have to take it all back again. You may say that all you have is mine to use: yes, but that means it is also mine to use in moderation.

29. Ummidius Quadratus

Avidius Quietus, whose good opinion of me I valued as much as his warm affection, had been a friend of Thrasea's[2] and used to tell me

1. Trajan returned from his victories in Dacia in 106.
2. Thrasea Paetus; see Introduction, page 21.

many of his sayings. One he often quoted was that there were three kinds of case which we should undertake: our friends', those which no one else would take on, and those which establish a precedent. No explanation is needed to show why we should help our friends; we should undertake the second type, he said, as the best means of showing our generosity and strength of mind, and the third because nothing is so important as establishing the right precedent. To these I will add a fourth type of case, though it may seem presumption on my part: cases which bring fame and recognition, for there is no reason why a speaker should not sometimes act for his honour and reputation's sake, and so plead his own case. These then (as you ask my opinion) are the limits I would lay down for a person of your high standing and discretion.

I am quite well aware that practice is generally held to be the best teacher of public speaking, and rightly so; I see plenty of people with small talent and no education who have acquired the art of speaking well simply by speaking, but at the same time I have found by experience that this saying (which I am told is Pollio's, or at any rate is attributed to him) comes nearest the truth: 'By pleading well I came to plead often, but this in turn led me to plead less well.' In fact excessive application is more likely to produce facility and foolhardiness than fluency and confidence. His shyness and weak voice prevented Isocrates from speaking in public; nevertheless he was judged to be an orator of the first rank. So read, write, and make all the preparations you can; you will then be able to speak when you wish and when duty calls you.

This was my own guiding principle on the whole, though there were times when I had to yield to necessity, which is one aspect of reason. I undertook certain cases at the bidding of the Senate, but some of these come under Thrasea's heading as establishing a precedent. I appeared for the people of Baetica against Baebius Massa,[1] when the question arose whether time should be granted them in which to collect evidence: it was granted. I acted for them again when they brought a charge against Caecilius Classicus;[2] this time the question was whether provincials should be penalized for being the governor's allies and accomplices: they were punished. I appeared for the prosecution when Marius Priscus[3] was found guilty of taking bribes and tried

1. In 93; see III: 4 and VII: 33. 2. In 101; see III: 9. 3. In 99–100; see II: 11.

to profit from the leniency of the law dealing with such cases, although the charges against him were too serious to be covered by the maximum penalty it allowed: he was banished. I defended Julius Bassus[1] on the ground that he had acted foolishly and without proper caution, but with no criminal intent: he was allowed to have his penalty assessed by special court and retained his place in the Senate. I spoke recently on behalf of Varenus[2] when he applied for permission to call witnesses from his province for his defence: his request was granted. As for the future, I hope I shall be required to take up cases only when I might suitably have done so unbidden.

30. To Calpurnius Fabatus, his wife's grandfather

I am bound indeed to celebrate your birthday like my own, when my enjoyment of life depends on you; for thanks to your careful management I can be happy here and have no worries about things at Comum.

Your Villa Camilla in Campania is certainly suffering from its age, but the more valuable parts of the building are still intact or else only very slightly damaged, so I will have it restored as reasonably as I can. Amongst my many friends I seem to have practically no one of the type you want for this post; they are all thorough townsfolk, whereas the management of country estates needs a stalwart countryman who will neither find the work too hard or beneath him, nor the lonely life depressing. You are quite right to consider Rufus, as he was your son's friend – I don't know quite what he can do for us there, but I am sure he intends to do his best.

31. To Cornelianus

I was delighted to be summoned by the Emperor to act as his assessor at Centum Cellae,[3] where I am now. Nothing could give me more pleasure than to have first-hand experience of our ruler's justice and wisdom and also to see him in lighter mood, as he can be when away from Rome. There were several different types of case which tested his judicial powers in various ways. The first one was that of Claudius

1. In 102–3; see IV:9.   2. In 106–7; see V:20, and VI:5 and 13.
3. On the coast of Etruria (now Civita Vecchia).

Aristion, the leading citizen of Ephesus, popular for his generosity and politically harmless; but he had roused the envy of people of a vastly different character who had suborned an informer against him. He was cleared of the charge and acquitted.

The case heard on the following day was that of Gallitta, charged with adultery. She was the wife of a military tribune who was just about to stand for civil office, and had brought disgrace on her own and her husband's position by an affair with a centurion. Her husband had reported it to the governor, and he had informed the Emperor. After sifting the evidence the Emperor cashiered the centurion and banished him. There still remained the second half of the sentence, for the charge could only have been made against two persons; but here the husband held back out of affection for his wife and was censured for condoning her conduct. Even after he had reported his wife's adultery he had kept her in his house, apparently satisfied once he had got rid of his rival. When summoned to complete his accusation he did so with reluctance, but it was essential that the woman should be convicted, however unwilling her accuser. She was duly found guilty and sentenced under the Julian law.[1] In pronouncing judgement the Emperor mentioned the name of the centurion and made a statement on military discipline, for he did not wish all cases of this kind to be referred to him.

On the third day began an inquiry into Julius Tiro's will, a case which had given rise to a good deal of discussion and conflicting rumours. Some of the additional clauses to the will were agreed to be genuine; the rest were said to be forged. The persons charged were a Roman knight, Sempronius Senecio, and Eurythmus, one of the Emperor's freedmen and procurators. The heirs had written a joint letter to the Emperor while he was in Dacia, begging him to conduct the inquiry. He had agreed to do so, and had fixed a day for the trial on his return. Then he found that some of the heirs were reluctant to appear against Eurythmus and intended to drop the case, but he had very properly declared that 'He is not Polyclitus[2] nor am I Nero.' He had however agreed to an adjournment, and took his seat to hear the case now that the time-limit had expired. Only two of the heirs were

1. Under the *lex Julia de adulteriis* a woman forfeited half her dowry and was banished to an island.
2. Nero's notorious freedman.

present, and they asked that either all the heirs should be compelled to appear, as all were responsible for the prosecution, or that they should themselves be allowed to drop the case. The Emperor's reply was restrained and impressive, but, when the counsel for Senecio and Eurythmus said that his clients were left under suspicion if they were not given a hearing, 'I am not concerned so much with their position,' he said, 'as with the fact that I am left under suspicion myself.' Then he turned to us. 'Consider what we ought to do. These people want to complain about being let off the charge against them.' Acting on our advice he then gave orders that all the heirs were to be summoned to carry on the case or else to give adequate reasons individually for dropping it: otherwise he would declare them guilty of instituting false charges.

As you see, our days were well spent on serious matters, but we enjoyed our relaxations in the evenings. The Emperor invited us to dinner every day, a simple affair if you consider his position. Sometimes we were entertained by recitations, or else the night was prolonged by pleasant conversation, and, on our last day, with his usual thoughtful generosity, he sent us all parting gifts. I took great pleasure in the importance of the cases, the honour of being an assessor, and the charm and informality of our social life, and I was no less delighted in the place itself. The house is really beautiful: it is surrounded by green fields and faces the sea-shore, where a natural bay is being converted with all speed into a harbour. The left arm has already been reinforced by a solid mole and the right is in process of construction. At the entrance to the harbour an island is rising out of the water to act as a breakwater when the wind blows inland, and so give a safe passage to ships entering from either side. Its construction is well worth seeing. Huge stones are brought by large barges and thrown out one on top of another facing the harbour; their weight keeps them in position and the pile gradually rises in a sort of rampart. A hump of rocks can already be seen sticking up, which breaks the waves beating against it and tosses them high into the air with a resounding crash, so that the sea all round is white with foam. Later on piers will be built on the stone foundation, and as time goes on it will look like a natural island. The harbour will be called after its maker, and is in fact already known by his name; and it will save countless lives by providing a haven on this long stretch of harbourless coast.

32. To Quintilianus[1]

I know your own tastes are of the simplest and that you have brought
up your daughter as befits a daughter of yours and a grandchild of
Tutilius; but as she is to marry so distinguished a person as Nonius
Celer, whose public duties oblige him to keep up a certain amount of
style, she ought to be provided with clothes and attendants in keeping
with her husband's position. These things cannot increase her worth,
but can give it the setting it needs. I know too that you are rich in
intellectual gifts but that your means are limited, so I want to share
your burden and play the part of a second father to your daughter. I
am therefore settling 50,000 sesterces on her, and would offer more
were I not sure that it is only the trifling nature of the gift which will
prevail on your sense of delicacy to accept it.

33. To Voconius Romanus

'Away with everything,' he said, 'and put aside whatever you have
begun!'[2] You may be reading something or writing – put it down and
take up my speech; like Vulcan's arms, it is divine. Could conceit go
farther? But, seriously, compared with my other speeches it is very
fine, and I am quite content to rival myself. It was delivered on behalf
of Attia Viriola, and its interest lies not only in the position of the
person concerned but also in the rarity of this type of case and the size
of the court which heard it. Here was a woman of high birth, the
wife of a praetorian senator, disinherited by her eighty-year-old
father ten days after he had fallen in love and brought home a stepmother for his daughter, and now suing for her patrimony in the
united Centumviral Court. One hundred and eighty judges were
sitting, the total for the four panels acting together; both parties were
fully represented and had a large number of seats filled with their
supporters, and a close-packed ring of onlookers, several rows deep,
lined the walls of the courtroom. The bench was also crowded, and
even the galleries were full of men and women leaning over in their
eagerness to see and also to hear, though hearing was rather more
difficult. Fathers, daughters and stepmothers all anxiously awaited the
verdict. This proved not to be united, for two divisions voted for us

1. Not the famous Quintilian, who was dead by this time.
2. *Aeneid*, VIII : 439.

and two against. Such divergence of opinion was particularly surprising in a single case, conducted by the same counsel before the same judges at the same hearing. By pure chance, though it might have been thought otherwise, the stepmother, who had been left a sixth of the estate, lost her case, and so did Suburanus, who had the extraordinary impudence to claim someone else's patrimony when he had been disinherited by his own father and dare not sue for his own.

I have told you this so that this letter shall explain anything you cannot understand from the speech, and also (for I don't conceal my guile) because I thought you would be more willing to read the speech if you imagined yourself present at the actual trial. It is long, but I feel sure it will be as popular as a short one, for the interest is kept up by the lively arrangement of the abundant material, the frequent use of short anecdotes, and the variety of oratorical style. Much of it is in the grand manner and full of fire (I wouldn't dare say this to anyone else) but there are long sections in a plainer style, where I was often obliged to introduce calculations into the midst of my impassioned and lofty arguments, and practically demand counters and a board for reckoning, as if my case had been transformed into a private one. I gave full play to my feelings of wrath and indignation, and steered by course through this vastly important case with the wind full in my favour. In fact some of my friends think that in comparison with my other speeches, this one is my '*De Corona*'.[1] Whether this is so or not, you can easily judge. You have all my speeches by heart, so you only have to read the one I am sending now to be able to make your comparison.

34. To Valerius (?) Maximus

You did well to put on a show of gladiators for our people of Verona, who have long shown their affection and admiration for you and have voted you many honours. Verona was also the home town of the excellent wife you loved so dearly, whose memory you owe some public building or show, and this kind of spectacle is particularly suitable for a funeral tribute. Moreover, the request came from so many people that a refusal would have been judged churlish rather than strong-minded on your part. You have also done admirably in giving the show so readily and on such a lavish scale, for this indicates a true spirit of generosity.

1. Demosthenes' most celebrated speech.

I am sorry the African panthers you had bought in such quantities did not turn up on the appointed day, but you deserve the credit although the weather prevented their arriving in time; it was not your fault that you could not show them.

BOOK SEVEN

1. *To Rosianus Geminus*

This persistent ill-health of yours is alarming, and, although I know that your self-control is generally excellent, I am afraid that your character may be affected. I can only advise you to be patient and endure; there is hope of recovery as well as merit in this, and it is not beyond human capacity. At any rate I personally, when in good health, have often spoken like this to my household: 'I hope that if I chance to fall ill, I shall not ask for anything which would be a reason, for subsequent shame and regret, but, if illness gets the upper hand, I warn you now not to give me anything without the doctors' permission, or else I shall punish you as anyone else would for refusing.' I was indeed once suffering from a raging fever: at last it began to abate, I was oiled and massaged and was just taking a drink from the doctor when I held out my hand for him to feel my pulse, and refused the cup which had been put to my lips. Later on, when I had been ill nearly three weeks, I was being prepared for a bath, but suddenly noticed the doctors whispering and asked the reason why. They replied that probably it was quite safe for me to take a bath, but they felt a little doubtful about it. 'Then is it necessary?' I asked, and so without protest quietly gave up hope of the bath which in my imagination I was already entering, and resigned myself again to do without it with the same inward and outward composure as when I was in a state of anticipation.

My initial reason for telling you this was to have an example to illustrate my advice, but I can also use this letter as a kind of pledge to bind me to practise the same self-control in future.

2. *To Fabius (?) Justus*

I don't see how you can say in the same breath that your time is taken up by incessant public duties and ask to see my speeches! I have difficulty enough when people have plenty of time in persuading them to give up a moment of their wasted hours. I will let you finish the summer, which I know is always a busy and trying time for you, and then in winter, when your nights at least are likely to be free, I will look through my efforts for something to send. Meanwhile I am more than satisfied if my letters are not a nuisance; but I expect they are and will make them shorter in future.

3. To Bruttius (?) Praesens

How much longer will you persist in dividing your time between Lucania[1] and Campania? I know you say that Lucania is your native district and Campania your wife's, but that can only justify a prolonged absence, not a perpetual one. Are you ever coming back to Rome, back to your honours and official duties, your influential friendships, and your clients' attentions? How much longer will you be your own master, stay up when you feel inclined, and sleep as long as you like? How long will your shoes go unworn and your toga stay on holiday, while all your day is your own? It is time you renewed acquaintance with our vexations, if only to prevent your pleasures diminishing through sheer surfeit. Come and pay your respects to use for a while so as to be better pleased to receive other peoples', and rub shoulders in the crowd here in order to appreciate your solitude the more.

But it is silly of me to risk discouraging the very person I am trying to persuade; my arguments may well induce you to sink deeper and deeper into retirement, though I am not asking you to give it up, only to interrupt it. If I were giving you a dinner, I should alternate the sweet dishes with piquant savouries to stimulate your palate when dulled by too much sweetness; and so I am asking you now to season your pleasant way of living with something a little more stimulating.

4. To Pontius Allifanus

You say that you have read my hendecasyllables, and you want to know how a serious man like me came to write them; and I am not frivolous, I admit. To start at the beginning, I was always interested in poetry and wrote a Greek tragedy at the age of fourteen. What it was like I can't say – anyway, I called it a tragedy. Later on I was weatherbound in the island of Icaria[2] while on my way home from

1. The region south-east of Campania.   2. In the Aegean (now Nicaria).

military service, and wrote some Latin elegiacs with the sea and island for theme. I have also occasionally tried my hand at epic verse, but this is my first attempt at hendecasyllables. This is how I came to make it. While I was staying in my house at Laurentum I had Asinius Gallus's works read aloud to me, in which he draws a comparison between his father and Cicero and quotes an epigram of Cicero's on his favourite Tiro. Then, when I had retired for my siesta (it was summer) and was unable to sleep, I began to reflect upon the fact that all the greatest orators had amused themselves with this kind of writing and had won fame thereby. I set my mind to it, and, to my surprise, in spite of being long out of practice, I had soon expressed the very thought which had inspired me to write. This was the result:

> Reading the works of Gallus, where he ventures
> To hand the palm of glory to his father,
> I found that Cicero could unbend his talent
> To play with polished wit on lighter theme.
> Tiro, he says, defrauds and cheats his lover
> Of kisses promised for a dinner eaten,
> Why then conceal my blushes, why not publish
> My Tiro's wiles and coy endearing favours
> Whereby he heaps the fuel on my passion?

Next I tried some elegiac verses, which I finished just as quickly, and finding them so easy I was tempted to add more. Afterwards, when I returned to Rome, I read them to my friends, who were appreciative. Then I made attempts in various other metres whenever I had time, especially when travelling. Finally I decided to do as many authors have done and complete a separate volume of hendecasyllables; and I have never regretted this. My verses are read and copied, they are even sung, and set to the cithara or lyre by Greeks who have learned Latin out of liking for my little book. But I must not boast (though poets can talk wildly!) even if it is not my own opinion I am quoting but other people's – which pleases me whether right or wrong. I only pray that posterity will be right or wrong in the same way.

5. *To his wife Calpurnia*

You cannot believe how much I miss you. I love you so much, and we are not used to separations. So I stay awake most of the night thinking of you, and by day I find my feet carrying me (a true word, carrying) to your room at the times I usually visited you; then finding it empty I depart, as sick and sorrowful as a lover locked out. The only time I am free from this misery is when I am in court and wearing myself out with my friends' lawsuits. You can judge then what a life I am leading, when I find my rest in work and distraction in troubles and anxiety.

6. To Caecilius Macrinus

A most extraordinary thing has happened to Varenus,[1] though it is not yet definitely settled. The Bithynians are reported to have dropped their case against him, as an ill-advised venture. I say 'reported', but the representative of the province is here with his Council's decree, copies of which he has presented to the Emperor, to a large number of prominent citizens and to us, as acting for Varenus. However, Magnus is being as obstinate as ever and keeps on harassing that excellent man Nigrinus, through whom he has approached the consuls with a demand for Varenus to be compelled to produce his accounts.

At this stage I was standing by Varenus in a friendly capacity only and decided to say nothing, for it could only have done him harm if the counsel given him by the Senate began by defending him as if he were on trial when the essential thing was to show that he was not on trial at all. But when Nigrinus had made his request and the consuls turned to me, I said that they would see that I had good reason for my silence as soon as they had heard the true representatives of the province. 'To whom have they been sent?' asked Nigrinus. 'To me, amongst others,' I replied: 'I have the Council's decree.' 'You may have your own information,' he said. 'If you have yours,' I retorted, 'surely I may have mine – of a better sort.' Then Polyaenus, the Bithynian spokesman, explained their reasons for dropping the prosecution and asked that no decision should be taken before the Emperor held an inquiry. Magnus replied to this, and Polyaenus spoke again. I threw in a few words now and then, but kept silent most of the time, for I have learned that there are occasions when silence is as effective a form of oratory as eloquence. I can indeed remember certain criminal cases when I did my clients more good by saying nothing than I could have done by the most elaborate speech.

1. See v : 20 and vi : 5 and 13.

For example (there is nothing to stop me from discussing my professional activities, though I had another purpose in writing this letter), a mother who had lost her son charged his freedmen, who were heirs to the estate with her, of poisoning their master and forging his will. She had brought her case before the Emperor and been granted Julius Servianus to judge it. I had defended the accused men before a large assembly, for the case was celebrated and there were distinguished personalities engaged on both sides. The inquiry was stopped after the court had come to a decision in favour of the defendants. Subsequently the mother approached the Emperor with a declaration that she had discovered fresh evidence. Suburanus was instructed to hear the case again, if she could produce any new material. The mother was represented by Julius Africanus, the grandson of the famous orator about whom Passienus Crispus said after hearing him speak 'Fine, by Jove, fine; but *why* so fine?' His grandson, an able young man but a bit too sharp, had said a good deal and come to the end of his time-limit, but then asked Suburanus for permission to add 'just one more word'. My turn came, and everyone was looking to me for a lengthy reply. 'I should have spoken in reply,' I said, 'if Africanus had added his "one more word", for this, I am sure, would have contained all the fresh evidence.' I can scarcely remember ever winning such applause for a speech as I did on that occasion for not making one.

The same sort of reception and applause has greeted my policy of saying nothing for Varenus. The consuls have granted Polyaenus's request and left the whole question open for the Emperor to decide. I am anxiously awaiting the result, for that day will determine whether we are to have some peace and respite from worry on Varenus's account or to renew our efforts with fresh anxiety.

7. *To Pompeius Saturninus*

I thanked our friend Priscus only the other day, but I was very glad to do so again at your bidding. It is a great pleasure to me that splendid men like yourselves, both friends of mine, should be so devoted and conscious of your mutual attachment. Priscus also declares that nothing gives him greater happiness than his friendship with you and vies with you in this best of rivalries, a reciprocated affection which will increase as time goes on.

I am sorry to hear that you are immersed in business, as it keeps you from your own work, but if you can settle one case by arbitration and the other, as you say, by your own efforts, you will begin to enjoy your leisure where you are; and then can return to us when you are tired of it.

8. *To Neratius (?) Priscus*

Words cannot express my pleasure on receiving letter after letter from our friend Saturninus, in which he expresses his warmest thanks to you. Go on as you have begun, love this splendid man as much as you can; his friendship will prove a source of long and lasting happiness for he is endowed with all the virtues, not least the gift of unfailing loyalty in his affections.

9. *To Fuscus Salinator*

You ask me what course of study I think you should follow during your present prolonged holiday. The most useful thing, which is always being suggested, is to translate Greek into Latin and Latin into Greek. This kind of exercise develops in one a precision and richness of vocabulary, a wide range of metaphor, and power of exposition, and, moreover, imitation of the best models leads to a like aptitude for original composition. At the same time, any point which might have been overlooked by a reader cannot escape the eye of a translator. All this cultivates perception and critical sense.

When you have read a passage sufficiently to remember the subject-matter and line of thought, there is no harm in your trying to compete with it; then compare your efforts with the original and consider carefully where your version is better or worse. You may well congratulate yourself if yours is sometimes better and feel much ashamed if the other is always superior to yours. You may also sometimes choose a passage you know well and try to improve on it. This is a daring attempt, but does not presume too far when it is made in private; and yet we see many people entering this type of contest with great credit to themselves and, by not lacking confidence, outstripping the authors whom they only intended to follow. You can also revise the speeches you have put aside, retaining much of the original, but leaving out still more and making other additions and alterations. This I know you will think a tedious labour, but its very difficulty makes it profitable to rekindle your fire and recover your enthusiasm when once its force is spent; to graft new limbs, in fact, on to a finished trunk without disturbing the balance of the original.

I know that your chief interest at the present time is forensic oratory, but that is not a reason for advising you to limit yourself to this provocative and somewhat pugnacious style. The soil is refreshed when sown with successive changes of seed, and so are our minds if cultivated by different subjects. I should like you sometimes to take a passage of historical narrative or turn your attention to letter-writing, for often even in a speech the subject calls for a narrative or a poetic style of description; and letters develop brevity and simplicity of style. It is permissible, too, to seek relaxation in writing poetry, by which I mean not a long continuous poem (which can only be finished if one has plenty of leisure), but one of those short, polished sets of verses which make a break in your duties and responsibilities, however pressing. This is called light verse, but it sometimes brings its authors as much fame as serious work. In fact (for why shouldn't I versify to encourage you to take to verse?)

> The beauty of wax is its power to yield
>   To the fingers' skilful touch;
> Thus taught, it can shape the god of War,
>   Chaste Wisdom or Love or her son.
> The secret springs can quench a flame,
>   Or gladden the flowers and fields;
> So the mind of man, through the gentle arts
>   Is taught the wisdom of change.

The greatest orators, and the greatest men, too, used to train or amuse themselves in this way – or rather, combine their training with amusement, for it is remarkable how the mind is both stimulated and relaxed by these trifles. They comprise our loves and hatreds, our indignation, compassion and wit, in fact every phase of life and every detail of our public and professional activities. They also offer the same advantages as other forms of poetry; when we have been bound by the restrictions of metre, we delight in the freedom of prose and gladly return to what comparison has shown to be the easier style.

Perhaps this is more than you wanted, but there is one more thing. I have said nothing about what I think you should read, though this was implied when I was telling you what to write. Remember to make a careful selection from representative authors in each subject, for the saying is that a man should be deeply, not widely, read. These authors are too well known and approved to need further indication; and, besides, I have let this letter run on so far that I am robbing you of time for work with all my advice on planning it. Back then to your books and writing – either something on the lines I suggest, or what you have already started.

10. To Caecilius Macrinus

If I have heard the beginning of a story I always want to pick up the thread and add the conclusion, so I expect you, too, would like to hear the end of the affair between Varenus and the Bithynians. Polyaenus spoke on one side and Magnus on the other. The Emperor listened to both speeches and then declared that neither party should have cause to complain of delay; he would undertake to find out the wishes of the province. Meanwhile Varenus has gained much, for the justice of the charge against him is all the more doubtful when it is still uncertain if he is being charged at all. We can only hope that the province will not decide again in favour of what it was reported to have rejected, not think better of its change of heart.[1]

11. To Calpurnius Fabatus, his wife's grandfather

You are surprised to hear that my freedman Hermes has sold to Corellia, without waiting for the public auction, the land which I inherited and ordered to be put up for sale, valuing my five-twelfths of the estate at 700,000 sesterces. It might have fetched 900,000 you say, and this makes you wonder all the more whether I shall confirm what he has done. Yes, I do; and here are my reasons, for I am anxious to have your approval and my fellow-heirs' forgiveness if I disassociate myself from them in obedience to a higher claim.

I have the greatest respect and affection for Corellia, first as the sister of Corellius Rufus, whose memory I always hold sacred, and then as my mother's dearest friend. Then I have old ties of friendship with her excellent husband Minicius Justus, as I did with her son, who presided over the games held during my praetorship. During my last visit to you, when Corellia told me that she would like to own some property on the shores of Lake Como, it was I who offered her any

1. Nothing more is heard of this case.

one of my estates she liked, at her own price, with the exception of what I inherited from my parents; for those I could not give up even to her. Consequently, when I inherited this property, which included the land you refer to, I wrote and told her it was for sale. Hermes took her the letter, and when she asked him to transfer my share to her at once, he did so.

I am bound then, as you see, to confirm an action of my own freed-man which was in accordance with my own wishes. The only thing now is for my fellow-heirs not to be annoyed with me for having allowed a separate sale of what I need not have sold at all. There is no necessity for them to follow my example, for they have not the same ties with Corellia; so they are permitted to consider their own interests, though friendship took priority over mine.

12. To Minicius Fundanus

Here is the short speech which you asked me to write, for your friend (or rather for our friend, as we have everything in common) to use if he needs it. I have sent it at the last minute, to leave you no time to correct, which means to spoil it. Doubtless though you *will* find time – for spoiling certainly, for correcting I can't say: you purists cut out all the best passages! But I shan't care, for I can pass the result off as my own some day, and take the credit for your fastidiousness, as I do for the passages you will find marked with an alternative version written between the lines. For I suspected that you would find its sonority and grandeur rather too pompous, so I thought it would be best to put you out of your misery by adding something shorter and plainer straight away – a meaner, inferior version, in fact, though you may think it an improvement. (Here's my chance to make a real attack on your ultra-refinement.) So far I have been trying to raise a smile from you in the midst of your responsibilities, but this is serious: be sure to re-fund my expenses for taking the trouble to send this by special messenger. Now you have read this request you will condemn the whole speech out of hand and not just the details, being unwilling to admit it is worth anything when you are asked to pay for it.

13. To Julius Ferox

The same letter of yours tells me that you are doing no work and yet you are working. I speak in riddles, you protest; so I do, until I make my meaning clear. You say you are not working, but your letter is so well phrased that it could only have been written by someone who worked at it; or else you are luckier than the rest of us in being able to produce work of such finish in your idle moments.

14. To Corellia

It is very generous of you to insist so warmly that I should give orders for the price you are to pay for my land to be raised from the 700,000 sesterces agreed by my freedman to 900,000, the real value on which you have had to pay the five-per-cent inheritance tax. But I must insist in my turn that you consider what is the right course for me, as well as for you, and allow me to oppose you on this one point in the same spirit in which I usually comply with all your wishes.

15. To Pompeius Saturninus

You want my news, but there is nothing new to tell; I am involved in public duties, active on behalf of my friends, and occasionally doing some work of my own. If I could describe the work as exclusive and continuous I should certainly be happier, though I would not like to say my time would be better spent. As for your news, I should be sorry to hear that your activities are the opposite of what you would choose were you not so honourably employed; for managing the affairs of one's city merits our highest praise no less than settling disputes between friends.

I felt sure that you would enjoy the company of our friend Priscus. I know what a frank and charming person he is, but I had yet to learn how grateful he could be: if, as you say in your letter, he has such happy memories of my services.

16. To Calpurnius Fabatus, his wife's grandfather

Calestrius Tiro is one of my dearest friends, and we have been closely associated in both personal and official relations. We did our military service together and were both quaestors serving the Emperor. He held the office of tribune before me, through the privilege granted to fathers of children, but I caught him up in the praetorship when the Emperor gave me a year's remission. I have often visited him in his country houses, and he has often spent times of convalescence in my home.

He is now setting out for Baetica as governor of the province, and will pass through Ticinum.[1] I hope, in fact I am sure, that I can easily persuade him to leave his direct route to pay you a visit, if you really intend to liberate formally the slaves you recently pronounced free before your friends. You need not fear that this will be a trouble to a man who would not find a journey round the world too far on my behalf. So be rid of your usual diffidence and consult your own inclinations. He will be as pleased to do my bidding as I am to do yours.

17. To Caecilius (?) Celer

Everyone has his own reasons for reading his work aloud; my own, as I have often said, is to be told of the slips I know I am sure to have made. So I am all the more surprised to read in your letter that there were people who criticized me for giving any reading of my speeches at all: unless they think that this is the only kind of writing which never needs correction. I should like to ask them why they allow (if they do allow) readings of history, whose authors aim at truth and accuracy rather than at displaying their talents, and tragedy, which needs a stage and actors rather than a lecture-room, and lyric poetry, which calls for a chorus and a lyre instead of a reader. They say that such readings are an established custom. Then is their originator to be blamed? Besides, there have been readings of speeches before, by some of our own orators as well as by the Greeks.

'But it is unnecessary to read a speech already delivered.' It would be if the audience and the speech were exactly the same, and you read the speech immediately after delivery; but if you make certain additions and alterations, if you invite new people along with those who heard you before, and after a certain interval, why should it be less suitable to read a speech than to publish it? 'It is difficult for a reading of a speech to be satisfactory.' That depends on the efforts of the reader and is no reason for not reading at all. Personally, I do not seek praise for my speech when it is read aloud, but when the text can be read after publication, and consequently I employ every possible method of correction. First of all, I go through my work myself; next, I read it to two or three friends and send it to others for comment. If I have any doubts about their criticisms, I go over them again with one or two people, and finally I read the work to a larger audience; and that

1. In Gallia Cisalpina, on the Po (now Pavia).

is the moment, believe me, when I make my severest corrections, for my anxiety makes me concentrate all the more carefully. Respect for an audience, modesty and anxiety are the best critics. Look at it in this way: if you are going to talk to a single individual, however well informed, won't you be less nervous than you are before large numbers who may be quite ignorant? When you rise to plead in court, isn't that the moment when you have least confidence in yourself, when you wish you could alter most of your speech or indeed the whole? Especially if the scene is imposing and the assembly large, for even the sight of dirty working clothes can be intimidating. If you feel that your opening words are badly received, don't you falter and break down? I imagine it is because there is some sort of sound collective wisdom in mere numbers, so that, though individual judgements may be poor, when combined they carry weight. Thus it was that Pomponius Secundus, the author of tragedies, if one of his close friends happened to think that some passage should be deleted when he wished to keep it, used to say that he 'appealed to the people': and according to the people's silence or applause he would act on his own judgement or that of his friend. Such was his faith in public opinion, whether rightly or wrongly it is not for me to say. For I do not invite the general public, but a select and limited audience of persons whom I admire and trust, whom I observe individually and fear as a whole; seeing that I apply to fear what Cicero said about the practice of writing. Fear is the sternest corrective – the prospect of giving a reading, our entry into the lecture-room, our white faces, our trembling, and our nervous glances, all prompt us to correct our work.

Consequently I do not regret my practice; experience has taught me its great advantages, and I am so far from being deterred by the idle comments of the people you quote that I should like you to suggest something else I can do. Nothing can satisfy my desire for perfection; I can never forget the importance of putting anything into the hands of the public, and I am positive that any work must be revised more than once and read to a number of people if it is intended to give permanent and universal satisfaction.

18. To Caninius Rufus

You want my advice on what provision to make for securing now and after your death the money you have offered to our native town to pay the cost of an annual feast. It is an honour to be consulted, but difficult to give an immediate opinion. You might hand over the capital to the town, but there is a danger of its being dissipated. Or you might make a gift of land, but it would be neglected as public property always is. Personally I can think of no better plan than the one I adopted myself. I had promised a capital sum of 500,000 sesterces for the maintenance of free-born boys and girls, but instead of paying this over I transferred some of my landed property (which was worth considerably more) to the municipal agent, and then had it reconveyed back to be charged with an annual rent payable of 30,000 sesterces. By this means the principal is secured for the town, the interest is certain, and the property will always find a tenant to cultivate it because its value greatly exceeds the rent charged. I am well aware that I appear to have paid out more than the sum I have given, seeing that the fixed rent charge has reduced the market value of a fine property, but one ought to make personal and temporary interests give place to public and permanent advantages, and consider the security of a benefaction more than one's own gains.

19. To Neratius (?) Priscus

I am very worried about Fannia's illness. She contracted it while nursing Junia, one of the Vestal Virgins, a duty she undertook voluntarily at first (Junia being a relative of hers) and then by order of the pontiffs. (For when sickness compels the Virgins to leave the hall of Vesta, they are always committed to the care of some married woman.) This service Fannia was faithfully performing when she fell a victim to her present illness. Her fever never leaves her, her cough grows worse, and she is painfully thin and weak. There remains only the courage and the spirit worthy of her husband Helvidius and her father Thrasea: in every other way she is failing, and my anxiety on her behalf is coupled with grief, grief that so great a woman will be lost to the sight of her country when her like may not be seen again: such are her purity and integrity, her nobility and loyal heart. Twice she followed her husband into exile, and a third time was banished herself on his account. For when Senecio was on trial for having written a life of Helvidius, and said in his defence that he had done so at Fannia's request, Mettius Carus then demanded in a threatening tone if this was true. She replied that it was. Had she lent Senecio her husband's diaries? 'Yes.' Did her mother know of this? 'No.' Not a word in fact did she utter through fear of danger. Moreover, although the Senate was driven through fear of the times to order the destruction of the books in question, she managed to save them when her possessions were confiscated, and took them with her into the exile they had caused.

At the same time she has such friendliness and charm, the rare gift, in fact, of being able to inspire affection as well as respect. Will there be anyone now whom we can hold up as a model to our wives, from whose courage even our own sex can take example, and whom we can admire as much as the heroines of history while she is still in our midst? To me it seems as though her whole house is shaken to its very foundations and is tottering to its fall, even though she may leave descendants; for how can their deeds and merits be sufficient to assure that the last of her line has not perished in her?

A further and more personal pain and grief for me is my feeling that I am losing her mother again – to whom I can pay no higher tribute than by calling her the famous mother of a great woman. The mother was restored to us in her daughter, but soon will be taken away with her, leaving me the pain of a re-opened wound to bear as well as this fresh blow. I honoured and loved them both – I cannot say which the more, nor did they wish a distinction to be drawn. My services were at their command alike in prosperity and adversity; I was their comfort in exile and their champion after their return. I could never make them an adequate return, and so I am all the more anxious for Fannia's life to be spared to give me time to pay my debt. These are my troubles at the time of writing to you; but, if one of the gods will turn them to joy, I shall make no complaint about my present fears.

20. To Cornelius Tacitus

I have read your book, and marked as carefully as I could the passages which I think should be altered or removed, for if it is my custom to tell the truth, you are always willing to hear it; no one accepts criticism so readily as those who best deserve praise. Now I am awaiting the return of my book from you, with your comments: a fair exchange which we both enjoy. I am delighted to think that if posterity takes any interest in us the tale will everywhere be told of the harmony, frankness, and loyalty of our lifelong relationship. It will seem both rare and remarkable that two men of much the same age and position, and both enjoying a certain amount of literary reputation (I can't say much about you when it refers to me too), should have encouraged each other's literary work.

I was still a young man when you were already winning fame and glory, and I aspired to follow in your footsteps and be 'far behind but still the nearest'[1] to you in fact and in repute. There were at the time many other distinguished men of talent, but a certain similarity in our natures made me feel that you were the person I could and should try to imitate. So I am all the happier to know that whenever conversation turns upon literature, our names are mentioned together, and that my name comes up when people talk about you. There may be writers who are ranked higher than either of us, but if we are classed together our position does not matter; for me the highest position is the one nearest to you. You must also surely have noticed in wills that unless someone has been a particular friend of one or the other of us we are left legacies of the same kind and value. All this shows that our love should be still warmer, seeing that there are so many ties to bind us in our work, character, and reputation, and, above all, in the last wishes of our friends.

21. *To Cornutus Tertullus*

I obey, dear colleague, and I am seeing to my eye trouble as you bid me. I travelled here in a closed carriage with the light completely excluded, so that I might have been at home in bed, and now that I am here I am neither writing nor reading – no easy sacrifice, but I have made it – and am working only by ear. I can darken my rooms by drawing the blinds, without making them too dark, and the light in the roofed arcade is reduced by half when the lower windows have their shutters closed. By this means I am gradually reaccustoming myself to full daylight. I take baths, as they do me good, and wine, which can do no harm, but only very sparingly; this has always been my way, and now I am under supervision. I was delighted to receive the pullet, especially as it was a gift from you. My eyes may still be inflamed, but they were sharp enough to see how plump it was.

1. *Aeneid,* v : 320.

22. *To Pompeius Falco*

You may have felt that I was rather pressing in my request for you to confer a military tribunate on a friend of mine, but you will be less surprised when you know who and what he is. Now that I have your promise I can give you his name and a full description. He is Cornelius Minicianus, in rank and character the pride of my native district. He is well born and rich, but cares for literature as a poor professional might; and he is remarkable too for his justice on the bench, courage at the bar, and loyalty in friendship. You will feel that it is you who are receiving the favour when you come to know him more intimately and find that he is equal to any official position or distinction; I don't want to say more in praise of the most modest of men.

23. *To Calpurnius Fabatus, his wife's grandfather*

I am delighted to hear that you are feeling well enough to meet Tiro at Mediolanum,[1] but I must ask you to conserve your strength and not take upon yourself a burden too heavy for your years. In fact I insist that you wait for him at home, indoors and without leaving your room; for as I love him like a brother, he must not demand from one I honour as a father an attention which he would not expect his own father to show.

24. *To Rosianus Geminus*

Ummidia Quadratilla is dead, having almost attained the age of seventy-nine and kept her powers unimpaired to her last illness, along with a sound constitution and sturdy physique which are rare in a woman. She died leaving an excellent will; her grandson inherits two-thirds of the estate, and her granddaughter the remaining third. I scarcely know the latter, but the grandson is a close friend of mine. He is a remarkable young man who inspires a sort of family affection amongst people in no way related to him. In the first place, though conspicuous for his good looks, he spent his youth and early manhood untouched by scandal; then he married before he was twenty-four and would have been a father had his prayers been granted. He lived in his grandmother's house, but managed to combine personal austerity with deference to her sybaritic tastes. She kept a troupe of mimic actors

1. Milan.

whom she treated with an indulgence unsuitable in a lady of her high position, but Quadratus never watched their performances either in the theatre or at home, nor did she insist on it. Once when she was asking me to supervise her grandson's education she told me that as a woman, with all a woman's idle hours to fill, she was in the habit of amusing herself playing draughts or watching her mimes, but before she did either she always told Quadratus to go away and work: which, I thought, showed her respect for his youth as much as her affection.

This incident will surprise you as it did me. The last Sacerdotal Games were opened by a performance of mime, and as we left the theatre together Quadratus said to me: 'Do you realize that today was the first time I have seen any of my grandmother's dancers?' So said her grandson; but meanwhile people who were nothing to Quadratilla were running to the theatre to pay their respects to her – though 'respect' is hardly the word to use for their fawning attentions – jumping up and clapping to show their admiration, and then copying every gesture of their mistress with snatches of song. Today there is only a tiny bequest as a gratuity for their hired applause, which they will receive from the heir who never watched them perform.

I have told you this because you are usually glad to hear of any news, and also because I like to dwell on my pleasure by writing about it. It is a joy to witness the family affection shown by the deceased and the honour done to an excellent young man, and I am happy to think that the house which once belonged to Gaius Cassius, the founder of the Cassian School of jurisprudence, will have a master no less distinguished. For my friend Quadratus will adorn it by his presence and restore its former grandeur, fame, and glory by rising to be as great an orator as Cassius was a jurist.

25. To Caninius (?) Rufus

What a number of scholars are hidden and lost to fame through their own modesty or retiring habits! And yet when we are about to make a speech or give a reading we are nervous only of those who parade their learning, whereas the others who say nothing prove themselves superior by paying a noble profession the tribute of silence. I can illustrate this from my own experience.

After Terentius Junior had held the military posts open to a knight and had also served as procurator in the province of Gallia Narbonensis, his conduct being irreproachable throughout, he retired to his estates, preferring a life of peace and leisure to the offices which could have been his. I looked upon him as a good father of his household and a hard-working farmer, so when he invited me to visit him I intended to talk on the subjects with which I imagined he was familiar; but when I began to do so the scholarly trend of his conversation led me back to literary topics. Everything he says is expressed in well-turned phrases in excellent Latin or Greek, and his proficiency in both languages is such that he always seems to speak best the one he happens to be using. He reads and remembers an immense amount; you would think Athens his home, not a country house. In short, he has increased my nervousness and made me respect these retired somewhat countrified people as much as the persons I know to be learned scholars. You should do likewise, for in the field of letters, as of battle, there are men who may be rustic in appearance, but are found on closer inspection to be well armed and equipped and full of spirit and fire.

26. To Valerius (?) Maximus

The poor health of a friend of mine has lately reminded me that we are never so virtuous as when we are ill. Has a sick man ever been tempted by greed or lust? He is neither a slave to his passions nor ambitious for office; he cares nothing for wealth and is content with the little he has, knowing that he must leave it. It is then that he remembers the gods and realizes that he is mortal: he feels neither envy, admiration, nor contempt for any man: not even slanderous talk can win his attention or give him food for thought, and his dreams are all of baths and cool springs. These are his sole concern, the object of all his prayers; meanwhile he resolves that if he is lucky enough to recover he will lead a sober and easy life in future, that is, a life of happy innocence.

So here for our guidance is the rule, put shortly, which the philosophers seek to express in endless words and volumes: in health we should continue to be the men we vowed to become when sickness prompted our words.

27. To Licinius Sura

Our leisure gives me the chance to learn and you to teach me; so I should very much like to know whether you think that ghosts exist, and have a form of their own and some sort of supernatural power, or whether they lack substance and reality and take shape only from our fears. I personally am encouraged to believe in their existence largely from what I have heard of the experience of Curtius Rufus.[1] While he was still obscure and unknown he was attached to the suite of the new governor of Africa. One afternoon he was walking up and down in the colonnade of his house when there appeared to him the figure of a woman, of superhuman size and beauty. To allay his fears she told him that she was the spirit of Africa, come to foretell his future: he would return to Rome and hold office, and then return with supreme authority to the same province, where he would die. Everything came true. Moreover, the story goes on to say that as he left the boat on his arrival at Carthage the same figure met him on the shore. It is at least certain that when he fell ill he interpreted his future by the past and misfortune by his previous success, and gave up all hope of recovery although none of his people despaired of his life.

Now consider whether the following story, which I will tell just as it was told to me, is not quite as remarkable and even more terrifying. In Athens there was a large and spacious mansion with the bad reputation of being dangerous to its occupants. At dead of night the clanking of iron and, if you listened carefully, the rattle of chains could be heard, some way off at first, and then close at hand. Then there appeared the spectre of an old man, emaciated and filthy, with a long flowing beard and hair on end, wearing fetters on his legs and shaking the chains on his wrists. The wretched occupants would spend fearful nights awake in terror; lack of sleep led to illness and then death as their dread increased, for even during the day, when the apparition had vanished, the memory of it was in their mind's eye, so that their terror remained after the cause of it had gone. The house was therefore deserted, condemned to stand empty and wholly abandoned to the spectre; but it was advertised as being to let or for sale in case someone was found who knew nothing of its evil reputation.

The philosopher Athenodorus came to Athens and read the notice. His suspicions were aroused when he heard the low price, and the whole story came out on inquiry; but he was none the less, in fact all the more, eager to rent the house. When darkness fell he gave orders that a couch was to be made up for him in the front part of the house,

1. The story is also told in Tacitus, *Annals*, XI: 21.

and asked for his notebooks, pen and a lamp. He sent all his servants to the inner rooms, and concentrated his thoughts, eyes and hand on his writing, so that his mind would be occupied and not conjure up the phantom he had heard about nor other imaginary fears. At first there was nothing but the general silence of night; then came the clanking of iron and dragging of chains. He did not look up nor stop writing, but steeled his mind to shut out the sounds. Then the noise grew louder, came nearer, was heard in the doorway, and then inside the room. He looked round, saw and recognized the ghost described to him. It stood and beckoned, as if summoning him. Athenodorus in his turn signed to it to wait a little, and again bent over his notes and pen, while it stood rattling its chains over his head as he wrote. He looked round again and saw it beckoning as before, so without further delay he picked up his lamp and followed. It moved slowly, as if weighed down with chains, and when it turned off into the courtyard of the house it suddenly vanished, leaving him alone. He then picked some plants and leaves and marked the spot. The following day he approached the magistrates, and advised them to give orders for the place to be dug up. There they found bones, twisted round with chains, which were left bare and corroded by the fetters when time and the action of the soil had rotted away the body. The bones were collected and given a public burial, and after the shades had been duly laid to rest the house saw them no more.

For these details I rely on the evidence of others, but here is a story I can vouch for myself. One of my freedmen, a man of some education, was sleeping in the same bed as his younger brother when he dreamed that he saw someone sitting on the bed and putting scissors to his hair, even cutting some off the top of his head. When day dawned he found this place shorn and the hair lying on the floor. A short time elapsed and then another similar occurrence confirmed the earlier one. A slave boy was sleeping with several others in the young slaves' quarters. His story was that two men clad in white came in through the window, cut his hair as he lay in bed, and departed the way they had come. Daylight revealed that his head had also been shorn and the hair was scattered about. Nothing remarkable followed, except perhaps the fact that I was not brought to trial, as I should have been if Domitian (under whom all this happened) had lived longer. For amongst the papers in his desk was found information laid against me by Carus;

from which, in view of the custom for accused persons to let their hair grow long, one may interpret the cutting of my slaves' hair as a sign that the danger threatening me was averted.

So please apply your learned mind to this question; it deserves your long and careful consideration, nor can I be called undeserving as a recipient of your informed opinion. You may argue both sides of the case as you always do, but lay your emphasis on one side or the other and do not leave me in suspense and uncertainty; my reason for asking your opinion was to put an end to my doubts.

28. To Septicius Clarus

You say that people have criticized me in your hearing for taking any opportunity for exaggerated praise of my friends. I accept the charge, in fact I welcome it, for there can be no more honourable fault than warmth of heart. But who are these people who know my friends better than I do myself? And, even if they do, why grudge me happiness in my delusion? My friends may not be all I proclaim them, but it makes me happy to think that they are. Let these people transfer their misplaced attentions to someone else; they will find all too many who think it a sign of good judgement to disparage their friends, but they will never persuade me to believe that I love mine too much.

29. To Montanus

You will think it a joke – or an outrage, but a joke after all – if you read this, which has to be seen to be believed. On the road to Tibur, less than a mile from Rome, as I noticed the other day, there is a monument to Pallas[1] with the following inscription: 'To him the Senate decreed in return for his loyal services to his patrons, the insignia of a praetor, and the sum of fifteen million sesterces, but he thought fit to accept the distinction only.'

Personally I have never thought much of these honours whose distribution depends on chance rather than on a reasoned decision, but this inscription more than anything makes me realize what a ridiculous farce it is when they can be thrown away on such dirt and filth, and that rascal could presume to accept and refuse them, all with a show of

1. Freedman and financial secretary of the Emperor Claudius; see also Tacitus, *Annals*, XII: 53.

setting posterity an example of moderation. But it isn't worth my indignation; better to laugh, or such people will think they have really achieved something when their lucky chance has brought them no more than ridicule.

30. To Julius Genitor

I am deeply distressed to hear that you have lost a pupil of such promise, and, knowing your readiness with kindly attentions and generous affection for anyone of whom you think highly, I cannot but feel that his illness and death have interfered with your own work.

As for me, I am pursued by city business even here, for there is no lack of people wanting me to act as judge or arbitrator, and then there are the peasants who claim their right after my long absence to vex my ears with their complaints. The necessity of letting my farms is also becoming urgent and giving a good deal of trouble, for suitable tenants can rarely be found. Consequently I can only beg a moment here and there for my own work, though I *am* working, for I write a little and read; though comparison with my reading only makes me realize how badly I write, however much you encourage me by comparing my speeches in vindication of Helvidius[1] with Demosthenes' speech against Meidias. I admit that I had this by me while I was writing my own speech, not with any idea of rivalling it – it would be madness to presume so far – but treating it as a model to follow as closely as the diversity of subject permitted, and the difference between my own small talent and Demosthenes' genius allowed.

31. To Cornutus Tertullus

Claudius Pollio is anxious for your friendship, which he deserves for that very reason, and also because he has a real affection for you himself – for few people expect this from others if they do not first feel it themselves. He is besides a man of honour and integrity, retiring and modest almost to excess, if that were possible. We did our military service together, when I came to know him more intimately than just as a fellow soldier. He was in command of a cavalry division, while I had been ordered by the consular legate to audit the accounts of the cavalry and infantry divisions; in several cases I found a great deal of

1. See IX : 13.

shocking rapacity and deliberate inaccuracy, by contrast with his accounts which had been kept with scrupulous care and complete honesty. On his subsequent promotion to important administrative posts he could never be tempted out of his deep-rooted dislike of personal gain; success never went to his head, and, in all the various posts he held, he preserved intact his reputation for humanity while applying the same strength of purpose to all his duties, as he now shows in his present retirement. He did indeed once (to his greater glory) return temporarily to active life when he was chosen by our friend Corellius to assist him in the purchase and distribution of land made possible through the generosity of the Emperor Nerva; and there could be no higher honour than to be the special choice of so great a man from such a wide field for selection.

You can also be assured of Pollio's respect and loyalty for his friends by the dying wishes of many people, amongst them Annius Bassus whose merit is well known, and whose memory Pollio preserves and perpetuates in the grateful tribute of a published biography; for he cultivates literature as he does every honest pursuit. Such splendid conduct deserves praise for its very rarity, seeing that the majority of people remember their dead friends only to complain about them. This, then, is the man who so much desires your friendship, so that you should, if you will trust me, welcome him with open arms and summon him to your side with affection so as to show your gratitude. For, according to the code of friendship, the one who takes the initiative puts the other in his debt and owes no more until he is repaid.

32. *To Calpurnius Fabatus, his wife's grandfather*

I am glad you enjoyed my friend Tiro's visit, and particularly pleased to hear that you took the opportunity of his presence with a governor's authority to liberate a number of your slaves. I am always anxious for the advancement of our native place, and above all through the increasing numbers of her citizens, for that is a tribute which sets a town on the surest of foundations.

One other thing pleases me I confess, not that I am courting popularity; you go on to say that you and I were both warmly praised in a vote of thanks, and, as Xenophon says, 'praise is the sweetest thing to hear',[1] especially if it is felt to be deserved.

1. *Memorabilia*, II, I, 31.

33. To Cornelius Tacitus

I believe that your histories will be immortal: a prophecy which will surely prove correct. That is why (I frankly admit) I am anxious to appear in them. We are usually careful to see that none but the best artists shall portray our features, so why should we not want our deeds to be blessed by a writer like yourself to celebrate them? So here is an account of an incident which can hardly have escaped your watchful eye, since it appeared in the official records; but I am sending it so that you may be assured of my pleasure if this action of mine, which gained interest from the risks attending it, shall be distinguished by the testimony of your genius.

The Senate had instructed me to act with Herennius Senecio as counsel for the province of Baetica against Baebius Massa,[1] and after Massa's conviction had passed the resolution that his property should be kept in official custody. Senecio then discovered that the consuls would be willing to hear Massa's claims for restitution, so sought me out and proposed that we should continue to act in unity as we had done in carrying out the prosecution entrusted to us: we should approach the consuls and ask them not to allow the dispersal of the property which they were responsible for holding in custody. I pointed out that we had acted as counsel by appointment of the Senate, and asked him to consider whether perhaps we had come to the end of our role now that the case was over. 'You can set what limit you like to your own responsibilities,' he said, 'for you have no connexion with the province except the recent one of the services you have rendered, but I was born in Baetica and served as quaestor there.' 'If your mind is made up,' I said, 'I will act with you, so that if any ill-will results, you will not have to face it alone.'

We went to the consuls. Senecio said what was necessary and I added a few words. We had scarcely finished speaking when Massa complained that Senecio had displayed the animosity of a personal enemy rather than a professional counsel's honour, and demanded leave to prosecute him for treason. Amidst the general consternation I began to speak: 'Most noble consuls, I am afraid that by not including me in his accusation Massa's very silence has charged me with collusion with himself.' These words were acclaimed at once and subsequently much talked about; indeed, the deified Emperor Nerva (who never failed to notice anything done for the good of the State even before he became Emperor) sent me a most impressive letter in which he congratulated not only me but our generation for being blessed with an example so much (he said) in the best tradition.

Whatever the merit of this incident, you can make it better known and even famous, but I am not asking you to go beyond what is due to the facts. History should always confine itself to the truth, which in its turn is enough for honest deeds.

BOOK EIGHT

1. To Septicius Clarus

I had an easy journey, apart from the fact that some of my people were taken ill in the intense heat. Indeed, my reader Encolpius (the one who is our joy for work or play) found the dust so irritating to his throat that he spat blood, and it will be a sad blow to him and a great loss to me if this makes him unfit for his services to literature when they are his main recommendation. Who else will read and appreciate my efforts or hold my attention as he does? But the gods promise happier things. The haemorrhage has stopped and the pain is less severe; and he is a good patient, we are taking every care of him, and the doctors are attentive. In addition, the healthy climate here and the complete rest and quiet can provide as much for a cure as for a holiday.

2. To Calvisius Rufus

Other people visit their estates to come away richer than before, but I go only to return the poorer. I had sold my grape harvest to the dealers, who were eager to buy, when the price quoted at the time was tempting and prospects seemed good. Their hopes were frustrated. It would have been simple to give them all the same rebate, but hardly fair, and I hold the view that one of the most important things in life is to practise justice in private as in public life, in small matters as in great, and apply it to one's own affairs no less than to other people's. For if we say with the Stoics that 'all offences are equal' the same applies to merits. Accordingly I returned to everyone an eighth of the sum he had spent so that 'none should depart without a gift of mine'.[1] Then I made a special provision for those who had invested very large

1. *Aeneid*, v : 305.

sums in their purchase, since they had been of greater service to me and theirs was the greater loss. I therefore allowed everyone whose purchases had cost him more than 10,000 sesterces a tenth of anything he had spent above the 10,000, in addition to the original eighth which was a sort of general grant.

I am afraid I have put it badly; let me try to make my calculations clearer. Suppose someone had offered the sum of 15,000 sesterces; he would receive an eighth of 15,000, plus a tenth of 5,000. Moreover, in view of the fact that some people had paid down large instalments of what they owed, while others had paid little or nothing, I thought it most unfair to treat them all with the same generosity in granting a rebate when they had not been equally conscientious in discharging their debts. Once more, then, I allowed another tenth of the sum received to those who had paid. This seemed a suitable way both of expressing my gratitude to each individual according to his past merits, and of encouraging them all not only to buy from me in the future but also to pay their debts.

My system – or my good nature – has cost me a lot, but it has been worth it. The whole district is praising the novelty of my rebate and the way in which it was carried out, and the people I classified and graded instead of measuring all with the same rod, so to speak, have departed feeling obliged to me in proportion to their honest worth and satisfied that I am not a person who 'holds in equal honour the wicked and the good'.[1]

3. To Julius Sparsus

You say that the book I sent you the other day has given you more pleasure than any of my other works. A learned friend of mine is of the same opinion, and this encourages me to think that neither of you is mistaken; for it is unlikely that you would both be wrong, and I like to flatter myself. In fact I always want my latest work to be thought my masterpiece; consequently I have turned against the one you have in favour of a speech which I have just published, and which you shall see as soon as I can find someone reliable to bring it. Now I have roused your expectations, but I fear they may be disappointed when you have the speech in your hands. Meanwhile wait for its arrival with the intention of liking it and you may find you do so after all.

1. *Iliad*, IX : 319.

4. To Caninius Rufus

It is an excellent idea of yours to write about the Dacian war. There is no subject which offers such scope and such a wealth of original material, no subject so poetic and almost legendary although its facts are true. You will describe new rivers set flowing over the land, new bridges built across rivers, and camps clinging to sheer precipices; you will tell of a king driven from his capital and finally to death, but courageous to the end; you will record a double triumph, one the first over a nation hitherto unconquered, the other a final victory.

There is only one difficulty, but a serious one. To find a style of expression worthy of the subject is an immense undertaking, difficult even for a genius like yours, though this is capable of attaining supreme heights and surpasses itself in each magnificent work you have produced. Another problem arises out of the barbaric names, especially that of the king himself where the uncouth sounds will not fit into Greek verse; but every difficulty can be reduced by skill and application even if it cannot be entirely resolved. Besides, if Homer is permitted to contract, lengthen, and modify the flexible syllables of the Greek language to suit the even flow of his verse, why should you be denied a similar licence, especially when it is a necessity and no affectation? So call the gods to your aid, as a poet may, without forgetting that divine hero whose exploits, achievements and wisdom you are going to celebrate; slacken your sheets, spread sail, and now, if ever, let the full tide of your genius carry you along. (Why shouldn't I be poetical with a poet?)

Now I have a stipulation to make; send me each section in turn as you finish it, or better still send it unfinished in its rough draught as it is first put together. You will object that a collection of incomplete fragments cannot give the same pleasure as the finished whole. But knowing this I shall judge them only as a beginning, examine them as parts of a whole, and keep them in my desk to await your final revision. Give me this further pledge of your affection – let me into the secrets you would prefer no one to know. To sum up, I may perhaps be better able to approve and admire your work if you are slow and cautious about sending it, but I shall love and value yourself the more if you can send it without delays and misgivings.

5. To Rosianus Geminus

Our friend Macrinus[1] has had a terrible blow; he has lost his wife, one who would have been exemplary even in former times, after they had lived together for thirty-nine years without a quarrel or misunderstanding. She always treated her husband with the greatest respect, while deserving the highest regard herself, and she seemed to have assembled in herself the virtues of every stage of life in the highest degree. Macrinus has indeed the great consolation of having possessed such a treasure so long, though it is this which makes his loss so hard to bear; for our enjoyment of pleasure increases the pain of deprivation. So I shall continue to be anxious about him, for I love him dearly, until he can permit himself some distraction and allow his wound to heal; nothing can do this but acceptance of the inevitable, lapse of time, and surfeit of grief.

6. To Montanus

You should have heard from my last letter[2] that I had recently seen a monument to Pallas with this inscription: 'To him the Senate decreed in return for his loyal services to his patrons, the insignia of a praetor and the sum of fifteen million sesterces, but he thought fit to accept the distinction only.' I took the trouble afterwards to look up the actual decree of the Senate, and found it so verbose and fulsome in tone that the insolence of this inscription seemed modest and positively humble by comparison. All our national heroes put together – and I don't mean those of the past, with their titles of Africanus, Achaicus, and Numantinus, but the Marii, Sullas, and Pompeys of recent times, to name no more – would still fall short of Pallas's fame. Am I to suppose this decree expresses the wit or the misery of its authors? Wit is unbecoming to the Senate; and no man's misery need bring him to this extremity. Then was it self-interest or desire for advancement? But who is so crazy as to desire advancement won through his own and his country's dishonour, in a State where the chief privilege of its highest office is that of being the first to pay compliments to Pallas in the Senate?

1. This is probably Minicius Macrinus, father of Minicius Acilianus, mentioned in I : 14.
2. VII : 29.

I say nothing of this offer of the praetorian insignia to a slave, for they were slaves themselves who made the offer, nothing of the resolution that he should not only be begged but even compelled to wear a gold ring (it would lower the prestige of the Senate for a praetorian to wear the slave's iron one): these are trivial details which may well be set aside. This is what must stand on record; on behalf of Pallas the Senate (and the House has not been subsequently purged of its shame) – on behalf of Pallas the Senate thanked the Emperor for his own recognition of the man in bestowing high honour, and for giving them the opportunity of testifying their appreciation. For what could be more splendid for the Senate than to show suitable gratitude to Pallas? The resolution continues: ' . . . that Pallas, to whom all to the utmost of their ability acknowledge their obligation, should reap the just reward of his outstanding loyalty and devotion to duty.' (One might suppose he had extended the boundaries of the Empire or brought home the armies he had commanded.) Then follows: 'Since the Senate and the Roman people could have no more gratifying occasion for liberality than the opportunity to add to the means of this self-denying and faithful custodian of the imperial finances. . . .' This then was the will of the Senate, the chief pleasure of the people, the highly gratifying occasion for liberality – to add to Pallas's fortune by squandering public funds.

What next? The Senate wished to vote him a grant of fifteen million sesterces from the Treasury, and, knowing how far removed he was from all desires of this kind, the more urgently besought the Father of the State to compel him to comply with their wishes. In fact the only thing lacking was for Pallas to be officially approached and begged to comply, for the Emperor himself to champion the cause and plead with that insolent self-denial in order that the fifteen million should not be rejected. But Pallas did reject it; a great fortune had been offered him in the name of the State, and this was his only means of showing greater contempt than if he had accepted it. Yet even this the Senate met with further compliments, this time in a reproachful tone: 'But inasmuch as the noble Emperor and Father of the State at Pallas's request has expressed his wish that the clause referring to the grant of fifteen million sesterces from the Treasury should be rescinded, the Senate declares that though it had freely and justly taken steps to grant this sum to Pallas amongst the other distinctions offered him on account of his loyalty and devotion to duty, yet since it holds that in nothing is it lawful to oppose the Emperor, in this matter also it must bow to his wishes.'

Picture Pallas interposing his veto, as it were, on the Senate's decree, setting limits to his own honours, and refusing fifteen million as excessive while accepting the praetorian insignia as if they meant less! Picture the Emperor before the assembled Senate carrying out his freedman's request or rather command – for this is what such a request made before the Senate amounts to. Picture the Senate going so far as to declare that it had freely and justly taken steps to grant Pallas this sum amongst his other honours, and that it would have carried out its intention but for the need of bowing to the Emperor's wishes which could not on any point be lawfully opposed. Thus, to permit Pallas to decline this fifteen million from the Treasury, it took the combined forces of his own discretion and the Senate's obedience, which it would never have shown on this occasion had it believed that disobedience were lawful on any point.

Is this all, do you think? Wait and hear something better still. 'Inasmuch as it is expedient that the Emperor's generous promptitude to praise and reward merit should everywhere be published and particularly in places where those entrusted with the administration of his affairs may be encouraged to follow the examples set them, and where the example of Pallas's proved loyalty and integrity may inspire others to honourable rivalry, it is resolved that the statement made by the noble Emperor before this distinguished House on 23 January last, together with the resolutions passed by the Senate concerning this matter, shall be engraved on a bronze tablet and that tablet shall be affixed to the mailed statue of the deified Julius Caesar.' So it was not enough for these disgraceful proceedings to be witnessed by the walls of the Senate house; the most frequented spot in Rome was chosen to display them, where they could be read by everyone, today and ever after. A resolution was passed that all the honours of this insolent slave should be inscribed on bronze, both those he had refused and those he had accepted as far as those who conferred them had the power to do so. The praetorian insignia granted to Pallas were engraved and cut on a public monument for all time as if they were an ancient covenant or a sacred law. To such lengths did the Emperor, the Senate, and Pallas himself push their – I can't think of a word to express their conduct – as if they intended to set up a record in the sight of all, Pallas of his insolence, the Emperor of his complaisance, the Senate of its degradation! Nor were they ashamed to find a reason to justify their disgrace, and a splendid reason too, 'so that by the reward given to Pallas others might be inspired to rival him'! Honours were then to be so cheap, the honours which Pallas did not disdain; and yet people of good family could be found who were fired by ambition for distinctions which they saw granted to freedmen and promised to slaves.

How glad I am that my lot did not fall in those days – for which I blush as if I had lived in them. I am sure you will feel the same, knowing your lively sympathy and honest mind; so that, though in some passages I may have let my indignation carry me beyond the bounds of a letter, you will readily believe that I have suppressed my feelings rather than exaggerated them.

7. To Cornelius Tacitus

It was not as one master to another, nor, as you say, as one pupil to another, but as a master to his pupil (for you are master, I am pupil, and so you call me back to school while I am still keeping the Saturnalia) that you sent me your book. Could I write a longer hyperbaton than that, and thereby prove that so far from being your master I do not even deserve to be called your pupil? But I will play the part of master and exercise the authority you have given me over your book; the more freely as for the moment I have nothing of my own to send you on which you can take your revenge.

8. To Voconius Romanus

Have you ever seen the source of the Clitumnus?[1] If not (and I fancy not, or you would have told me) do visit it as I did the other day. I am only sorry I put off seeing it so long.

There is a fair-sized hill which is densely wooded with ancient cypresses; at the foot of this the spring rises and gushes out through several channels of different size, and when its eddies have subsided it broadens out into a pool as clear as glass. You can count the coins which have been thrown in and the pebbles shining at the bottom. Then it is carried on, not by any downward slope of the land but by

1. In Umbria, between Trevi and Spoleto (Clitunno).

its own volume and weight of water: one minute it is still a spring and the next a broad river navigable for boats to which it can give a passage even when two are moving in opposite directions and must pass each other. The current is so strong that although the ground remains level, a boat travelling downstream is hurried along without needing its oars, while it is very difficult to make any headway upstream with oars and poles combined. Anyone boating for pleasure can enjoy hard work alternating with easy movement simply by a change of course.

The banks are clothed with ash trees and poplars, whose green reflections can be counted in the clear stream as if they were planted there. The water is as cold and as sparkling as snow. Close by is a holy temple of great antiquity in which is a standing image of the god Clitumnus himself clad in a magistrate's bordered robe; the written oracles lying there prove the presence and prophetic powers of his divinity. All round are a number of small shrines, each containing its god and having its own name and cult, and some of them also their own springs, for as well as the parent stream there are smaller ones which have separate sources but afterwards join the river. The bridge which spans it marks the sacred water off from the ordinary stream: above the bridge boats only are allowed, while below bathing is also permitted. The people of Hispellum,[1] to whom the deified Emperor Augustus presented the site, maintain a bathing place at the town's expense and also provide an inn; and there are several houses picturesquely situated along the river bank. Everything in fact will delight you, and you can also find something to read: you can study the numerous inscriptions in honour of the spring and the god which many hands have written on every pillar and wall. Most of them you will admire, but some will make you laugh – though I know you are really too charitable to laugh at any of them.

9. To Cornelius Ursus

It is a long time since I have had a book or a pen in my hand, a long time since I have known what peace and quiet are or even known that lovely, lazy state of doing and being nothing; so completely has the pressure of my friends' business kept me from either leaving Rome or working at my books. For no such work is important enough to

1. Spello.

justify neglect of the claims of friendship, a duty which these same books tell us to observe with scrupulous care.

10. To Calpurnius Fabatus, his wife's grandfather

I know how anxious you are for us to give you a great-grandchild, so you will be all the more sorry to hear that your granddaughter has had a miscarriage. Being young and inexperienced she did not realize she was pregnant, failed to take proper precautions, and did several things which were better left undone. She has had a severe lesson, and paid for her mistake by seriously endangering her life; so that although you must inevitably feel it hard for your old age to be robbed of a descendant already on the way, you should thank the gods for sparing your granddaughter's life even though they denied you the child for the present. They will surely grant us children later on, and we may take hope from this evidence of her fertility though the proof has been unfortunate.

I am giving you the same advice and encouragement as I use on myself, for your desire for great-grandchildren cannot be keener than mine for children. Their descent from both of us should make their road to office easy; I can leave them a well-known name and an established ancestry, if only they may be born and turn our present grief to joy.

11. To Calpurnia Hispulla

Remembering how you love your brother's daughter more tenderly than a mother, I feel that I ought to begin with the second half of my news, so that happiness may come first and leave no room for anxiety. And yet I am afraid your relief will turn to fear again, and your joy at hearing that your niece is out of danger will be tempered by your alarm at her narrow escape. By now her good spirits are returning as she feels herself restored to herself and to me, and she is beginning to measure the danger she has been through by her progress towards recovery. The danger was indeed grave – I hope I may safely say so now – through no fault of her own, but perhaps of her youth. Hence her miscarriage, a sad proof of unsuspected pregnancy. So though you are still without a grandchild of your brother's to comfort you for his loss, you must remember that this consolation is postponed, not denied us. We build our hopes on her, and she has been spared. Meanwhile, explain this accident to your father, as it is the sort women can more easily understand.

12. To Cornelius Minicianus

Today is the one day I must be free: Titinius Capito is giving a reading, which it is my duty – or perhaps my urgent desire – to attend. He is a splendid personality who should be numbered among the shining lights of our generation; a patron of literature and admirer of literary men, whom he supports and helps in their careers. To many who are authors he is a haven of refuge and protection, while he is an example to all; it is he in fact who has restored and reformed literature itself when it was on the decline. He lends his house for public readings, and is wonderfully generous about attending those which are held elsewhere; at any rate he has never missed one of mine, provided that he was in Rome at the time. It would then be all the more disgraceful in me to fail to show the gratitude I have every good reason to feel. If I were engaged in a lawsuit I should feel bound to the man who stood bail for me; so now when literature is absorbing all my thoughts, shall I feel less bound to the one whose unfailing attentiveness to me gives him a special – if I mayn't say a sole – claim on me? But even if I owed Capito no return, no exchange of services, I should still be persuaded by the greatness of his noble genius which can combine tenderness with austerity, or else by the dignity of his theme. He is writing on the deaths of famous men, some of whom were very dear to me; so I feel that I am performing a pious duty in being present at something like their funeral orations when I could not attend their funerals: a tribute no less sincere for being thus delayed.

13. To Genialis

I am glad to hear that you have been reading my published speeches with your father. It will help your own progress if you learn from a man of his accomplishments what to admire and what to criticize, and at the same time are taught the habit of speaking the truth. You have your model before you, in whose footsteps you should tread, and are fortunate indeed to be blessed with a living example who is both the best possible and your close relative: in short, to have for imitation the very man whom Nature intended you to resemble most.

14. *To Titius Aristo*

As you are such an authority on civil and constitutional law, including senatorial procedure, I am particularly anxious to hear whether or not you think I made a mistake at a recent meeting of the Senate. It is too late to be put right about past events, but I should like to know what to do in future should any similar situation arise. You will wonder why I am asking a question I ought to be able to answer myself. The fact is we have forgotten our knowledge of senatorial procedure, as of other honest practices, in the servitude of former times; very few people have the patience and will-power to learn what is never likely to be of any practical use, and it is besides difficult to remember what you have learned unless you put it into practice. So, now that Liberty is restored, she finds us awkward and inexperienced; carried away by her charms we are compelled to act in certain ways before we understand them.

In ancient times it was the recognized custom for us to learn from our elders by watching their behaviour as well as listening to their advice, thus acquiring the principles on which to act subsequently ourselves and to hand on in our turn to our juniors. Hence young men began their early training with military service, so that they might grow accustomed to command by obeying, and learn how to lead by following others; hence as candidates for office they stood at the door of the Senate house and watched the course of State councils before taking part in them. Everyone had a teacher in his own father, or, if he was fatherless, in some older man of distinction who took his father's place. Thus men learned by example (the surest method of instruction) the powers of the proposer, the rights of expressing an opinion, the authority of office, and the privileges of ordinary members; they learned when to give way and when to stand firm, how long to speak and when to keep silence, how to distinguish between conflicting proposals and how to introduce an amendment, in short the whole of senatorial procedure. For our own generation it was different. Though our early manhood was spent in camp, it was at a time when merit was under suspicion and apathy an asset, when officers lacked influence and soldiers respect, when there was neither authority nor obedience, and the whole system was slack, disorganized and chaotic, better forgotten than remembered. We too were spectators in the Senate, but in a Senate which was apprehensive and dumb since it was dangerous to voice a genuine opinion and pitiable to express a forced one. What could be learned at that time, what profit could there be in learning, when the Senate was summoned to idle away its time or to perpetuate some vile crime, and was kept sitting for a joke or its own humiliation; when it could never pass a serious resolution, though often one with tragic consequences? On becoming senators we took part in these evils and continued to witness and endure them for many years, until our spirits were blunted, broken and destroyed with lingering effect; so that it is only a short time (the happier the time the shorter it seems) since we began to want to know our own powers and put our knowledge into practice.

I have then all the more reason to ask you first to forgive any mistake I may have made, and then to remedy it with your expert knowledge; for you have always made a special study of civil and constitutional law, ancient and modern, with reference to exceptional as well as current problems. Personally I think that the kind of question I am putting to you would be unfamiliar even to people whose constant dealing with large numbers of cases makes them conversant with most possibilities; it might be entirely outside their experience. So there will be the more excuse for me, if perhaps I was at fault, and the more credit to you if you can instruct me on a point on which you may not have been informed yourself.

The case at issue concerned the freedmen of the consul Afranius Dexter, who had been found dead; it was not known whether he had killed himself or his servants were responsible, and, if the latter, whether they acted criminally or in obedience to their master. After the proceedings one opinion (whose? – mine, but that is irrelevant) was that they should be acquitted, another that they should be banished to an island, and a third that they should be put to death. Such diversity of sentences meant that they had to be considered singly; for what have death and banishment in common? Obviously no more than banishment and acquittal, though a vote for acquittal is nearer banishment than a vote for death, for the first two leave a man his life while death removes it. Meanwhile those who voted for the death penalty and banishment respectively were sitting together and shelving their differences by a temporary show of unity.

I asked for the three sentences to be reckoned as three, and that two should not join forces under a momentary truce. Therefore I insisted that the supporters of the death penalty should move away from the proposers of banishment, and that the two parties should not combine to oppose those asking for acquittal when they would afterwards disagree amongst themselves; for it mattered little that they took the same negative view when their positive proposals were so different. Another point I found extraordinary was that the member who proposed banishment for the freedmen and death for the slaves should have been obliged to divide his vote, while one who was for executing the freedmen could be counted as voting with the proposer of banishment. For if one person's vote had to be divided because it covered two distinct sentences, I could not see how the votes of two people making such different proposals could be taken together.

Now, although the case is over let me treat it as still open; let me explain to you, as I did to the Senate, why I held this view; and let me assemble now in my own time the points I had then to make piecemeal amidst considerable interruption. Let us suppose that three judges only have been appointed for this case, one of whom has said that the freedmen should die, the second that they should be banished, and the third that they should be acquitted. Is the combined weight of the first two sentences to defeat the third, or is each one to be weighed against the others and the first and second to be combined no more than the second and third? Similarly, in the Senate, all different opinions expressed ought to be counted as conflicting. But if one and the same person proposed both death and banishment could the prisoners suffer both punishments by one person's sentence alone? Could it be considered as one sentence at all when it combined such different proposals? Then, when one person proposes death and another banishment, how can these be held to be a single sentence because expressed by two people when they were not a single sentence if expressed by one person?

Well; the law clearly states that sentences of death and banishment should be considered separately, in its formula for taking a division: 'All who agree go to this side, all who support any other proposal to the side you support.' Take the words one by one and consider them. 'Who agree' means 'Who think the prisoners should be banished'; 'to this side' is the side of the House where the proposer of banishment is sitting. It is clear from this that those who want death for the prisoners cannot stay on that side. 'Who support any other proposal'

– you will observe that the law is not content with saying 'other' but has added the word 'any'. Can it be doubted that those who would put the prisoners to death 'support any other proposal' in comparison with those who would banish them? 'Go to the side you support': surely the wording of the law seems to summon and positively compel those who disagree to take different sides? The consul also indicates not only by the established formula, but by a movement of the hand where everyone is to remain or to what side to cross.

But it can be argued that if the sentences of death and banishment are taken separately it will result in the acquittal having a majority. That is no concern of the voters, and it certainly ill becomes them to use every weapon and device to defeat a more lenient sentence. Or, again, it can be said that those voting for death and banishment should first be matched against those supporting acquittal, and then against each other. In some of the public games one gladiator draws a lot which entitles him to stand aside and wait to fight the victor; so I suppose there are to be first and second rounds in the Senate, too, and the third sentence is to wait and meet the victor of the other two. What about the rule that if the first sentence is approved all the others are defeated? On what principle can these sentences not start on the same footing, seeing that they may all subsequently cease to count? I will put this again more clearly. As soon as the proposal of banishment is made, unless those in favour of execution immediately cross over to the other side, it will be useless their afterwards opposing what they agreed with a short time before.

But I should not be the one to give instruction, when I really wanted to learn whether the two sentences should have been subsequently divided, or all three voted on separately. I carried my point, but none the less I want to know whether I should have made it. How did I manage this? The proposer of the death sentence was convinced by the justice of my request (whether or not it was legal), dropped his own proposal, and supported that of banishment. He was afraid, no doubt, that if the sentences were taken separately (which seemed likely if he did not act) the acquittal would have a majority, for there were many more people in favour of this than of either of the other two proposals. Then, when those who had been influenced by him found themselves abandoned by his crossing the floor and the proposal thrown over by its author, they dropped it too, and deserted after their leader. So the three sentences became two, and the second carried the day by elimination of the third which could not defeat both the others, and therefore chose to submit to one.

15. To Terentius Junior

I must be overwhelming you by sending so many books at once; but you asked for them, and, as you write that your grape harvest is so poor, I can be sure that if you can't be picking grapes you will have time, as they say, to pick up a book. I have the same news from my own farms, so I shall have time, too, to write something for your 'picking' so long as I can still afford to buy paper. Otherwise I shall have to erase all I write, good or bad, and use the paper again.

16. To Plinius Paternus

I have been much distressed by illness amongst my servants, the deaths, too, of some of the younger men. Two facts console me somewhat, though inadequately in trouble like this: I am always ready to grant my slaves their freedom, so I don't feel their death is so untimely when they die free men, and I allow even those who remain slaves to make a sort of will which I treat as legally binding. They set out their instructions and requests as they think fit, and I carry them out as if acting under orders. They can distribute their possessions and make any gifts and bequests they like, within the limits of the household: for the house provides a slave with a country and a sort of citizenship.

But though I can take comfort from these thoughts, I still find my powers of resistance weakened by the very feelings of humanity which led me to grant this privilege. Not that I would wish to be harder of heart; and I am well aware that some people look upon misfortunes of this kind as no more than a monetary loss, and think themselves fine men and philosophers for doing so. Whether they are in fact fine and philosophic I can't say, but they are certainly not men. A true man is affected by grief and has feelings, though he may fight them; he allows himself to be consoled, but is not above the need of consolation. I may perhaps have said more on this subject than I ought, but not so much as I would like. Even grief has its pleasure, especially if you can weep in the arms of a friend who is ready with approval or sympathy for your tears.

17. *To Caecilius Macrinus*

Can the weather be as bad and stormy where you are? Here we have nothing but gales and repeated floods. The Tiber has overflowed its bed and deeply flooded its lower banks, so that although it is being drained by the canal cut by the Emperor, with his usual foresight, it is filling the valleys and inundating the fields, and wherever there is level ground there is nothing to be seen but water. Then the streams which it normally receives and carries down to the sea are forced back as it spreads to meet them, and so it floods with their water the fields it does not reach itself. The Anio, most delightful of rivers – so much so that the houses on its banks seem to beg it not to leave them – has torn up and carried away most of the woods which shade its course. Where the banks rise high they have been undermined, so that its channel is blocked in several places with the resultant landslides; and in its efforts to regain its lost course it has wrecked buildings and forced out its way over the debris.

People who were hit by the storm on higher ground have seen the valuable furniture and fittings of wealthy homes, or else all the farm stock, yoked oxen, ploughs and ploughmen, or cattle left free to graze, and amongst them trunks of trees or beams and roofs of houses, all floating by in widespread confusion. Nor have the places where the river did not rise escaped disaster, for instead of floods they have had incessant rain, gales, and cloudbursts which have destroyed the walls enclosing valuable properties, rocked public buildings and brought them crashing to the ground. Many people have been maimed, crushed, and buried in such accidents, so that loss of life is added to material damage.

My fears that you have been through something like this are proportionate to the danger – if I am wrong, please relieve my anxiety as soon as possible; and let me know in any case. Whether disaster is actual or expected the effect is much the same, except that suffering has its limits but apprehension has none; suffering is confined to the known event, but apprehension extends to every possibility.

18. *To Fadius Rufinus*

There is certainly no truth in the popular belief that a man's will is a mirror of his character, for Domitius Tullus has proved himself to be much better in death than life. Although he had encouraged legacy hunters, he left as heiress the daughter he shared with his brother (he had adopted his brother's child). He also left a great many welcome legacies to his grandsons and to his great-granddaughter; in fact the whole will is ample proof of his affection for his family, and so all the more unexpected.

Consequently the city is full of conflicting opinions; some accuse him of hypocrisy, ingratitude and fickleness, and in attacking him betray themselves by their own disgraceful admissions, for they complain about a man who was a father, grandfather, and great-grandfather as if he were childless. Others applaud him for the very reason that he has disappointed the shameless expectations of men whose frustration in this way accords with the spirit of the times. They also say that Tullus was not free to leave any other will, for he did not bequeath his wealth to his daughter so much as restore what he had acquired through her. For when Curtilius Mancia took a violent dislike to his son-in-law Domitius Lucanus (brother of Tullus), he made his granddaughter, Lucanus's daughter, his heiress on condition that she was freed from her father's control. The father set her free, but the uncle adopted her; thus the purpose of the will was defeated, for, as the brothers held their property jointly, the daughter, once freed, was brought back under her father's control by the device of adoption, and with her came a large fortune. Indeed, these brothers seemed destined to be made rich by people who intended otherwise. Even Domitius Afer, who adopted them into his family, left a will which had been drawn up eighteen years previously and was subsequently so far removed from his intentions that he had taken steps to procure the confiscation of their father's property. His severity in removing from the citizen roll the man whose children he had shared is no less remarkable than their good fortune in finding a second father in the man who ruined their first. However, this inheritance from Afer was also destined to go to Lucanus's daughter along with the rest of the brothers' joint acquisitions; for Lucanus had made Tullus his sole heir in preference to his own daughter, with the idea of bringing them together.

So this will is all the more creditable for being dictated by family affection, honesty, and feelings of shame; and in it Tullus acknowledges his obligations to all his relatives in return for their services to him, as he does to the excellent wife who had borne with him so long. She has inherited his beautiful country houses and a large sum of money, and deserved all the more from her husband for having been so severely criticized for marrying him. It was thought most unsuitable that a woman of her high birth and blameless character, who was no longer young, had borne children in the past and long been widowed, should marry a wealthy old man and a hopeless invalid, whom even a wife who had known him when young and healthy might have found an object of disgust. Crippled and deformed in every limb, he could only enjoy his vast wealth by contemplating it and could not even turn in bed without assistance. He also had to have his teeth cleaned and brushed for him – a squalid and pitiful detail – and when complaining about the humiliations of his infirmity was often heard to say that every day he licked the fingers of his slaves. Yet he went on living, and kept his will to live, helped chiefly by his wife, whose devoted care turned the former criticism of her marriage into a tribute of admiration.

That is all the city gossip, as Tullus is all we talk about. We are looking forward to the sale of his effects, for he had so many possessions that on the very day he bought a large garden he was able to beautify it with quantities of antique statues from the splendid works of art he had stored away and forgotten. If you have any local news worth sending in return, don't grudge me it. Not only is it always a pleasure to hear something new, but also through examples we study the art of living.

19. To Maximus

Literature is both my joy and my comfort: it can add to every happiness and there is no sorrow it cannot console. So worried as I am by my wife's ill-health and the sickness in my household and death of some of my servants, I have taken refuge in my work, the only distraction I have in my misery. It may make me more conscious of my troubles, but helps me to bear them with patience.

It is, however, my habit to test everything I propose to submit to the general public by the judgement of my friends, especially your own. Will you then give your attention to the book you will receive with this letter, now as never before? I fear my distress will have impaired my own concentration, for I could control my feelings enough to write, but not to write freely and happily, and if one's work is to give pleasure it must have its inspiration in happiness.

20. To Clusinius (?) Gallus

We are always ready to make a journey and cross the sea in search of things we fail to notice in front of our eyes, whether it is that we are naturally indifferent to anything close at hand while pursuing distant objects, or that every desire fades when it can easily be granted, or that we postpone a visit with the idea that we shall often be seeing what is there to be seen whenever we feel inclined. Whatever the reason, there are a great many things in Rome and near by which we have never seen nor even heard of, though if they were to be found in Greece, Egypt or Asia, or any other country which advertises its wealth of marvels, we should have heard and read about them and seen them for ourselves.

I am a case in point. I have just heard of something (and seen it, too) which I had neither seen nor heard of before. My wife's grandfather had asked me to look at his property in Ameria.[1] While going round I was shown a lake at the foot of the hills called Lake Vadimon,[2] and at the same time told some extraordinary facts about it. I went down to look at it, and found it was perfectly round and regular in shape, like a wheel lying on its side, without a single irregular bend or curve, and so evenly proportioned that it might have been artificially shaped and hollowed out. It is subdued in colour, pale blue with a tinge of green, has a smell of sulphur and a mineral taste, and the property of healing fractures. It is of no great size, but large enough for the wind to raise waves on its surface. There are no boats on it, as the waters are sacred, but floating islands, green with reeds and sedge and the other plants which grow more profusely on the marshy ground at the edge of the lake. Each island has its peculiar shape and size, and all have their edges worn away by friction, as they are constantly knocking against each other and the shore. They all have the same height and buoyancy, each shallow base dipping into the water like the keel of a boat; and this has the same appearance from all sides, both the part above and the part under water. Sometimes the islands join together to look like a continuous piece of land, sometimes they are driven apart by conflicting winds, while in calm weather they are left to float about separately. The small islands often attach themselves to the larger, like small boats to a merchant ship, and both large and small sometimes

1. In Umbria (now Amelia).   2. Lago di Bassano, north-west of Orte.

appear to be racing each other; or they are all driven to one side of the lake to create a headland where they cling to the shore; they remove or restore stretches of the lake on one side or the other, so that its size is unaltered only when they all keep to the centre. Cattle are often known to walk on to the islands while grazing, taking them for the edge of the lake, and only realize that they are on moving ground when carried off from the shore as if forcibly put on board ship, and are terrified to find themselves surrounded by water; then, when they land where the wind has carried them, they are no more conscious of having ended their voyage than they were of embarking on it. Another feature of the lake is the river leading from it, which is visible for a short distance before it enters a cave and continues its course at a great depth; anything thrown in before it disappears is carried along and reappears with it.

I have given you these details because I imagine they are as new and interesting to you as they were to me; natural phenomena are always a great source of interest to us both.

21. To Maturus Arrianus

In literature, as in life, I think it a becoming sign of humanity to mingle grave and gay, lest the one becomes too austere and the other indelicate; and this is the principle which leads me to intersperse my more serious works with trifles for amusement. Some of these I had ready to bring out, so I chose the most suitable time and place, and to accustom them from now onwards to being received by a leisured audience in the dining-room, I gathered my friends together in the month of July (which is usually a quiet time in the law courts) and settled them in chairs in front of the couches. It so happened that on the morning of that very day I was unexpectedly summoned to court to give legal assistance, and this gave me a subject for my introductory remarks. For I began by hoping that no one would accuse me of irresponsibility when, on the day I was to give a reading (though this was limited to a small circle of friends), I had not kept myself free from professional duties – that is, the claims of other friends. I went on to say that I kept to the same order in my writing; I put duty before

pleasure and serious work before amusement, and wrote primarily for my friends and after them for myself.

The work itself consisted of short pieces in different metres, for that is how those of us with no great confidence in our abilities avoid the risk of boring our public. The reading lasted for two days, at the request of my audience, in spite of the fact that, whereas other people omit passages and expect credit for doing so, I make it clear that I am leaving nothing out. I read every word so as to correct every word: a thing which is impossible for readers of selected passages. It may be said that theirs is the more restrained and possibly more considerate practice, but mine is more guileless and affectionate; for the confidence in your friends' affection which makes you have no fear of boring them is proof of your own feeling. Besides, what is the good of having friends if they meet only for their own amusement? It is the dilettante and indifferent listener who would rather listen to a good book by his friend instead of helping to make it so. I don't doubt that your affection for me will make you eager to read this work of mine as soon as possible, before it has lost its freshness; and so you shall, but not until after revision, as this was the purpose of my reading it aloud. Parts of it you have seen already, but after these have been corrected (or changed for the worse, as does sometimes happen after a long delay) you will find new life and style in them. For when the greater part of a book is recast the remainder appears to share in the change.

22. To Rosianus Geminus

You must know people who are slaves to every sort of passion while they display a sort of jealous resentment against the faults of others, and show least mercy to those they most resemble; though there are other people who need no man's forgiveness but are best known for their tolerance. My own idea of the truly good and faultless man is one who forgives the faults of others as if he was daily committing them himself, and who keeps himself free of faults as if he could never forgive them. This then should be our rule at home and abroad, in every walk of life: to show no mercy to ourselves and be ready with it for others, even for those who can excuse no failings but their own. Let us always remember what was so often said by Thrasea, whose gift of sympathy made him the great man he was: 'Anyone who hates faults hates mankind.'

You may wonder what has provoked me to write like this. Someone recently – but I can tell you better when we meet, or better still, not at all, for I am afraid that if I offer any hostile criticism or even tell you what I dislike, it will conflict with this principle to which I attach such importance. The man and his character shall not be told; to expose him would point no moral, but not to do so is a true sign of generosity.

23. To Aefulanus Marcellinus

Work, cares and distractions – all are interrupted, cut short, and driven out of my mind, for the death of Junius Avitus has been a terrible blow. He had assumed the broad stripe of the senator in my house and had my support when standing for office, and such moreover was his affectionate regard for me that he took me for his moral guide and mentor. This is rare in the young people of today, few of whom will yield to age or authority as being their superior. They are born with knowledge and understanding of everything; they show neither respect nor desire to imitate, and set their own standards.

Avitus was not like this. His wisdom consisted in his belief that others were wiser than himself, his learning in his readiness to be taught. He always sought advice for his studies or his duties in life, and always went away feeling he was made better; and indeed he *was* better, either from the advice given him or from the very fact that he had asked for it. What deference he showed to the high standards of Servianus! They first met when Servianus was legate of Germany, and Avitus, when serving as military tribune, so won his heart that on his transfer to Pannonia he took the young man with him, not as a serving soldier so much as a companion and member of his personal staff. Think of the industry and unassuming manner which won him the liking and affection of the many consuls who found him so useful as a quaestor, and the energy and concentration he applied to canvassing for the office of aedile, from which he has been thus prematurely taken away. This is what I find hardest to bear; his useless efforts, his fruitless prayers, the position he deserved but never held, are always in my mind's eye; the senator's stripe he assumed in my home, the first time, and now this last time I supported his election, our talks and discussions, all come back to me.

I mourn his youth and the plight of his family, for he leaves an elderly mother, a wife he married only a year ago, and a daughter not long born. So many hopes and joys are thus reversed in a single day. He had just been elected aedile, and for a short time he was husband and father: now he has left the post he never held, his mother is childless and his wife a widow, and his daughter is left an orphan, never to know a father's love. I weep the more to think that I was away and knew nothing of the fate hanging over him – the news of his illness and death reached me at the same moment, before fear could accustom me to this cruel sorrow. I am in such anguish as I write that this must be all; I can think and speak of nothing else just now.

24. To Valerius (?) Maximus

I know you need no telling, but my love for you prompts me to re-mind you to keep in mind and put into practice what you know already, or else it would be better for you to remain ignorant. Remember that you have been sent to the province of Achaea, to the pure and genuine Greece, where civilization and literature, and agriculture, too, are believed to have originated; and you have been sent to set in order the constitution of free cities, and are going to free men who are both men and free in the fullest sense, for they have maintained their natural rights by their courage, merits, and friendly relationships, and finally by treaty and sanction of religion. Respect the gods their founders and the names they bear, respect their ancient glory and their very age, which in man commands our veneration, in cities our reverence. Pay regard to their antiquity, their heroic deeds, and the legends of their past. Do not detract from anyone's dignity, independence, or even pride, but always bear in mind that this is the land which provided us with justice and gave us laws, not after con-quering us but at our request; that it is Athens you go to and Sparta you rule, and to rob them of the name and shadow of freedom, which is all that now remains to them, would be an act of cruelty, ignorance and barbarism. (Illness is the same in a slave as in a free man, but you will have observed how a doctor will treat the free man with more kindness and consideration.) Remember what each city was once, but without looking down on it for being so no longer; do not allow yourself to be hard or domineering, and have no fear that you will be despised for this. No one who bears the insignia of supreme authority is despised unless his own meanness and ignobility show that he must be the first to despise himself. It is a poor thing if authority can only test its powers by insults to others, and if homage is to be won by terror; affection is far more effective than fear in gaining you your ends. Fear disappears at your departure, affection remains, and, whereas fear engenders hatred, affection develops into genuine regard.

Never, never forget (I must repeat this) the official title you bear, and keep clearly in mind what it means and how much it means to establish order in the constitution of free cities, for nothing can serve a city like ordered rule and nothing is so precious as freedom; nor can anything equal the disgrace should order be overthrown and freedom give place to servitude. You are moreover your own rival; you bring with you the excellent reputation you won during your quaestorship in Bithynia, you bring the Emperor's recognition and your experience as tribune, praetor, and holder of your present office, given you as a reward for your services. You must then make every effort not to let it appear that you were a better, kinder, and more experienced administrator in a remote province than in one nearer Rome and when dealing with servile rather than free men, when you were elected by lot instead of being the Emperor's choice, and at a time when you were raw and unknown before being tested and proved by experience. And, besides, as you have often heard and read, it is far more shameful to lose a reputation than not to win one.

Please believe, as I said at the start, that this letter was intended not to tell, but to remind you of your duties – though I know I am really telling you as well, as I am not afraid of letting my affection carry me too far; there is no danger of excess where there ought to be no limits.

BOOK NINE

1. To Novius (?) Maximus

I have often urged you to be as quick as you can about publishing the articles you wrote in your own defence or against Planta[1] – or rather, with both ends in view as the subject demanded. Now that I have news of his death, I am even more anxious for you to do this. I know you have read them to a number of people and lent them to others to read, but I don't want anyone to imagine that you waited for his death to begin what you had in fact completed during his lifetime. You must keep up your reputation for standing by your convictions, and can do so if it is known to your friends and enemies alike that you did not pluck up courage to write as a result of your enemy's death, but that your work was already finished for publication when his death intervened. At the same time you will avoid Homer's 'impiety of boasting over the dead';[2] for anything written and read about a man in his lifetime can still be published against him after death as if he were still alive, so long as it is published at once. So, if you have anything else in hand, lay it aside for the present and put the finishing touch to these speeches; although those of us who have read them think they reached perfection long ago. You should think the same, for the subject calls for action and the circumstances should cut short your hesitation.

2. To Statius Sabinus

It is kind of you to ask me to make my letters long as well as frequent. I have been rather doubtful about doing so, partly out of consideration

1. Pompeius Planta, prefect of Egypt in 97–9 (see X:7).
2. *Odyssey*, XXII:412.

for your busy life, partly because my own time has been much taken
up, mostly with trivial duties which interrupt concentration and make
it difficult to resume it. Besides, I lacked subject-matter for writing
more. You want me to follow Cicero's example, but my position is
very different from his. He was not only richly gifted but was supplied
with a wealth of varied and important topics to suit his abilities, though
you know without my telling you the narrow limits confining me.
I might decide to send you a sort of pupil's exercise for a letter, but
I can imagine nothing less suitable, when I think of your life under
arms, the camps, bugles and trumpets, sweat and dust and heat of
the sun.

There is my excuse, a reasonable one I think, though I'm not sure
if I want you to accept it; it is a sign of true affection to refuse to forgive a friend for the shortness of his letters although you know he has
good reason for them.

3. *To Valerius Paulinus*

Opinions differ, but my idea of the truly happy man is of one who
enjoys the anticipation of a good and lasting reputation, and, confident
in the verdict of posterity, lives in the knowledge of the fame that is to
come. Were my own eyes not fixed on the reward of immortality I
could be happy in an easy life of complete retirement, for everyone,
I think, must choose between two considerations: that fame is im-
perishable or man is mortal. The former will lead him to a life of toil
and effort, the latter will teach him to relax quietly and not to wear
out his short existence with vain endeavours, as I see many doing,
though their semblance of industry, as wretched as it is unrewarding,
only brings them to despise themselves. I tell you this as I tell it to myself every day, so that I can stop if you disagree; but I doubt if you
will, when you have some great and immortal project always in mind.

4. *To Caecilius Macrinus*

With this letter I am sending a speech which I might fear you would
find too long, were it not the kind which gives the impression of repeated starts and conclusions; for each separate charge is treated as a
separate case. So, wherever you begin and leave off, you will be able
to read what follows either as a new subject or as part of the whole,

and judge me long-winded over the complete speech but brief enough in each section.

5. To Calestrius Tiro

I am told you are doing splendidly (and I hope this will continue) in your administration of justice in your province; by your tact you make it accepted by the people, a tact which consists mainly in making every honest man your friend, and winning the affection of the humble without losing the regard of their superiors. Yet most people in their fear of appearing to allow too many concessions to the influence of the great, acquire the reputation of being clumsy and even offensive. You are quite free from this fault I know, but I cannot help sounding as if I were proffering advice when I mean to congratulate you on the way in which you preserve the distinctions of class and rank; once these are thrown into confusion and destroyed, nothing is more unequal than the resultant 'equality'.

6. To Calvisius Rufus

I have been spending all the last few days amongst my notes and papers in most welcome peace. How could I – in the city? The Races were on, a type of spectacle which has never had the slightest attraction for me. I can find nothing new or different in them: once seen is enough, so it surprises me all the more that so many thousands of adult men should have such a childish passion for watching galloping horses and drivers standing in chariots, over and over again. If they were attracted by the speed of the horses or the drivers' skill one could account for it, but in fact it is the racing-colours they really support and care about, and if the colours were to be exchanged in mid-course during a race, they would transfer their favour and enthusiasm and rapidly desert the famous drivers and horses whose names they shout as they recognize them from afar. Such is the popularity and importance of a worthless shirt – I don't mean with the crowd, which is worth less than the shirt, but with certain serious individuals. When I think how this futile, tedious, monotonous business can keep them sitting endlessly in their seats, I take pleasure in the fact that their pleasure is not mine. And I have been very glad to fill my idle hours with literary work during these days which others have wasted in the idlest of occupations.

7. To Voconius Romanus

I am delighted to hear you are building; now I can count on you to plead my case, and be justified in my own plans if you are building too. We have a further point in common – you are building by the sea and I on the shores of Lake Como. There I have several houses, two of which give me a lot of pleasure but a corresponding amount of work. One is built on the rocks with a view over the lake, like the houses at Baiae,[1] the other stands on the very edge of the water in the same style, and so I have named one Tragedy, because it seems to be raised on actor's boots, and the other Comedy, because it wears low shoes. Each has its special charm and seems the more attractive to the occupant by contrast with the other. The former has a wider view of the lake, the latter a closer one, as it is built to curve gradually round a single bay, following its line by a broad terrace; while the other stands on a high ridge dividing two bays, where a straight drive extends for some distance above the shore. One is untouched by the water and you can look down from its height to the fishermen below, while the waves break against the other and you can fish from it yourself, casting your line from your bedroom window and practically from your bed as if you were in a boat. All these existing amenities give me a reason for building necessary additions on to both houses; though I know I need not explain myself to you, when this is no more than you are doing yourself.

8. To Sentius Augurinus

If I begin praising you after your praise of me, I fear I shall look as though I am only showing gratitude instead of giving a true opinion. All the same, I do think all your written works are very fine, but especially those which deal with me. For this there is one and the same reason – you are at your best in writing about your friends, and I find it your best when it is about myself.

9. To Colonus

I very much appreciate your grief at the death of Pompeius Quintianus, and can understand how your love for him is increased by your sense of loss; unlike most people who feel affection only for the living, or

1. The popular resort on the Campanian coast.

rather make a show of doing so, and not even that unless they see their friends prospering: the unfortunate they forget as quickly as the dead. But your loyalty is unfailing, and your constancy in love too great for anything short of your own death to end it; and Quintianus was indeed a man who deserved affection through the example he gave of it. He loved his friends in success, helped them in misfortune, and mourned them in death. Think, too, of his honest countenance and deliberate speech, the happy balance he kept between reserve and friendliness, and his enthusiasm for literature combined with his critical powers: think how he lived dutifully with a father very unlike himself, and though an excellent son was never prevented from showing his merits as a man!

But I must not aggravate your suffering, though I know you loved the young man so dearly that you find suffering preferable to silence about him; and least of all do you want silence from me, when I can voice the praise which you feel can do honour to his life, prolong his memory, and give back to him the years taken from him.

10. To Cornelius Tacitus

I should like to obey your orders, but when you tell me I ought to honour Diana along with Minerva I find it impossible – there is such a shortage of boars. So I can only serve Minerva, and even her in the lazy way to be expected during a summer holiday. On my way here I made up some bits of nonsense (not worth keeping) in the conversational style one uses when travelling, and I added something to them once I was here and had nothing better to do; but peace reigns over the poems which you fancy are only too easy to finish in the woods and groves. I have revised one or two short speeches, though this is the sort of disagreeable task I detest and is more like one of the hardships of country life than its pleasures.

11. To Rosianus Geminus

I have your letter, a specially welcome one as you want me to write you something which can be included in your published work. I will find a subject, either the one you suggest or something preferable, for yours may give offence in certain quarters – use your eyes and you will see. I didn't think there were any booksellers in Lugdunum,[1] so

1. Lyons.

I was all the more pleased to learn from your letter that my efforts are being sold. I'm glad they retain abroad the popularity they won in Rome, and I'm beginning to think my work must really be quite good when public opinion in such widely different places is agreed about it.

12. To Terentius Junior

Someone was reproving his son for spending rather too much buying horses and dogs. When the young man had left us I said to his father: 'Well, have *you* never done anything your father could complain about? Or rather, don't you still sometimes do things which your son could criticize as severely if he suddenly became father and you his son? Surely everyone is liable to make mistakes and everyone has his own foibles?' I took warning myself from this instance of undue severity, and am writing to you as one friend to another so that you, too, may never be too harsh and strict with your son. Remember that he is a boy and you have been a boy yourself, and use your rights as a father without forgetting that you are only human and so is your son.

13. To Ummidius Quadratus

The more thoroughly you apply yourself to reading my speeches in vindication of Helvidius,[1] the more pressing becomes your demand that I should give you a full account of the particulars not covered by the speeches as well as those arising out of them – in fact you want the whole sequence of the events which you were too young to witness yourself.

Once Domitian was dead I decided on reflection that this was a truly splendid opportunity for attacking the guilty, avenging the injured, and making oneself known. Moreover, though many crimes had been committed by numerous persons, none seemed so shocking as the violent attack in the Senate-house made by a senator on a fellow senator, by a praetorian acting as judge on a consular who had been brought to trial. I had also been the friend of Helvidius, as far as friendship was possible with one who had been driven through fear of the times to hide his famous name and equally famous virtues in re-tirement, and the friend of his stepmother Fannia and her mother Arria. But I was not moved to act so much by personal obligations as by the demands of common justice, the enormity of the deed, and the

1. The son of Helvidius Priscus. See Introduction, page 22.

thought of establishing a precedent. Now, in the early days after liberty was restored, everyone had acted for himself, brought his personal enemies to trial (if they were not too powerful), and had them condemned amid the general confusion and chaos. By contrast I believed that the proper course, as well as the more effective, was to deal with this atrocious criminal not through the universal hatred of Domitian's time, but by bringing a specific charge against him at a moment when the first outburst had spent itself and the fury which was daily abating had yielded to justice. So though I was greatly distressed at the time by the recent death of my wife,[1] I sent a message to Anteia (widow of Helvidius) asking her to visit me, as I was kept indoors by my recent bereavement. When she came I told her I had determined not to leave her husband unavenged. 'Tell this to Arria and Fannia,' I said (for they were back from exile). 'Talk it over with them and see whether you wish to be associated with this case. I don't need support, but I am not so jealous for my own glory as to grudge you a share in it.' Anteia did as I asked and the women acted promptly.

Fortunately the Senate met on the next day but one. I was in the habit of referring everything to Corellius Rufus, whom I knew to possess the greatest foresight and wisdom of our time, but on this occasion I was satisfied with my own judgement; for I was afraid he might forbid me to proceed, being rather cautious and hesitant. However, I could not bring myself not to tell him of my intended action on the actual day, when my decision was made. (I have learned from experience that, if your mind is already made up, you should not consult people whose advice you should take if you ask for it.) I entered the Senate, asked for permission to speak, and for a while won warm approval for what I was saying, but as soon as I mentioned the charge and indicated (though not yet by name) who was to be accused, there was a general outcry against me. 'Tell us who is the object of this irregular attack!' 'Who is being charged before notice is served?' 'Let us survivors remain alive!' and so on. I listened, calm and unafraid; such is the strength to be won from an honest cause, and so much does confidence or fear depend on whether one's conduct meets with active opposition or no more than disapproval. It would take too long to recount all the arguments on both sides, but finally the consul told me that if I had anything to say I could speak in my proper turn.

1. His second wife, daughter of Pompeia Celerina.

I pointed out that I had only been granted the permission which was never refused anyone, and then sat down while other business was dealt with. Meanwhile, one of my friends amongst the consulars took me aside privately and seriously rebuked me for coming forward so rashly and recklessly, advised me to desist, and added that I had made myself a marked man in the eyes of future Emperors. 'Never mind,' said I, 'as long as they are bad ones.' Scarcely had he left me when another began: 'What are you doing? Where are you heading? What about the risks you are running? Why such confidence in the present when the future is uncertain? You are challenging a man who is already a Treasury official and will soon be consul, and has besides such influence and friends to support him!' (He named someone[1] who was then in the east, at the head of a powerful and celebrated army, and about whom serious though unconfirmed rumours were circulating.) To this I replied, '"All have I foreseen and gone through in my mind";[2] if it is to be my fate, I am prepared to face the penalty for an honest deed while punishing a criminal one.'

By now it was time for members to give their opinions. Domitius Apollinaris the consul-elect, Fabricius Veiento, Fabius Postuminus, Bittius Proculus, colleague of Publicius Certus (the subject of the debate) and stepfather of my late wife, all spoke, and were followed by Ammius Flaccus. All defended Certus as if I had named him (though I had not yet done so), and set about refuting a charge as yet unspecified. What else they said I needn't tell you, as you have it all in the published speeches – I gave it all in full, in the words of the speakers.

Avidius Quietus and Cornutus Tertullus then spoke on the opposite side. Quietus argued that it was quite unjust to refuse to hear the complaints of injured parties, and that therefore Arria and Fannia should not be denied their right of protest; what mattered was not a man's position but the case he had to answer. Cornutus said that the consuls had appointed him guardian to Helvidius's daughter at the request of her mother and stepfather, and even at the present time he could not think of giving up his responsibilities; however, he would set a limit to his personal indignation and comply with the very moderate sentiments of these excellent women, who asked no more than to remind the Senate of the bloodstained servility of Publicius Certus and to petition that if such flagrant crime were to go unpunished, he might at

1. Unidentified.   2. *Aeneid,* VI : 105.

least be branded with some degradation like the former censors' mark. Then Satrius Rufus made a vague and ambiguous sort of speech. 'In my opinion,' he said, 'injustice will be done to Publicius Certus if he is not acquitted; for his name was only mentioned by the friends of Arria and Fannia, and by his own friends. We need not be apprehensive, for it is we, who have confidence in the man, who will be his judges. If he is innocent, as I hope and wish and shall continue to believe until something is proved against him, you will be able to acquit him.'

These were the views expressed as the speakers were called upon in order. Then my turn came. I rose to my feet with the opening words you see in the published speech, and replied to them one by one. It was remarkable to see the attention and applause with which all I said was received by those who had previously shouted me down: a change of front produced either by the importance of the issue, the success of the speech, or the firmness of the speaker. I came to an end, and Veiento began to reply. No one would allow it, and the interruption and uproar increased until he said, 'I beg you, Conscript Fathers, not to compel me to appeal for the protection of the tribunes.' At once the tribune Murena retorted, 'The honourable member has my permission to proceed.' Again there was an outcry, and meanwhile the consul called out names, took a division, and dismissed the Senate, leaving Veiento still standing and trying to speak. He has complained bitterly about this insult (as he calls it) in a line of Homer's: 'My lord, the young fighters are surely too much for your age.'[1]

Almost the entire Senate embraced me with open arms and overwhelmed me with enthusiastic congratulations for having revived the practice, long fallen into disuse, of bringing measures for the public good before the Senate at the risk of incurring personal enmities; I had in fact freed the Senate from the odium in which it was held amongst the other classes for showing severity to others while sparing its own members by a sort of mutual connivance. Certus was not present at these proceedings; either he suspected something of the sort or he was ill – the excuse he gave. It is true that the Emperor brought no motion against him before the Senate, but I won my point. The consulship was given to Certus's colleague, and Certus was removed from his Treasury post, so that my concluding demand was fulfilled that 'he

1. *Iliad*, VIII: 102.

should give back under the best of Emperors the reward he received from the worst'.

Afterwards I set down what I could remember of my speech, and made several additions. By coincidence, though it seemed no mere coincidence, a few days after the speech was published Certus fell ill and died. I have heard it said that always in his mind's eye he had a vision of me threatening him with a sword. Whether this is true I shouldn't like to say, but it helps to point a moral if it is accepted as true.

Here you have a letter as long as the speeches you have read, if you think what the length of a letter should be – but you weren't satisfied with the speeches and have only yourself to blame.

14. *To Cornelius Tacitus*

You are never satisfied with yourself, but I never write with such confidence as when I write about you. Whether posterity will give us a thought I don't know, but surely we deserve one – I don't say for our genius, which sounds like boasting, but for our application, hard work, and regard for future generations. Only let us continue along the path we have chosen; if it leads few to the full light of fame, it brings many out of the shades of obscurity.

15. *To Pompeius Falco*

I took refuge in Tuscany to be free to do as I liked, but even there it has been impossible. I am beset on all sides by the peasants with all their petitions full of complaints, and these I read rather more unwillingly than my own writings, which I really have no wish to read either. (I am revising some minor speeches of mine, and after a lapse of time it is a tedious and exasperating task.) My accounts are neglected, as if I had not come here to do them. I do, however, take a horse sometimes and play the part of proprietor, but only to the extent of riding round part of the estate for exercise. Don't you drop your habit of sending me the city news while I am rusticating in this way!

16. *To Pomponius Mamilianus*

I'm not surprised you enjoyed your hunting so much, with all that in the bag – you write as the historians do that the numbers couldn't be counted. Personally I have neither time nor inclination for hunting;

no time because I am busy with the grape harvest, and no inclination because it is a bad one. But I am bringing in some new verses instead of new wine, and, as you are kind enough to ask for them, I will send them when the fermenting stage is over.

17. *To Julius Genitor*

Thank you for your letter. You complain about a dinner party, a grand affair which filled you with disgust at the mimes and clowns and the male 'dancers' going the round of the tables. Please don't be for ever frowning – I have nothing of that kind in my own house, but I can put up with those who do. The reason why I don't have them is that I find nothing novel or amusing to attract me in that sort of 'dancer's' charms, in a mime's impudence, or a clown's folly. But you see I am not pleading my principles but my personal taste; and think how many people there are who dislike the entertainments which we find fascinating, and think them either pointless or boring. How many take their leave at the entry of a reader, a musician, or an actor, or else lie back in disgust, as you did when you had to endure those monstrosities as you call them! Let us then be tolerant of other people's pleasures so as to win indulgence for our own.

18. *To Statius Sabinus*

The devoted concentration with which you read and remember my small efforts is clear from your letter; so you are to blame for the task you set yourself by begging and coaxing me to send you as much of my work as I can. I can't refuse, but I shall send it bit by bit in small doses – grateful though I am to that memory of yours, I don't want to confuse it by application to too much material at a time and leave it overwhelmed and surfeited, so that it has to sacrifice the parts for the whole and the earlier items for the later.

19. *To Cremutius Ruso*

You say you have read in a letter of mine[1] that Verginius Rufus ordered this inscription for his tomb:

> Here lies Rufus, who once defeated Vindex and set free the imperial
>   power
> Not for himself, but for his country.

I. VI: IO.

You dislike this; Frontinus, you say, showed a better and nobler spirit in forbidding any monument at all to be set up to himself; finally, you want my opinion on both men.

I loved them both, but I admired more the man you criticize, admired him so much that I thought he could never be praised enough. Yet now the time has come when I must undertake his defence. Everyone who has done some great and memorable deed should, I think, not only be excused but even praised if he wishes to ensure the immortality he has earned, and by the very words of his epitaph seeks to perpetuate the undying glory of his name. And I cannot easily think of anyone except Verginius whose fame in action is matched by his modesty in speaking of it. I can bear witness to this myself; I enjoyed his confidence and close friendship, but only once in my hearing did he go so far as to make a single reference to what he had done. This was the occasion when Cluvius[1] said, 'You know how a historian must be faithful to facts, Verginius, so, if you find anything in my histories which is not as you would like it, please forgive me.' To this he replied, 'Don't you realize, Cluvius, that I did what I did so that the rest of you should be at liberty to write as you please?'

Now let us consider Frontinus, on the very point in which you find him more moderate and restrained. Frontinus forbade any monument to be set up, but what were his words? 'A monument is money wasted; my memory will live on if my life has deserved it.' Do you really think that it shows more reticence to publish throughout the world that your memory will live on, than to record your achievement in a single place in a mere couple of lines? However, my intention was not to criticize Frontinus but to defend Verginius; though there could be no better defence of him for your ears than a comparison with the man you prefer. My own feeling is that neither should be blamed, for both hoped for fame though they sought it by different roads, one by claiming the epitaph which was his due, the other by professing to despise it.

20. To Venator

Your letter pleased me all the more for being a long one, especially as it was all about my own books. I can't be surprised that you enjoy

1. Cluvius Rufus, the historian of the early Empire and one of Tacitus's sources.

them, since you care almost as much for my efforts as you do for myself. As for me, at this very moment I am gathering in the grape harvest, which is poor, but better than I had expected; if you can call it 'gathering' to pick an occasional grape, look at the press, taste the fermenting wine in the vat, and pay a surprise visit to the servants I brought from the city – who are now standing over the peasants at work and have abandoned me to my secretaries and readers.

21. To Sabinianus

The freedman of yours with whom you said you were angry has been to me, flung himself at my feet, and clung to me as if I were you. He begged my help with many tears, though he left a good deal unsaid; in short, he convinced me of his genuine penitence. I believe he has reformed, because he realizes he did wrong. You are angry, I know, and I know too that your anger was deserved, but mercy wins most praise when there was just cause for anger. You loved the man once, and I hope you will love him again, but it is sufficient for the moment if you allow yourself to be appeased. You can always be angry again if he deserves it, and will have more excuse if you were once placated. Make some concession to his youth, his tears, and your own kind heart, and do not torment him or yourself any longer – anger can only be a torment to your gentle self.

I'm afraid you will think I am using pressure, not persuasion, if I add my prayers to his – but this is what I shall do, and all the more freely and fully because I have given the man a very severe scolding and warned him firmly that I will never make such a request again. This was because he deserved a fright, and is not intended for your ears; for maybe I *shall* make another request and obtain it, as long as it is nothing unsuitable for me to ask and you to grant.

22. To Herennius (?) Severus

I have been very worried about the illness of Passennus Paulus – and with every just reason, for he is the best of men, the soul of honesty, and my devoted friend. His literary work is modelled on that of the ancients whom he imitates and brings back to life, Propertius in particular, from whom he traces his descent; and he is indeed a true descendant, resembling the poet most in the qualities which were his greatest. Take up his elegiacs and you will find them exquisitely finished, full of sensuous charm, and truly in Propertius's style. He has lately turned to lyric poetry, and here he recalls Horace as successfully as he does Propertius elsewhere: if kinship has any influence on literature, you would think he was related to Horace too. He is highly versatile, with many changes of mood; he can love like a true lover and portray grief in all its passion; his tributes are generous and his wit is brilliant: in fact he can do everything with a specialist's perfection.

This is the friend and genius for whom I have been as sick at heart as he was in body, but now at last he is restored, and I with him. Congratulate me, congratulate literature itself, for the danger to his life has brought it through hazards as great as the glory his recovery will ensure for it.

23. To Maximus

It has often happened to me when speaking in the Centumviral Court that my hearers have preserved their judicial dignity and impassivity for a while and then suddenly jumped to their feet with one accord to congratulate me as if driven by some compelling force. From the Senate, too, I have often had all the applause my heart could desire; but never have I felt such pleasure as I did recently at something Tacitus said. He was describing how at the last Races he had sat next to a Roman knight who engaged him in conversation on several learned subjects and then asked if he came from Italy or the provinces. 'You know me,' said Tacitus, 'from your reading.' At which the man said, 'Then are you Tacitus or Pliny?' I can't tell you how delighted I am to have our names assigned to literature as if they belonged there and not to individuals, and to learn that we are both known by our writing to people who would otherwise not have heard of us.

A similar thing happened to me a day or two ago. I had a distinguished neighbour at dinner, Fadius Rufinus, and on his other side was someone from his native town who had come to Rome on his first visit that same day. Pointing to me, Rufinus said to him, 'Do you see my friend here?' Then he spoke at length about my work, and the man exclaimed, 'It must be Pliny!'

I confess I feel well rewarded for my labours. If Demosthenes had the right to be pleased when the old woman of Attica recognized him with the words 'That's Demosthenes!'[1] I may surely be glad when my

1. Cicero, *Tusculanae Disputationes*, v : 103.

name is well known. In fact I *am* glad and admit it. For I'm not afraid of appearing too boastful when I have other people's opinions to quote and not only my own, especially when talking to you; for you are never envious of anyone's reputation and are always furthering mine.

24. To Sabinianus

You have done the right thing in taking back into your home and favour the freedman who was once dear to you, with my letter to mediate between you both. You will be glad of this, and I am certainly glad, first because I see you are willing to be reasonable and take advice when angry, and then because you have paid me the tribute of bowing to my authority, or, if you prefer, granting my request. So accept my compliments as well as my thanks, but, at the same time, a word of advice for the future: be ready to forgive the faults of your household even if there is no one there to intercede for them.

25. To Pomponius Mamilianus

You grumble about being beset with military affairs, and yet you can read my bits of nonsense as if you had all the leisure in the world – you even enjoy them, clamour for them, and are insistent that I produce more like them. I am in fact beginning to think that I can look for more than mere amusement from this kind of writing, and now that I have the opinion of one who is both learned and serious, and above all sincere, I may even think of fame.

At the moment I have some legal work to do, not much, but enough to occupy my time. When this is finished I will entrust something inspired by the same Muse to your kindly care. If you think well of my little sparrows and doves, as they do of themselves, let them fly among your eagles; and if you don't, please shut them in a cage or keep them in their nest.

26. To Lupercus

One of our contemporary orators is a sound and sober speaker while lacking in grandeur and eloquence, so that I think my comment on him has point: his only fault is that he is faultless.

The orator ought in fact to be roused and heated, sometimes even to boiling-point, and to let his feelings carry him on till he treads the edge of a precipice; for a path along the heights and peaks often skirts the sheer drop below. It may be safer to keep to the plain, but the road lies too low to be interesting.[1] A runner risks more falls than a man who keeps to a snail's pace, but he wins praise in spite of a stumble, whereas there is no credit in walking without a fall. Eloquence is in fact one of the skills which gain most from the risks they run. You have seen tightrope walkers and the applause they win as they move along the length of the rope and every minute look as though they are going to fall; for it is the most unexpected and dangerous feats which win most admiration: ventures which the Greeks can define so well in a single word. Consequently the courage demanded of a helmsman to steer his course through a stormy sea is quite different from what he needs when the sea is calm and he reaches harbour unnoticed, to find no praise and congratulations awaiting him. It is when the sheets creak, the mast bends, and the rudder groans that he is covered with glory and stands almost equal to the gods of the sea!

I write as I do because I had an idea that you had criticized some passages in my writings for being pompous, though I thought them splendid, and what I imagined to be a full treatment of a bold enterprise you dismissed as redundant and exaggerated. But it is important to determine whether you are attacking genuine faults or only striking phrases; for, though anyone can see what stands out above the average, it needs a keen judgement to decide whether this is extravagant and disproportionate or lofty and sublime. Homer provides the best examples; no one can fail to notice (whatever he feels about them) such expressions as 'high heaven's trumpet rang out', 'his spear rested on a cloud', and 'neither the sea's breakers roar so loud',[2] but they must be weighed with care before judging if they are meaningless phantasies or noble creations of a divine inspiration. Not that I think that these are the times and I am the person to have written words like these, nor that I have the ability to do so: I am not so foolish. But I want to make the point that eloquence should be given its head, and the pace of genius should not be confined within too narrow a ring.

You may say that orators are different from poets – as if indeed Cicero lacked daring! However, let us leave out Cicero, since in his case I think there is no dispute. But there is surely no curb nor restraint

---

1. See Horace, *Ars Poetica*, 28.
2. *Iliad*, XXI : 388, V : 356, and XIV : 394.

holding back Demosthenes, the true model and exemplar of oratory, when he delivers the famous 'Abominable men, flatterers and evil spirits' and 'neither with stones nor bricks did I fortify this city', and later, 'Was it not to make Euboea the bulwark of Attica on the seaward side?'[1] Elsewhere he says 'For my part, men of Athens, by the gods I believe that Philip is drunk with the magnitude of his achievements',[2] and there can hardly be anything bolder than the magnificent long digression beginning 'For a disease . . .'[3] The following passage may be shorter but is no less daring: 'Then when Python swaggered and poured out a torrent of abuse on us, I stood firm';[4] and this bears the same stamp: 'But when a man has grown strong, as Philip has, by rapacity and crime, then the first pretext, some trifling slip, overthrows and shatters all.'[5] In the same style are the expressions 'Cordoned off from every right which holds sacred in the city' and 'You have thrown away their claim to pity, Aristogeiton, indeed you have destroyed it once and for all. Do not then seek anchorage in harbours which you have yourself blocked up and filled with stakes.' In the same speech he had said 'But I cannot see that any one of these topics gives a sure foothold to the defendant; he has nothing before him but precipices, gulfs, and pitfalls', and also 'I am afraid that to some you will appear to have set up as a trainer of any citizen with a taste for wickedness'. There is also 'I cannot believe that your ancestors built you these law courts as a hotbed for rascals of this sort' and 'If he is a jobbing dealer, a pedlar, and retailer of wickedness',[6] and innumerable such instances, not counting those which Aeschines called 'not words but wonders'.[7]

This is an argument on the wrong side, and you will retort that Demosthenes is at fault in the same way as you say I am. But you must see how much greater he is than Aeschines, his critic, and greater in these very passages; he can show vigour elsewhere, but here he stands out as sublime. Besides, was Aeschines himself free from the faults he finds in Demosthenes? 'For it is essential, men of Athens, that the orator and the law should speak the same language; but when the law

1. *De Corona*, 296, 299, and 301.
2. *Philippic*, 1:49.   3. *De Falsa Legatione*, 259.
4. *De Corona*, 136.   5. *Olynthiac*, 11:9.
6. *In Aristogeitonem* 1:28, 84, 76, 7, 48, and 46.
7. *In Ctesiphontem*, 167.

says one thing, and the orator another . . .' Elsewhere he says that 'Then he displays himself as especially concerned with the decree', and again 'But keep watch and lie in ambush as you listen to him, so that you drive him to keep within the limits of the charge of illegality',[1] and he is so pleased with this metaphor that he repeats it: 'But as in the race track, drive him to keep to the relevant course.'[2] Nor is his style any more controlled and restrained in this example: 'But you reopen old wounds, and are more concerned with today's speeches than with the welfare of the State'; and he aims high when he asks: 'Will you not dismiss this man as a public menace to Greece? Or arrest him as a pirate who infests politics by cruising around the State in his brig of words, and then bring him to justice?'[3]

I am waiting for you to strike out certain expressions in this letter (such as 'the rudder groans' and 'equal to the gods of the sea') by the same rule as you attack the passages I am quoting; for I am well aware that in seeking indulgence for my past offences I have fallen into the very errors you condemn. Strike then – as long as you will fix an early date for us to discuss both past and present in person. Then you can make me more cautious or I shall teach you to be venturesome.

27. To Plinius Paternus

I have often been conscious of the powers of history, its dignity and majesty and inspired authority, but never more so than on a recent occasion. An author had begun a reading of a work of exceptional candour, and had left part to be read another day. Up came the friends of someone I won't name, begging and praying him not to read the remainder; such is the shame people feel at hearing about their conduct, though they felt none at the time of doing what they blush to hear. The author complied with their request, as he could well do without loss of sincerity, but the book, like their deeds, remains and will remain; it will always be read, and all the more for this delay, for information withheld only sharpens men's curiosity to hear it.

28. To Voconius Romanus

Your letters have reached me after a long delay, three in fact at once, all beautifully expressed, warmly affectionate, and such as I ought to

1. *In Ctesiphontem*, 16, 101, and 206.   2. *In Timarchum*, 176.
3. *In Ctesiphontem*, 208 and 253.

have from you, especially when I had been waiting for them. In one you entrust me with the very welcome commission of forwarding your letter to the august lady Plotina:[1] it shall be done. The same letter introduces Popilius Artemisius. I carried out his request at once. You also say that you have had a poor grape harvest, and I can join you in this complaint, although we live so far from each other.[2]

The second letter tells me you are setting down or dictating your impressions of myself. Thank you – I would thank you more if you had been willing for me to read the actual pages as they are finished; as you read my work, in common justice I should read yours, even when someone else is the subject. At the end you promise that, once you have some definite news of my arrangements, you will escape from your domestic affairs and take refuge here with me, where I am already forging you fetters which you will never manage to break.

Your third letter mentions that you have received my speech on behalf of Clarius and thought it seemed fuller than when you heard me deliver it. It *is* fuller, for I made several additions afterwards. You then want to know if I have had the other letter you sent, which was composed with special care. No, I haven't, and I can't wait for it. So send it as soon as you can, and pay me full interest: I work it out at twelve per cent per annum, and can't be expected to let you off more lightly than that.

29. To Fabius (?) Rusticus[3]

It is better to excel in one thing than do several moderately well, but moderate skill in several things is better if you lack ability to excel in one. Bearing this in mind, I have tried my hand at various styles of composition as I have never felt confident in any one. So when you read anything of mine you must be indulgent to each style I use in consideration of its not being my only one; quantity is an excuse for lack of quality in the other arts, so why should there be a harsher law for literature where success is even more difficult? But I mustn't talk about indulgence as if I were ungrateful – if you receive my latest efforts as kindly as you did my earlier work I should be looking for praise rather than begging indulgence, though this would be enough.

1. Wife of Trajan.
2. See 11:13. Voconius Romanus was a native of Hither Spain.
3. The historian (see Tacitus, *Agricola*, 10).

30. To Rosianus Geminus

I have often heard you praise your friend Nonius in person, as you do
in your last letter, for his generosity to certain people, and I will add
my own praises if his generosity is not confined to these individual
cases. I should like to see the truly generous man giving to his country,
neighbours, relatives, and friends, but by them I mean his friends
without means; unlike the people who bestow their gifts on those best
able to make a return. Such persons do not seem to me to part with
anything of their own, but use their gifts as baits to hook other
people's possessions. Other smart characters rob one person to give to
another, hoping their rapacity will bring them a reputation for generous giving. But the first essential is to be content with your own lot,
the second to support and assist those you know to be most in need,
embracing them all within the circle of your friendship.

If your friend can achieve all this he is wholly to be praised, if part
only he is still praiseworthy in a lesser degree; so few instances are
there even of partial generosity. Greed for ownership has taken such
a hold of us that we seem to be possessed by wealth rather than to
possess it.

31. To Sardus

I am still enjoying your company as much as before we parted, for I
have been reading your book, and, to be honest, rereading again and
again the passages about myself, where you have indeed been eloquent!
The wealth of your material and variety of treatment, and the skill
whereby you avoid repetition without loss of consistency, makes me
wonder whether I should mingle congratulations with my thanks. I
can do neither adequately, and if I could I should be afraid it would
look conceited to congratulate you on the very thing for which I am
thanking you. I will only add that my pleasure in your work increased
its merit for me, while its merit added to my pleasure.

32. To Cornelius Titianus

What are you doing, and what are your plans? As for me, I'm enjoying life to the full, which means I am thoroughly idle. Consequently I
can't be bothered with writing longer letters in my pampered state,
though I should welcome some to read in my idle hours. No one is

so lazy as a pampered man, and nothing so inquisitive as a man with nothing to do.

33. To Caninius Rufus[1]

I have come across a true story which sounds very like fable, and so ought to be a suitable subject for your abundant talent to raise to the heights of poetry. I heard it over the dinner table when various marvellous tales were being circulated, and I had it on good authority – though I know that doesn't really interest poets. However, it was one which even a historian might well have trusted.

The Roman town of Hippo[2] is situated on the coast of Africa. Near by is a navigable lagoon, with an estuary like a river leading from it which flows into the sea or back into the lagoon according to the ebb and flow of the tide. People of all ages spend their time here to enjoy the pleasures of fishing, boating and swimming, especially the boys who have plenty of time to play. It is a bold feat with them to swim out into deep water, the winner being the one who has left the shore and his fellow-swimmers farthest behind. In one of these races a particularly adventurous boy went farther out than the rest. A dolphin met him and swam now in front, now behind him, then played round him, and finally dived to take him on its back, then put him off, took him on again, and first carried him terrified out to sea, then turned to the shore and brought him back to land and his companions.

The tale spread through the town; everyone ran up to stare at the boy as a prodigy, ask to hear his story and repeat it. The following day crowds thronged the shore, watched the sea, and anything like the sea, while the boys began to swim out, amongst them the same boy, but this time more cautious. The dolphin punctually reappeared and approached the boy again, but he made off with the rest. Meanwhile the dolphin jumped and dived, coiled and uncoiled itself in circles as if inviting and calling him back. This was repeated the next day, the day after, and on several more occasions, until these people, who are bred to the sea, began to be ashamed of their fears. They went up to the dolphin and played with it, called it, and even touched and stroked it when they found it did not object, and their daring increased with experience. In particular the boy who first met it swam up when it

1. The poet of VIII : 4.
2. Hippo Diarrhytus (now Bizerta), north-west of Carthage.

was in the water, climbed on its back, and was carried out to sea and brought back; he believed it knew and loved him, and he loved it. Neither was feared nor afraid, and the one grew more confident as the other became tamer. Some of the other boys used to go with him on either side, shouting encouragement and warnings, and with it swam another dolphin (which is also remarkable), but only to look on and escort the other, for it did not perform the same feats nor allow the same familiarities, but only accompanied its fellow to shore and out to sea as the boys did their friend. It is hard to believe, but as true as the rest of the story, that the dolphin who carried and played with the boys would even come out on to the shore, dry itself in the sand, and roll back into the sea when it felt hot.

Then, as is generally known, the governor Octavius Avitus was moved by some misguided superstition to pour scented oil on the dolphin as it lay on the shore, and the strange sensation and smell made it take refuge in the open sea. It did not reappear for many days, and then seemed listless and dejected; but as it regained strength it returned to its former playfulness and usual tricks. All the local officials used to gather to see the sight, and their arrival to stay in the little town began to burden it with extra expense, until finally the place itself was losing its character of peace and quiet. It was then decided that the object of the public's interest should be quietly destroyed.

I can imagine how sadly you will lament this ending and how eloquently you will enrich and adorn this tale – though there is no need for you to add any fictitious details; it will be enough if the truth is told in full.

34. To Suetonius Tranquillus

Please settle my doubts. I am told that I read badly – I mean when I read verse, for I can manage speeches, though this seems to make my verse reading all the worse. So, as I am planning to give an informal reading to my personal friends, I am thinking of making use of one of my freedmen. This is certainly treating them informally, as the man I have chosen is not really a good reader, but I think he will do better than I can as long as he is not nervous. (He is in fact as inexperienced a reader as I am a poet.) Now, I don't know what I am to do myself while he is reading, whether I am to sit still and silent like a mere spectator, or do as some people and accompany his words with lips, eye, and gesture. But I don't believe I am any better at mime that at reading aloud. Once more, then, settle my doubts and give me a straight answer whether it would be better to read myself, however badly, than to do or leave undone what I have just said.

35. To Atrius (?)

I have received the book you sent, for which many thanks. I am very busy just now, so I haven't read it yet in spite of my impatience. But I hold literature in general and your writings in particular in such high regard that I should feel it sacrilege to handle them, unless I could give my undivided attention.

I very much approve of the trouble you take over revising your work, but there should be a limit to this; first because too much application blurs the outline instead of improving the details, and then because it distracts us from more recent subjects and prevents us from starting on new work and also from finishing off the old.

36. To Fuscus Salinator

You want to know how I plan the summer days I spend in Tuscany. I wake when I like, usually about sunrise, often earlier but rarely later. My shutters stay closed, for in the stillness and darkness I feel myself surprisingly detached from any distractions and left to myself in freedom; my eyes do not determine the direction of my thinking, but, being unable to see anything, they are guided to visualize my thoughts. If I have anything on hand I work it out in my head, choosing and correcting the wording, and the amount I achieve depends on the ease or difficulty with which my thoughts can be marshalled and kept in my head. Then I call my secretary, the shutters are opened, and I dictate what I have put into shape; he goes out, is recalled, and again dismissed. Three or four hours after I first wake (but I don't keep to fixed times) I betake myself according to the weather either to the terrace or the covered arcade, work out the rest of my subject, and dictate it. I go for a drive, and spend the time in the same way as when walking or lying down; my powers of concentration do not flag and are in fact refreshed by the change. After a short sleep and another walk I read a Greek or Latin speech aloud and with emphasis, not so much for the sake of my voice as my digestion, though of course both are strengthened by this. Then I have another walk, am oiled, take exercise, and have a bath. If I am dining alone with my wife or with a few friends, a book is read aloud during the meal and afterwards we listen to a comedy or some music; then I walk again with the members of my household, some of whom are well educated. Thus the evening is prolonged with varied conversation, and, even when the days are at their longest, comes to a satisfying end.

Sometimes I vary this routine, for, if I have spent a long time on my couch or taking a walk, after my siesta and reading I go out on horseback instead of in a carriage so as to be quicker and take less time. Part of the day is given up to friends who visit me from neighbouring towns, and sometimes come to my aid with a welcome interruption when I am tired. Occasionally I go hunting, but not without my notebooks so that I shall have something to bring home even if I catch nothing. I also give some time to my tenants (they think it should be more) and the boorishness of their complaints gives fresh zest to our literary interests and the more civilized pursuits of town.

37. *To Valerius Paulinus*

It is not your nature to demand the conventional formalities from your personal friends when they are likely to be inconvenienced, and I love you too surely to fear you will misinterpret my intentions if I am not present when you take up your consulship on the first of the month; especially when I must stay here to arrange for letting my farms on long leases and I shall have to adopt a new system for this. During the past five years, despite the large reductions I made in the rents, the arrears have increased and as a result most of my tenants have lost interest in reducing their debt because they have no hope of being able to pay off the whole; they even seize and consume the produce of the land in the belief that they will gain nothing themselves by conserving it.

I must therefore face this growing evil and find a remedy. One way would be to let the farms not for a money rent but for a fixed share of the produce, and then make some of my servants overseers to keep a watch on the harvest. There is certainly no more just return than what is won from the soil, climate and seasons, but this method requires strict honesty, keen eyes, and many pairs of hands. However, I must make the experiment and try all possible changes of remedy for an obstinate complaint.

You see that it is not pure selfishness on my part which prevents my attending you on the first day of your consulship, and I shall celebrate it here with prayers, rejoicing and congratulations as if I were with you.

38. *To Pompeius Saturninus*

I do indeed congratulate Rufus, not at your request but because he merits praise. I have read his book, a finished performance in every way, my pleasure in which was much increased by my affection for its author. I did however read it critically; for criticism is not confined to those who read only to find fault.

39. *To Mustius*

I am told by the soothsayers that I must rebuild the temple of Ceres which stands on my property; it needs enlarging and improving, for it is certainly very old and too small considering how crowded it is on its special anniversary, when great crowds gather there from the whole district on 13 September and many ceremonies are performed and vows made and discharged. But there is no shelter near by from rain or sun, so I think it will be an act of generosity and piety alike to build as fine a temple as I can and add porticoes – the temple for the goddess and the porticoes for the public.

Will you then please buy me four marble columns, any kind you think suitable, and marble for improving the floor and walls; and we shall also have to have made a statue of the goddess, for several pieces are broken off the original wooden one as it is so old. As for the porticoes, at the moment I can't think of anything I want from you, unless you will draw me a plan suitable for the position. They cannot be built round the temple, for the site has a river with steep banks on one side and a road on the other. On the far side of the road is a large meadow where they might quite well stand facing the temple; unless you can think of a better solution from your professional experience of overcoming difficulties of terrain.

40. *To Fuscus Salinator*

You say you were delighted with my letter describing how I spend my summer holidays in Tuscany, and you want to know what change I make at Laurentum in winter. None, except that I cut out my siesta

and shorten my nights a good deal by using the hours before dawn or
after sunset; and, if I have an urgent case pending, as often happens in
winter, instead of having comedy or music after dinner I work again
and again over what I have dictated, and so fix it in my memory by
repeated revision.

Now that you have my habits in summer and winter you can add
spring and autumn, the intermediate seasons, during which none of
the day is wasted and so very little is stolen from the night.

BOOK TEN

1. *Pliny to the Emperor Trajan*

Your filial feelings, august Emperor, prompted your desire to succeed your father at the latest possible moment, but the immortal gods have hastened to put our country in your hands, a task to which you had already been assigned. Therefore I pray that you, and through you all mankind, may enjoy every prosperity, as befits your reign; and as an individual no less than as an official, noble Emperor, I wish you health and happiness.

2. *Pliny to the Emperor Trajan*

I have no words to tell you, Sir, how much pleasure you have given me by thinking me fit for the privileges granted to parents of three children. I know that you have granted this at the request of your worthy and devoted servant Julius Servianus, but from the wording of your decision I understand that you were the more willing to do so as his petition was on my behalf. For you to think me worthy of your personal favour at the opening of your auspicious reign is the realization of my highest hopes. Still more now do I long for children of my own, though I wanted them even during those evil days now past, as you may know from my having married twice. The gods knew better when they reserved my good fortune wholly for your generosity. Now is the time I would wish to be a father, when my happiness need know no fear.

3a. *Pliny to the Emperor Trajan*

When the kind interest of your father and yourself, Sir, promoted me to take charge of the Treasury of Saturn, I gave up my practice in the courts (though I had never taken on cases indiscriminately) so that I could be free to give my whole attention to the duties assigned me. Thus when the province of Africa asked me to act for them against Marius Priscus,[1] I begged to be excused the honour, and my excuse was accepted. Subsequently the consul-elect proposed that those of us who had been granted exemption should be prevailed on to remain at the Senate's disposal and to permit our names to be included in the ballot for advocates. I then thought I should best accord with the peaceful atmosphere of your reign if I did not oppose that distinguished body, especially when they were so reasonable in their request. I trust that you will think my obedience was correct, for I am anxious for every word and deed of mine to receive the sanction of your supreme authority.

3b. Trajan to Pliny

You have acted rightly both as a citizen and as a member of the Senate in obeying the just demands of that distinguished body, and I am sure that you will perform the duties you have undertaken in accordance with the trust placed in you.

4. Pliny to the Emperor Trajan

Your kindness, noble Emperor, of which I have full personal experience, encourages me to venture to ask you to extend it to my friends, amongst whom Voconius Romanus has the highest claim. He has been my friend from our early years when we were at school together, and for this reason I petitioned your late father, the Emperor, to raise him to the dignity of senatorial rank. However, I await your generosity for my wish to be granted; for, although Romanus's mother had written to your father to state that she was making a gift of four million sesterces to her son, she had failed to complete the legal formalities. She has since done so after a reminder from me, has transferred some property to him, and completed the necessary forms for the conveyance.

Now that the obstacle to our hopes is removed, I can vouch for the character of my friend Romanus with complete confidence, a character signalized by his cultivated interests and the devotion to his parents to which he owes this gift from his mother, as well as his inheritance from his father soon afterwards and his adoption by his stepfather.

1. In 99–100; see II: 11 and 12.

He comes, moreover, from a distinguished family, and his father was a wealthy man. In addition to this I trust that my own plea on his behalf will be a further recommendation to your kind interest. I pray you then, Sir, to enable me to congratulate Romanus as I so much wish to do, and to gratify what I hope is a worthy affection. I can then be proud to think that your recognition of myself extends to my friend.

5. Pliny to the Emperor Trajan

When I was seriously ill last year, Sir, and in some danger of my life, I called in a medical therapist whose care and attentiveness I cannot adequately reward without the help of your kind interest in the man. I pray you therefore to grant him Roman citizenship. He is a resident alien, Arpocras by name, and was given his freedom by his mistress, also alien. She was Thermuthis, wife of Theon, and died some time ago.

I also pray you to grant full Roman citizenship to Hedia and Antonia Harmeris, the freedwomen of the noble lady Antonia Maximilla. It is at her desire that I make the request.

6. Pliny to the Emperor Trajan

Thank you, Sir, for your promptitude in granting full citizenship to the freedwomen of my friend Antonia, and Roman citizenship to my therapist Arpocras. But when I was supplying his age and property according to your instructions, I was reminded by people more experienced than I am that, since the man is an Egyptian, I ought not to have asked for Roman citizenship for him before he became a citizen of Alexandria. I had not realized that there was any distinction between Egyptians and other aliens, so I had thought it sufficient to inform you only that he had been given his freedom by an alien and that his patron had died some time ago. I shall not regret my ignorance if it means that I can be further indebted to you on behalf of the same person; I pray you therefore to make him a citizen of Alexandria too so that I may lawfully enjoy the favour you have conferred. To prevent any further delay to your generous interest I have given the details of his age and property to your freedmen, as instructed.

7. Trajan to Pliny

Following the rule of my predecessors, I do not intend to grant Alexandrian citizenship except in special cases; but as you have already obtained Roman citizenship for your medical therapist Arpocras, I cannot refuse this further request. You must inform me of the man's district so that I can write you a letter for my friend Pompeius Planta, the prefect of Egypt.

8. Pliny to the Emperor Trajan

Your late father, Sir, the deified Emperor, had encouraged liberal giving among his subjects in his fine public speeches and by his own noble example. I therefore sought his permission to transfer to the town of Tifernum the statues of former Emperors which I had inherited through various bequests and had kept as I received them on my estate some distance away; I also asked if I might add to them a statue of himself. He had given his permission with his full approval. I had then written at once to the town council to ask them to allocate me a site where I could set up a temple[1] at my own expense, and they had honoured my proposal by leaving the choice of a site to me. But first my own ill-health, then your father's illness, and subsequently the responsibilities of the post you have both assigned me, have caused delays, so that this seems the first convenient opportunity for me to go there in person. My month on duty finished at the end of August, and there are a great many public holidays in September.

I pray you then first to permit me to add your statue to the others which will adorn the temple I propose to build, then to grant me leave of absence so that it can be built as soon as possible. But I should fail in sincerity if I concealed from your kindness the fact that my personal affairs will incidentally benefit very much. The farms I own in the district bring in more than 400,000 sesterces, and I cannot postpone letting them, especially as the new tenants should be there to see to the pruning of the vines, and this must be done soon. Moreover, the series of bad harvests we have had are forcing me to consider reducing rents, and I cannot calculate these unless I am on the spot.

If then, Sir, you will grant me thirty days' leave of absence on both accounts, I shall be indebted to your generosity both for the speedy accomplishment of my act of loyalty and the setting in order of my private affairs. I cannot manage with less than a month, as the town and farms I am talking about are more than 150 miles from Rome.

1. See III: 4 and IV: 1.

9. Trajan to Pliny

You have given me many reasons, as well as every official explanation, for your application for leave of absence, though I should have been satisfied with the mere expression of your wishes. I do not doubt that you will return as soon as possible to your exacting official duties.

You have my permission to set up my statue in the place you have chosen for it; I am generally very reluctant to accept honours of this kind, but I do not wish it to seem that I have put any check on your loyal feelings towards me.

10. Pliny to the Emperor Trajan

Words cannot express my gratitude, Sir, for your letter telling me that you have given my therapist Arpocras the additional grant of Alexandrian citizenship, although you had intended to follow the rule of your predecessors and grant it only in special cases. His district is Memphis. I pray you then, gracious Emperor, to send me your promised letter to Pompeius Planta, the prefect of Egypt.

I hope to meet you, Sir, to enjoy the sooner the pleasure of your return[1] which is eagerly awaited here; I beg your permission to join you as far out from Rome as I can go.

11. Pliny to the Emperor Trajan

My recent illness, Sir, put me under an obligation to my doctor, Postumius Marinus, to whom I can make an adequate return with your help, if you will grant my petition with your usual kindness. I pray you therefore to confer citizenship on his relatives, Chrysippus, son of Mithridates, and on Stratonice, wife of Chrysippus, daughter of Epigonus, and on Chrysippus's two sons, Epigonus and Mithridates, with the privilege of retaining the rights of a patron over their freedmen, while remaining under their father's authority. I pray you further to grant full Roman citizenship to Lucius Satrius Abascantus, Publius Caesius Phosphorus, and Pancharia Soteris; I make this request at the desire of their patrons.

12. Pliny to the Emperor Trajan

I know, Sir, that my petitions are not forgotten, for your memory never lets an opportunity pass for doing good. But as you have hitherto

1. From Germany and Pannonia in late 99.

shown me indulgence, may I remind you and at the same time add urgency to my request that you honour Attius Sura with a praetorship now that there is a vacancy? This is his only ambition, and it is fostered by the distinction of his family, his honourable conduct in times of poverty, and, above all, by the happiness of your reign which encourages any of your subjects who know their own merit to hope that they may benefit by your kind interest.

13. Pliny to the Emperor Trajan

I am well aware, Sir, that no higher tribute can be paid to my reputation than some mark of favour from so excellent a ruler as yourself. I pray you, therefore, to add to the honours to which I have been raised by your kindness by granting me a priesthood, either that of augur[1] or member of the septemvirate as there is a vacancy in both orders. By virtue of my priesthood I could then add official prayers on your behalf to those I already offer in private as a loyal citizen.

14. Pliny to the Emperor Trajan

May I congratulate you, noble Emperor, in your own name and that of the State, on a great and glorious victory[2] in the finest tradition of Rome? I pray the gods to grant that all your designs meet with such a happy issue, and that the glory of your Empire be renewed and enhanced by your outstanding virtues.

*

15. Pliny to the Emperor Trajan

I feel sure, Sir, that you will be interested to hear that I have rounded Cape Malea[3] and arrived at Ephesus with my complete staff, after being delayed by contrary winds. My intention now is to travel on to my province partly by coastal boat and partly by carriage. The intense heat prevents my travelling entirely by road and the prevailing Etesian winds make it impossible to go all the way by sea.

1. See IV: 8. 2. In Dacia, either in 102 or 106.
3. The southernmost tip of the Greek Peloponnese.

16. Trajan to Pliny

You did well to send me news, my dear Pliny, for I am much interested to know what sort of journey you are having to your province. You are wise to adapt yourself to local conditions and travel either by boat or carriage.

17a. Pliny to the Emperor Trajan

I kept in excellent health, Sir, throughout my voyage to Ephesus, but I found the intense heat very trying when I started to travel by road and developed a touch of fever which kept me at Pergamum. Then, when I had resumed my journey by coastal boat, I was further delayed by contrary winds, so that I did not reach Bithynia until 17 September[1]. I had hoped to arrive earlier, but I cannot complain of the delay as I was in time to celebrate your birthday in my province, and this should be a good omen.

I am now examining the finances of the town of Prusa, expenditure, revenues, and sums owing, and finding the inspection increasingly necessary the more I look into their accounts; large sums of money are detained in the hands of private individuals for various reasons, and further sums are paid out for quite illegal purposes. I am writing this letter, Sir, immediately after my arrival here.

17b. Pliny to the Emperor Trajan

I entered my province, Sir, on 17 September, and found there the spirit of obedience and loyalty which is your just tribute from mankind.

Will you consider, Sir, whether you think it necessary to send out a land surveyor? Substantial sums of money could, I think, be recovered from contractors of public works if we had dependable surveys made. I am convinced of this by the accounts of Prusa, which I am handling with all possible care.

18. Trajan to Pliny

I wish you could have reached Bithynia without any illness yourself or in your party, and that your journey from Ephesus had been as easy

1. In III.

as your voyage there. The date of your arrival in Bithynia, my dear Pliny, I have noted from your letter. The people there will appreciate, I think, that I am acting in their own interests, and you too will see that it is made clear to them that you were chosen as my representative for a special mission. Your first task must be to inspect the accounts of the various towns, as they are evidently in confusion.

As for land surveyors, I have scarcely enough for the public works in progress in Rome or in the neighbourhood, but there are reliable surveyors to be found in every province and no doubt you will not lack assistance if you will take the trouble to look for it.

19. *Pliny to the Emperor Trajan*

I pray you, Sir, to advise me on the following point. I am doubtful whether I ought to continue using the public slaves in the various towns as prison warders, as hitherto, or to put soldiers on guard-duty in the prisons. I am afraid that the public slaves are not sufficiently reliable, but on the other hand this would take up the time of quite a number of soldiers. For the moment I have put a few soldiers on guard alongside the slaves, but I can see that there is a danger of this leading to neglect of duty on both sides, when each can throw the blame on the other for a fault they may both have committed.

20. *Trajan to Pliny*

There is no need, my dear Pliny, for more soldiers to be transferred to guard-duty in the prisons. We should continue the custom of the province and use public slaves as warders. Their reliability depends on your watchfulness and discipline. For, as you say in your letter, if we mix soldiers with public slaves the chief danger is that both sides will become careless by relying on each other. Let us also keep to the general rule that as few soldiers as possible should be called away from active service.

21. *Pliny to the Emperor Trajan*

Gavius Bassus, Sir, the prefect of the Pontic Shore, has called on me with due ceremony and respect, and has been here several days. As far as I could judge he is an excellent man who merits your kind interest. I told him that you had given orders that he must limit himself to ten picked soldiers, two mounted soldiers, and one centurion from the troops which you had assigned to me. He replied that this number was insufficient and that he would write to you himself; so I thought it best not to recall for the present the soldiers he has in excess of that number.

22. Trajan to Pliny

I have also heard from Gavius Bassus direct that the number of soldiers assigned him by my order was inadequate. I have ordered a copy of my answer to him to be sent with this letter for your information. It is important to distinguish between the needs of a situation and the likelihood of his wishing to extend his privileges because of it. The public interest must be our sole concern, and as far as possible we should keep to the rule that soldiers must not be withdrawn from active service.

23. Pliny to the Emperor Trajan

The public bath at Prusa, Sir, is old and dilapidated, and the people are very anxious for it to be rebuilt. My own opinion is that you could suitably grant their petition. There will be money available for building it, first from the sums I have begun to call in from private individuals, and secondly because the people are prepared to apply to building the bath the grants they usually make towards financing the distribution of olive oil. This is, moreover, a scheme which is worthy of the town's prestige and the splendour of your reign.

24. Trajan to Pliny

If building a new bath at Prusa will not strain the city's finances, there is no reason why we should not grant their petition; provided that no new tax is imposed and there is no further diversion of funds of theirs intended for essential services.

25. Pliny to the Emperor Trajan

My assistant, Servilius Pudens, Sir, arrived in Nicomedia on 24 November, to my great relief as I had long been expecting him.

26. Pliny to the Emperor Trajan

As a result of your generosity to me, Sir, Rosianus Geminus became one of my closest friends; for when I was consul he was my quaestor.

I always found him devoted to my interests, and ever since then he has treated me with the greatest deference and increased the warmth of our public relations by many personal services. I therefore pray you to give your personal attention to my request for his advancement; if you place any confidence in my advice you will bestow on him your favour. He will not fail to earn further promotion in whatever post you place him. I am sparing in my praises because I trust that his sincerity, integrity and application are well known to you already from the high offices he has held in Rome beneath your own eyes, as well as from his service in the army under your command.

I still feel that I have not given adequate expression to the warmth of my affection, and so once more I pray you, Sir, most urgently, to permit me to rejoice as soon as possible in the due promotion of my quaestor – that is to say, in my own advancement in his person.

27. Pliny to the Emperor Trajan

Your freedman and procurator Maximus, assures me, Sir, that he too must have six soldiers, in addition to the ten picked men whom I had assigned in accordance with your instructions, to that excellent official Gemellinus. I thought it best to leave him meanwhile the soldiers I found in his service, especially as he was just setting out to collect corn from Paphlagonia, and at his request I also gave him two mounted soldiers as an escort. I pray you to let me know your instructions for the future.

28. Trajan to Pliny

You did quite right to supply my freedman Maximus with soldiers for his present requirements, when he was setting out to procure corn and so acting on a special mission. When he has returned to his former post the two soldiers you have assigned him should be enough, plus another two from Virdius Gemellinus, the procurator under whom he serves.

29. Pliny to the Emperor Trajan

Sempronius Caelianus, who is an excellent young man, has discovered two slaves among his recruits and has sent them to me. I have postponed judgement on them until I could ask your advice on what would be a suitable sentence, knowing that you are the founder and upholder of military discipline. My chief reason for hesitating is the fact that the men had already taken the oath of allegiance but had not yet been enrolled in a unit. I therefore pray you, Sir, to tell me what course to follow, especially as the decision is likely to provide a precedent.

30. Trajan to Pliny

Sempronius Caelianus was carrying out my instructions in sending you the slaves. Whether they deserve capital punishment will need investigation; it is important to know if they were volunteers or conscripts, or possibly offered as substitutes. If they are conscripts, then the blame falls on the recruiting officer; if substitutes, then those who offered them as such are guilty; but if they volunteered for service, well aware of their status, then they will have to be executed. The fact that they were not yet enrolled in a legion is immaterial, for the truth about their origin should have come out on the actual day they were accepted for the army.

31. Pliny to the Emperor Trajan

You may stoop when necessary, Sir, to give ear to my problems, without prejudice to your eminent position, seeing that I have your authority to refer to you when in doubt.

In several cities, notably Nicomedia and Nicaea, there are people who were sentenced to service in the mines or the arena, or to other similar punishments, but are now performing the duties of public slaves and receiving an annual salary for their work. Since this was told me I have long been debating what to do. I felt it was too hard on the men to send them back to work out their sentences after a lapse of many years, when most of them are old by now, and by all accounts are quietly leading honest lives, but I did not think it quite right to retain criminals in public service; and though I realized there was nothing to be gained by supporting these men at public expense if they did not work, they might be a potential danger if they were left to starve. I was therefore obliged to leave the whole question in suspense until I could consult you.

You may perhaps want to know how they came to be released from the sentences passed on them. I asked this question myself, but received no satisfactory answer to give you, and although the records of their sentences were produced, there were no documents to prove their release. But people have stated on their behalf that they had been released by order of the previous governors or their deputies, and this is confirmed by the unlikelihood that any unauthorized person would take this responsibility.

32. Trajan to Pliny

Let us not forget that the chief reason for sending you to your province was the evident need for many reforms. Nothing in fact stands more in r eed of correction than the situation described in your letter, where criminals under sentence have not only been released without authority but are actually restored to the status of honest officials. Those among them who were sentenced within the last ten years and were released by no proper authority must therefore be sent back to work out their sentences. But if the men are elderly and have sentences dating back farther than ten years, they can be employed in work of a penal nature, cleaning public baths and sewers, or repairing streets and highways, the usual employment for men of this type.

33. Pliny to the Emperor Trajan

While I was visiting another part of the province, a widespread fire broke out in Nicomedia which destroyed many private houses and also two public buildings (the Elder Citizens' Club and the Temple of Isis) although a road runs between them. It was fanned by the strong breeze in the early stages, but it would not have spread so far but for the apathy of the populace; for it is generally agreed that people stood watching the disaster without bestirring themselves to do anything to stop it. Apart from this, there is not a single fire engine anywhere in the town, not a bucket nor any apparatus for fighting a fire. These will now be provided on my instructions.

Will you, Sir, consider whether you think a company of firemen might be formed, limited to 150 members? I will see that no one shall be admitted who is not genuinely a fireman, and that the privileges granted shall not be abused: it will not be difficult to keep such small numbers under observation.

34. Trajan to Pliny

You may well have had the idea that it should be possible to form a company of firemen at Nicomedia on the model of those existing elsewhere, but we must remember that it is societies like these which have been responsible for the political disturbances in your province, particularly in its towns. If people assemble for a common purpose, whatever name we give them and for whatever reason, they soon turn into a political club. It is a better policy then to provide the equipment necessary for dealing with fires, and to instruct property owners to make use of it, calling on the help of the crowds which collect if they find it necessary.

35. Pliny to the Emperor Trajan

We have made our annual vows,[1] Sir, to ensure your safety and thereby that of the State, and discharged our vows for the past year, with prayers to the gods to grant that they may be always thus discharged and confirmed.

36. Trajan to Pliny

I was glad to hear from your letter, my dear Pliny, that you and the provincials have discharged your vows to the immortal gods on behalf of my health and safety, and have renewed them for the coming year.

37. Pliny to the Emperor Trajan

The citizens of Nicomedia, Sir, have spent 3,318,000 sesterces on an aqueduct which they abandoned before it was finished and finally demolished. Then they made a grant of 200,000 sesterces towards another one, but this too was abandoned, so that even after squandering such enormous sums they must still spend more money if they are to have a water supply.

I have been myself to look at the spring which could supply pure water to be brought along an aqueduct, as originally intended, if the supply is not to be confined to the lower lying parts of the town. There are very few arches still standing, but others could be built out of the blocks of stone taken from the earlier construction, and I think some ought to be made of brick, which would be easier and cheaper.

The first essential is for you to send out an engineer or an architect to prevent a third failure. I will add only that the finished work will combine utility with beauty, and will be well worthy of your reign.

1. 3 January 112.

38. Trajan to Pliny

Steps must be taken to provide Nicomedia with a water supply, and I am sure you will apply yourself to the task in the right way. But for goodness' sake apply yourself no less to finding out whose fault it is that Nicomedia has wasted so much money up to date. It may be that people have profited by this starting and abandoning of aqueducts. Let me know the result of your inquiry.

39. Pliny to the Emperor Trajan

The theatre at Nicaea, Sir, is more than half built but it is still unfinished and has already cost more than ten million sesterces, or so I am told – I have not yet examined the accounts. I am afraid it may be money wasted. The building is sinking and showing immense cracks, either because the soil is damp and soft or the stone used was poor and friable. We shall certainly have to consider whether it is to be finished or abandoned, or even demolished, as the foundations and substructure intended to hold up the building may have cost a lot but look none too solid to me. There are many additions to the theatre promised by private individuals, such as a colonnade on either side and a gallery above the auditorium, but all these are now held up by the stoppage of work on the main building which must be finished first.

The citizens of Nicaea have also begun to rebuild their gymnasium (which was destroyed by fire before my arrival) on a much larger and more extensive scale than before. They have already spent a large sum, which may be to little purpose, for the buildings are badly planned and too scattered. Moreover, an architect – admittedly a rival of the one who drew up the designs – has given the opinion that the walls cannot support the superstructure in spite of being twenty-two feet thick, as the rubble core has no facing of brick.

The people of Claudiopolis are also building, or rather excavating, an enormous public bath in a hollow at the foot of a mountain. The money for this is coming either from the admission fees already paid by the new members of the town council elected by your gracious favour, or from what they will pay at my demand. So I am afraid there is misapplication of public funds at Nicaea and abuse of your generosity at Claudiopolis, though this should be valued above any money. I am therefore compelled to ask you to send out an architect to inspect both theatre and bath and decide whether it will be more practicable, in view of what has already been spent, to keep to the original plans and finish both buildings as best we can, or to make any necessary alterations and changes of site so that we do not throw away more money in an attempt to make some use of the original outlay.

40. Trajan to Pliny

The future of the unfinished theatre at Nicaea can best be settled by you on the spot. It will be sufficient for me if you let me know your decision. But, once the main building is finished, you will have to see that private individuals carry out their promises of adding to the theatre.

These poor Greeks all love a gymnasium; so it may be that they were too ambitious in their plans at Nicaea. They will have to be content with one which suits their real needs.

As for the bath at Claudiopolis, which you say has been started in an unsuitable site, you must decide yourself what advice to give. You cannot lack architects: every province has skilled men trained for this work. It is a mistake to think they can be sent out more quickly from Rome when they usually come to us from Greece.

41. Pliny to the Emperor Trajan

In consideration of your noble ambition which matches your supreme position, I think I should bring to your notice any projects which are worthy of your immortal name and glory and are likely to combine utility with magnificence.

There is a sizeable lake[1] not far from Nicomedia, across which marble, farm produce, wood, and timber for building are easily and cheaply brought by boat as far as the main road; after which everything has to be taken on to the sea by cart, with great difficulty and increased expense. To connect the lake with the sea[2] would require a great deal of labour, but there is no lack of it. There are plenty of people in the countryside, and many more in the town, and it seems certain that they will all gladly help with a scheme which will benefit them all.

It remains for you to send an architect or an engineer, if you think fit, to make an accurate survey and determine whether the lake is

1. Lake Sophon (now Lake Sabanja), eighteen miles south-east of the town.
2. The text is defective, but this seems to be the general sense.

above sea-level. The local experts say that it is forty cubits[1] above. I have looked at the site myself and find there is a canal dug by one of the former kings of Bithynia, though whether this was intended to drain the surrounding fields or to connect the lake with the river I am not sure; it was left unfinished, and again I cannot say if this was because the king died suddenly or despaired of finishing the work. This, however, only fires me with enthusiasm to see you accomplish what kings could only attempt: you will forgive my ambition for your greater glory.

42. Trajan to Pliny

I may perhaps be tempted to think of connecting this lake of yours with the sea, but there must first be an accurate survey to find how much water the lake contains and from what source it is filled, or else it might be completely drained once it is given an outlet to the sea. You can apply to Calpurnius Macer[2] for an engineer, and I will send you out someone who has experience of this sort of work.

43. Pliny to the Emperor Trajan

When I was inspecting the accounts of the city of Byzantium, Sir, where expenditure has been very heavy, I was informed that a delegate was sent annually to offer you a loyal address and allowed 12,000 sesterces for his expenses. Remembering your wishes, I decided to send on the address but no delegate to convey it, so that the citizens could reduce expenses without failing in their official duty towards you. In the same accounts there is an entry of another 3,000 sesterces under the head of annual travelling expenses for the delegate sent with an official greeting to the governor of Moesia. This, too, I thought should be cut down in future.

I pray you, Sir, to think fit to give me your opinion, and either confirm my decision or correct me if I am at fault.

44. Trajan to Pliny

You were quite right, my dear Pliny, to remit the 12,000 sesterces which the citizens of Byzantium were spending on a delegate to convey their loyal address to me. Their duty will be fulfilled if their

1. Now about 120 feet. Nothing is known of this canal.
2. See x: 61–2. He is known to have been legate of Lower Moesia in 112.

resolution is forwarded through you. The governor of Moesia will also forgive them if they spend less on paying their respects to him.

45. Pliny to the Emperor Trajan

Are permits to use the Imperial Post valid after their date has expired, and, if so, for how long? I pray you, Sir, to tell me your wishes and settle my doubts. I am anxious not to make the mistake through ignorance of sanctioning illegal documents, or alternatively of holding up essential dispatches.

46. Trajan to Pliny

Permits to use the Post must not be used once their date has expired. I therefore make it a strict rule to see that new permits are sent out to every province before the date they can be needed.

47. Pliny to the Emperor Trajan

When, Sir, I wished to inspect the finances of Apamea, sums owing, revenue, and expenditure, I was told that the citizens were all quite willing for me to see the accounts, but as Apamea was a Roman settlement[1] none of the senatorial governors had ever done so; and it was their long-established custom and privilege to manage their internal affairs in their own way. I told them to set down their statements and authorities quoted in the form of a petition, and this I am sending to you just as I received it though I realize that much of it is irrelevant to the point at issue.

I pray you to think fit to instruct me how I ought to act. I am anxious for it not to seem that I have exceeded or fallen short of my duty.

48. Trajan to Pliny

Having received the petition from the citizens of Apamea which you sent with your letter, I think I need not look into the reasons why they wish it to be known that the senatorial governors of the province refrained from inspecting their accounts; seeing that they raise no objection to an inspection by you. I think then that you should reward their honesty and assure them that on this occasion you are making a special inspection at my express wish, and that it will be carried out without prejudice to their existing privileges.

1. Colonia Julia Concordia Augusta Apamea.

49. Pliny to the Emperor Trajan

Before my arrival, Sir, the citizens of Nicomedia had begun to build a new forum adjacent to their existing one. In one corner of the new area is an ancient temple of the Great Mother,[1] which needs to be rebuilt or moved to a new site, mainly because it is much lower than the buildings now going up. I made a personal inquiry whether the temple was protected by any specific conditions, only to find that the form of consecration practised here is quite different from ours.

Would you then consider, Sir, whether you think that a temple thus unprotected can be moved without loss of sanctity? This would be the most convenient solution if there are no religious objections.

50. Trajan to Pliny

You need have no religious scruple, my dear Pliny, about moving the temple of the Mother of the Gods to a more convenient place if a change of site seems desirable; nor need you worry if you can find no conditions laid down for consecration, as the soil of an alien country is not capable of being consecrated according to our laws.

51. Pliny to the Emperor Trajan

It is difficult, Sir, to find words to tell you how happy you have made me by your kindness to my mother-in-law and myself in transferring her relative Caelius Clemens to this province. I begin to realize to the full the extent of your generosity when it is thus graciously extended to my whole family: I could not venture to repay it, whatever my ability to do so might be. I can only have recourse to vows taken on your behalf and pray the gods that I may never prove unworthy of the favours you continually bestow.

52. Pliny to the Emperor Trajan

We have celebrated with appropriate rejoicing, Sir, the day of your accession[2] whereby you preserved the Empire; and have offered prayers to the gods to keep you in health and prosperity on behalf of the human race, whose security and happiness depends on your safety. We have also administered the oath of allegiance to the troops in the usual form, and found the provincials eager to take it, too, as a proof of their loyalty.

1. The Phrygian goddess Cybele. 2. 28 January.

53. Trajan to Pliny

I was glad to hear from your letter, my dear Pliny, of the rejoicing and devotion with which under your guidance, the troops and provincials have celebrated the anniversary of my accession.

54. Pliny to the Emperor Trajan

Thanks to your foresight, Sir, the sums owed to public funds have been paid in under my administration, or are in process of being so; but I am afraid the money may remain uninvested. There is no opportunity, or practically none, of purchasing landed property, and people cannot be found who will borrow from public funds, especially at the rate of twelve per cent, the same rate as for private loans.

Would you consider, Sir, whether you think that the rate of interest should be lowered to attract suitable borrowers, and, if they are still not forthcoming, whether the money might be loaned out amongst the town councillors upon their giving the State proper security? They may be unwilling to accept it, but it will be less of a burden to them if the rate of interest is reduced.

55. Trajan to Pliny

Neither can I see any other solution myself, my dear Pliny, to the problem of investing public funds, unless the rate of interest on loans is lowered. You can fix the rate yourself, according to the number of potential borrowers. But to force a loan on unwilling persons, who may perhaps have no means of making use of it themselves, is not in accordance with the justice of our times.

56. Pliny to the Emperor Trajan

May I express my deepest gratitude, Sir, that in the midst of your important preoccupations you have seen fit to direct me on matters on which I have sought your advice; I pray that you will do so once again.

A man has approached me with the information that certain enemies of his, who had been sentenced to three years banishment by the distinguished senator Publius Servilius Calvus,[1] are still in the province. They on the other hand insist that their sentences were reversed by

1. Senatorial Governor of Bithynia 109-10.

Calvus, and have quoted his edict of restitution. I therefore thought it necessary to refer the whole question to you, seeing that your official instructions were that I should not recall anyone banished by one of the governors or by myself, but I can find no ruling on the situation where a governor has passed sentence of banishment and subsequently reversed it. Consequently, Sir, I felt I must ask you what course you wish me to follow, and also what I am to do with people found still to be in the province, although they were sentenced to banishment and never had their sentences reversed.

A further type of case has also come to me for trial. A man was brought before me who had been sentenced to banishment for life by the governor Julius Bassus.[1] Knowing that all Bassus's acts had been annulled, and that the Senate had granted anyone sentenced by him the right to have a new trial so long as the appeal was made within two years, I asked this man if he had brought his case to the notice of the succeeding governor. He said he had not. So now I am obliged to ask whether you think that the man should be exiled on his original sentence, or if some heavier sentence, and if so, what, should be given him, and any others we may find in a similar situation.

I append copies of the sentence passed by Calvus and his edict of reversal, and the sentence passed by Bassus.

57. Trajan to Pliny

I will let you know my decision about the legal position of the persons who were banished for three years by the governor Publius Servilius Calvus and subsequently had their sentences reversed, as soon as I have found out from Calvus the reason why he did this.

As for the man who was banished for life by Julius Bassus, he had two years in which he could have asked for a re-trial if he thought his sentence was unjust, but, as he took no steps to do so, and remained in the province, he must be sent in chains to the officers in command of my imperial guards.[2] It is not sufficient to restore his former sentence when he evaded it by contempt of court.

58. Pliny to the Emperor Trajan

When, Sir, I was summoning jurors to attend assizes, Flavius Archippus tried to claim exemption on the grounds that he was a teacher of

1. See IV:9.   2. To await trial; as St Paul in Acts XXVIII:16.

philosophy. At this some people declared that it was not a question of excusing him from acting as a juror, but of removing his name altogether from the register and sending him back to complete the sentence he had evaded by breaking out of prison. The sentence pronounced by the governor Velius Paulus was quoted, whereby Archippus had been condemned to the mines for forgery. He could produce nothing to prove that this sentence had been reversed, but as evidence of his reinstatement he cited a petition he had presented to Domitian, letters written by Domitian testifying to his character, and a decree voted by the people of Prusa. To these he added a letter written by him to you, and an edict and letter of your father, all confirming the benefits granted him by Domitian.

Notwithstanding the nature of the charges made against this man, I thought I should make no decision until I had asked your advice; the case seemed to me to need your official ruling. I append the documents cited on both sides.

(a) Domitian's Letter to Terentius Maximus

At the petition of Flavius Archippus the philosopher, I have given instructions that up to 100,000 sesterces is to be spent on buying him a farm near his native town, Prusa; from the income whereof he may support his family. I wish this to be done on his behalf, and the full cost charged to me as a personal gift to him.

(b) Domitian's Letter to Lappius Maximus

Archippus the philosopher is an honest man, his character in accordance with his profession. I wish to recommend him to your notice, my dear Maximus, and trust that you will show him every courtesy in acceding to such modest demands as he may make of you.

(c) Edict of the Deified Emperor Nerva[1]

There are some matters, citizens, which need no edict in happy times like ours, nor should a good ruler have to give evidence of his intentions where they can be clearly understood. Every one of my subjects can rest assured without a reminder that, in sacrificing my retirement to the security of the State, it was my intention to confer new benefits and to confirm those already granted. However, to prevent your public rejoicing being marred by misgivings, through the doubts of any who have received favours, or the memory of the Emperor who bestowed them, I have thought it necessary and desirable to meet your anxieties

1. 'Pompous, grandiloquent and obscure' (E. G. Hardy).

by a proof of my generosity. It is my wish that no one should think that I shall withdraw any public or private benefactions conferred by any of my predecessors, so as to claim credit for restoring them myself. Everything shall be assured and ratified: no one on whom the fortune of the Empire has smiled, shall need to renew his petitions in order to confirm his happiness. Let my subjects then permit me to devote myself to new benefactions, and be assured that they need ask only for what they have not hitherto been granted.

(*d*) The Deified Emperor Nerva's Letter to Tullius Justus
Any regulations laid down for matters begun or concluded in the last reign are to hold good; consequently letters of Domitian must also remain valid.

59. Pliny to the Emperor Trajan

Flavius Archippus has charged me by your prosperity and immortal name, to forward a petition which he has placed in my hands. I thought it my duty to grant a request made in this way, provided that I informed Furia Prima, his accuser, of my intention. She has also handed me a petition which I am sending with this letter, so that you can hear both sides of the case and be better able to decide what is to be done.

60. Trajan to Pliny

It is possible that Domitian was unaware of Archippus's position when he wrote all these letters of recommendation, but I personally find it more natural to believe that Archippus was restored to his former status by the Emperor's intervention. This seems more likely because the people of Prusa so often voted Archippus the honour of having his statue set up, though they must have known about the sentence passed by the governor Paulus. But none of this means, my dear Pliny, that if any new charge is brought against him you must not give it a hearing.

I have read the petitions from Archippus and his accuser, Furia Prima, which you sent me in your second letter.

61. Pliny to the Emperor Trajan

You very wisely express the fear, Sir, that the lake near Nicomedia might be drained away if connected with the river and then to the sea, but since I have been on the spot I think I have found a way of avoiding this danger. The lake can be brought right up to the river by means of a canal without actually joining it, if a sort of dyke is left between to keep the two apart; it will not actually flow into the river (and so be drained of water) but the effect will be almost the same as if it did. It will be easy to bring cargoes along the canal and then transfer them to the river across the narrow strip of land between.

This would be a solution if necessary, but I am hopeful that it will not be needed; for the lake is in fact fairly deep, and has a river flowing out at the opposite side which can be dammed and diverted wherever we like, so that it would carry off no more water than at present and do no damage to the lake. There are, moreover, several streams along the course of the proposed canal, and if their water is carefully conserved it will augment the supply from the lake. Again, if we decide to cut a longer canal, deepen it and bring it down to sea-level so that the water will flow direct into the sea, instead of via the river, the counter-pressure from the sea will check the outflow from the lake. Even if we had none of these natural advantages we could manage to regulate the flow of water by sluices.

But these and other details can be much more accurately worked out in a survey by the engineer, whom you must assuredly send, Sir, as you promised. The scheme deserves your attention, and will prove worthy of your eminent position. Meanwhile, I have written to the distinguished senator Calpurnius Macer, as you directed, and asked him to send the most suitable engineer he has.

62. Trajan to Pliny

I can see, my dear Pliny, that you are applying all your energy and intelligence to your lake; you have worked out so many ways of avoiding the danger of its water draining away, and so increasing its usefulness to us in future. You choose then the way which best suits the situation. I am sure Calpurnius Macer will not fail to send you an engineer, and there is no lack of such experts in the provinces where you are.

63. Pliny to the Emperor Trajan

I have received a letter, Sir, from your freedman Lycormas, telling me to detain, pending his arrival, any embassy which may come here from the Bosporos on its way to Rome. None has come to Nicaea as yet, at least while I have been here, but a courier has arrived from King Sauromates. I thought I should seize this unforeseen opportunity to send him on with the courier who travelled here ahead of Lycormas, so that you could have both letters together in case they contained news of equal importance to you.

64. *Pliny to the Emperor Trajan*

King Sauromates has written to me to say that he has news which you should know as soon as possible. I have accordingly given a permit for the Post to the courier who is bringing his letter to you, in order to speed up his journey.

65. *Pliny to the Emperor Trajan*

A serious problem, Sir, which affects the whole province, concerns the status and cost of maintenance of the persons generally known as foundlings. I have looked at the orders of your predecessors, but was unable to find either a particular case or a general rule which could apply to Bithynia; so I decided I must ask you for directions, as I felt it was not sufficient to be guided only by precedents in a matter which required your authoritative opinion.

An edict referring to Andania[1] was quoted to me, which was said to be one issued by the deified Emperor Augustus, also letters of the deified Emperors Vespasian and Titus to the Spartans, and another from Titus to the Achaeans. There were also letters from Domitian to the governors Avidius Nigrinus and Armenius Brocchus, and yet another to the Spartans from Domitian. I have not sent copies of them to you as they seemed to be inaccurate, and some of them of doubtful authenticity; and I felt sure that you had accurate and genuine versions amongst your official files.

66. *Trajan to Pliny*

The question you raise of free persons who were exposed at birth, then brought up in slavery by those who rescued them, has often been discussed, but I can find nothing in the records of my predecessors which could have applied to all provinces. There are, it is true, the letters

---

1. The former capital of the kings of Messenia (now Androssa) in the Peloponnese.

from Domitian to Avidius Nigrinus and Armenius Brocchus, which ought possibly to give us guidance, but Bithynia is not one of the provinces covered by his ruling. I am therefore of the opinion that those who wish to claim emancipation on this ground should not be prevented from making a public declaration of their right to freedom, nor should they have to purchase their freedom by refunding the cost of their maintenance.

67. *Pliny to the Emperor Trajan*

An ambassador from King Sauromates, Sir, saw me at Nicaea, and waited there of his own accord for two days; after which I thought I ought not to delay him further, seeing that I still had no idea when your freedman Lycormas would arrive, and official duties compelled me to leave myself for another part of the province.[1] I thought I should bring this to your notice in view of my recent letter saying that Lycormas had asked me to detain pending his arrival any embassy which might come from the Bosporos. I could think of no good reason for keeping him any longer, especially as the letters from Lycormas, which (as I said in my earlier letter) I did not want to delay, seemed likely to reach you some days before this ambassador.

68. *Pliny to the Emperor Trajan*

Certain persons have asked me to follow the practice of the senatorial governors and permit them to move the remains of their deceased relatives, either because their monuments have suffered through lapse of time or the flooding of the river or for other similar reasons. Knowing that when cases of this kind arise in Rome application must be made to the College of Pontiffs, I thought I should consult you, Sir, as Chief Pontiff, to learn what course you wish me to follow.

69. *Trajan to Pliny*

It makes things difficult for provincials if we enforce the rule of applying to the Pontiffs when they have good reason for wanting to transfer the remains of their deceased from one site to another. I think it would be best to follow the example of former governors of your province and grant or refuse permission on the merits of each individual case.

1. Pontus. In letter 77 he is at Juliopolis.

70. Pliny to the Emperor Trajan

I have looked around Prusa, Sir, in search of a possible site for the new bath for which you have graciously given your permission, and chosen one which is occupied at present by the unsightly ruins of what I am told was once a fine house. We could thus remove this eyesore and embellish the city without pulling down any existing structure; indeed, we should be restoring and improving what time has destroyed.

But these are the facts about the house. It was left to the Emperor Claudius by the will of a certain Claudius Polyaenus, who also left instructions that a shrine to the Emperor was to be set up in the garden-court and the rest of the house was to be let. For some time the city drew rent for this; then, partly through pillage and partly through neglect, the whole house, court and garden gradually fell into ruins, so that now little but the site remains. The citizens would esteem it as a great favour, Sir, if you would either make them a present of this or give orders for it to be sold, as it is so conveniently situated. My own plan, if you approve, is to build the bath on what is already an open space, and to use the site of the original buildings for a hall and colonnades, to be dedicated to you as benefactor, for it will be a splendid public monument well worthy of your name. I am sending a copy of the will, though an imperfect one, from which you will see that Polyaenus left a good deal of furniture for the house. This has disappeared as well; but I shall make all possible inquiries about it.

71. Trajan to Pliny

There is no reason why we should not use the open space and the ruined house, which you say is unoccupied, for the new bath at Prusa. But you did not make it clear whether the shrine to Claudius had actually been set up in the garden-court. If so, the ground is still consecrated to him even if the shrine has fallen into ruins.

72. Pliny to the Emperor Trajan

Certain persons have requested that cases concerning acknowledgement of children and granting of free-born rights to former slaves should come to me personally for settlement. This, they say, would be in accordance with a letter written by Domitian to Minicius Rufus, and with the practice of former governors. I have looked up the decree of the Senate referring to cases of these types, but it covers only provinces under senatorial governors. I have therefore left the whole question in suspense until I have received your instructions, Sir, on what course to take.

73. *Trajan to Pliny*

If you will send me the decree of the Senate which is giving you difficulty, I shall be able to judge whether you ought to settle these cases of acknowledging children and restoring free-born rights.

74. *Pliny to the Emperor Trajan*

A soldier named Appuleius, Sir, stationed at Nicomedia, has sent me this report about a certain Callidromus. This man had been forcibly detained by his employers, Maximus and Dionysius (who are bakers), but had escaped and taken refuge before one of your statues. When brought before the magistrates, he made the following statement. He had once been a slave of Laberius Maximus,[1] was captured in Moesia by Susagus, and sent by Decebalus as a gift to Pacorus, King of Parthia, in whose service he remained for several years until he escaped and so made his way to Nicomedia.

As he repeated the same story when brought before me, I thought I ought to send him on to you; and I have delayed doing so only while I made inquiries about a jewel engraved with a portrait of Pacorus wearing his royal robes, which the man declared had been stolen from him. I should have liked to send this too, if it could have been found, along with the small nugget of gold I am sending now; he says he brought it from one of the mines in Parthia. I have sealed it with my signet ring, the chariot-and-four.

75. *Pliny to the Emperor Trajan*

Julius Largus of Pontus, Sir – a person whom I have never seen nor heard of, but presumably relying on your opinion of me – has entrusted me with the duty of administering, so to speak, his loyal sentiments towards you. He has left a will asking me to take formal possession of his estate and, after deducting 50,000 sesterces for my own use, to pay over the remainder to the cities of Heraclea and Tium, either for the erection of public buildings to be dedicated in your honour or

1. One of Trajan's generals in command of the Dacian war. Susagus is a general serving under Decebalus, King of Dacia.

for the institution of five-yearly games to be called by your name, whichever I think best. I thought I should bring this to your notice, mainly because I hope that you will guide my decision.

76. Trajan to Pliny

Julius Largus chose you for your sense of duty as if he had known you personally. Consider what will suit the conditions of both places, and also what will best perpetuate his memory, and make your own decision; you can adopt whichever plan you think best.

77. Pliny to the Emperor Trajan

It was a very wise move, Sir, to direct the distinguished senator Calpurnius Macer to send a legionary centurion to Byzantium. Would you now consider giving the same assistance to Juliopolis? Being such a small city it feels its burdens heavy, and finds its wrongs the harder to bear as it is unable to prevent them. Any relief you grant to Juliopolis would benefit the whole province, for it is a frontier town of Bithynia with a great deal of traffic passing through it.

78. Trajan to Pliny

Byzantium is in an exceptional position, with crowds of travellers pouring into it from all sides. That is why I thought I ought to follow the practice of previous reigns and give its magistrates support in the form of a garrison under a legionary centurion. If I decide to help Juliopolis in the same way I shall burden myself with a precedent, for other cities, especially the weaker ones, will expect similar help. I rely on you, and am confident that you will be active in every way to ensure that the citizens are protected from injustice.

If people commit a breach of the peace they must be arrested at once; and, if their offences are too serious for summary punishment, in the case of soldiers you must notify their officers of what is found against them, while you may inform me by letter in the case of persons who are passing through on their way back to Rome.

79. Pliny to the Emperor Trajan

Under the code of law, Sir, which Pompey drew up for Bithynia, it was laid down that no one could hold civil office or sit in the senate under the age of thirty. The same law stated that all ex-officials should

become members of the local senate. Then followed the edict of the
deified Emperor Augustus permitting the minor posts to be held from
the age of twenty-two. The question therefore arises whether anyone
who has held office under the age of thirty can be admitted to the
senate by the censors, and, if so, whether the law can be similarly interpreted so that persons who have not actually held office can be admitted to the senate at the age when they were eligible to do so. This
has been the practice hitherto, and is considered unavoidable because
it is so much more desirable to choose senators from the sons of better-
class families than from the common people.

When asked my opinion by the censors-elect, I told them that I
thought it would be in accordance with both the edict of Augustus
and the law of Pompey if anyone who had held civil office under the
age of thirty were admitted to the senate, seeing that the edict allowed
office to be held before the age of thirty, and the law laid down that
all ex-officials should become senators; but that in the case of persons
who had never held a civil office, although they had reached the age
of eligibility, I had some doubts. That is why, Sir, I am asking your
advice on what you wish me to do. I append the relevant sections of
the law of Pompey, and also the edict of Augustus.

80. Trajan to Pliny

I agree with your interpretation, my dear Pliny, that the law of Pompey was modified by the edict of Augustus to the extent that any
person not under the age of twenty-two was eligible to hold civil
office, and, having done so, could be admitted to the senate of his own
town. But no one, I think, under the age of thirty who has not held
office, can be elected to the senate of any place merely because he has
reached the age of eligibility.

81. Pliny to the Emperor Trajan

On the last day, Sir, of my stay at Prusa near Mount Olympus, I was
finishing my official business in the governor's residence when I was
informed by the magistrate Asclepiades that Claudius Eumolpus had
a request to make. It seems that at a meeting of the local senate
Dio Cocceianus[1] had applied for the transfer to the city of some

1. Better known as Dio Chrysostom, the orator and philosopher, whose
speeches *On the Duty of a Ruler* are addressed to Trajan.

public work which he had undertaken, but Eumolpus, representing Flavius Archippus, had opposed the transfer until Dio should produce his accounts for the building, as he was suspected of dishonest conduct. He also declared that your statue had been set up in the building although the bodies of Dio's wife and son were buried there, and he requested me to hold a judicial inquiry.

I agreed to postpone my departure and do so immediately, but he then wanted me to give him longer to prepare his case and asked me to hold the inquiry in another town. I arranged to hold it at Nicaea, but, when I took my seat to hear the case, Eumolpus again began to beg for an adjournment on the grounds that he was still insufficiently prepared, whereas Dio demanded an immediate hearing. After much argument on both sides, some of it referring to the actual case, I decided to grant an adjournment in order to ask your advice, as the case is likely to create a precedent. I told both parties to present their demands in writing as I wanted to enable you to judge their statements from their own words. Dio agreed to do this, but Eumolpus said he would confine his written statement to his request for accounts made on behalf of his town; as regards the bodies of Dio's relatives, he said that he was not instigating any charge, but was representing Flavius Archippus and carrying out his instructions. Archippus, who was supported by Eumolpus here as at Prusa, then said that he would draw up the statement himself. I have waited several days, but neither Archippus nor Eumolpus has given me any statement up to now. Dio has handed in the statement which I am sending with this letter.

I have visited the building myself, and have seen your statue in position in a library; the alleged burial-place of Dio's wife and son is in an open space surrounded by a colonnade. I pray you, Sir, to think fit to guide me, especially in an inquiry of this kind; it has aroused great public interest, as is inevitable when the facts are admitted and defended by precedents on both sides.

82. Trajan to Pliny

You need not have had any doubts, my dear Pliny, about the matter on which you thought it necessary to consult me. You know very well that it is my fixed rule not to gain respect for my name either from people's fears and apprehensions or from charges of treason. You must dismiss this side of the question, which I would not tolerate even if it has precedents to support it, and then see that Dio Cocceianus produces accounts for all the work carried out under his management as the public interest demands. Dio ought not to object and in fact has not done so.

83. Pliny to the Emperor Trajan

The people of Nicaea, Sir, have officially charged me by your immortal name and prosperity, which I must ever hold most sacred, to forward their petition to you. I felt that I could not rightly refuse, and so it has been handed to me to dispatch with this letter.

84. Trajan to Pliny

The Nicaeans state that they have the right granted by the deified Emperor Augustus to claim the property of any of the citizens of Nicaea who die intestate. You must therefore examine this assertion with care, summon all the persons concerned, and call on the procurators Virdius Gemellinus and Epimachus, my freedman, to help you; so that after weighing their arguments against those on the other side you can reach the best decision.

85. Pliny to the Emperor Trajan

Your freedman and procurator Maximus, throughout the time we have been associated, has always proved honest, hard-working, and conscientious, as devoted to your interests, Sir, as he is a strict maintainer of discipline. I gladly give him this testimonial in all good faith, as demanded by my duty to you.

86a. Pliny to the Emperor Trajan

Gavius Bassus, Sir, the prefect of the Pontic Shore, has always proved high-principled, honest, and hard-working in his official duties, and has shown me every respect. I give him my full support and recommendation, in all good faith, as demanded by my duty to you.

86b. Pliny to the Emperor Trajan

I warmly recommend. . . .[1] He has served in the army under you, and to this training he owes any claim he has on your generosity. While I have been here both soldiers and civilians, who have had close

1. The beginning of this letter is lost.

experience of his justice and humanity, have vied with each other to pay personal and public tribute to him. I bring these facts to your notice in all good faith, as demanded by my duty to you.

87. Pliny to the Emperor Trajan

Nymphidius Lupus, Sir, the former chief centurion and I were in the army together, when he was commanding a cohort and I was a tribune. I liked him very much from the start, and our friendship begun then has increased in warmth with the passage of time. I therefore sent him a summons to bring him out of retirement and induce him to join me in Bithynia as my assessor. Like a good friend he postponed his plans for a peaceful old age and consented; and he intends to remain with me. Consequently, I look upon his relatives as my own, especially his son Nymphidius Lupus, an honest, hard-working young man, well worthy of his excellent father. He will prove equal to any mark of your favour, as you may judge from his first military appointment as commander of a cohort, for which he has won the highest praise from the distinguished senators, Julius Ferox and Fuscus Salinator. Any promotion which you confer on my friend's son, Sir, will give me also an occasion for personal rejoicing.

88. Pliny to the Emperor Trajan

It is my prayer, Sir, that this birthday[1] and many others to come will bring you the greatest happiness, and that in health and strength you may add to the immortal fame and glory of your reputation by ever new achievements.

89. Trajan to Pliny

I write in acknowledgement of your prayers, my dear Pliny, that I may spend many birthdays made happy by the continued prosperity of our country.

90. Pliny to the Emperor Trajan

The town of Sinope, Sir, is in need of a water supply. I think there is plenty of good water which could be brought from a source sixteen miles away, though there is a doubtful area of marshy ground stretching for more than a mile from the spring. For the moment I have

1. 18 September 112.

only given orders for a survey to be made, to find out whether the ground can support the weight of an aqueduct. This will not cost much, and I will guarantee that there will be no lack of funds so long as you, Sir, will approve a scheme so conducive to the health and amenities of this very thirsty city.

91. Trajan to Pliny

See that the survey you have begun is thoroughly carried out, my dear Pliny, and find out whether the ground you suspect can support the weight of an aqueduct. There can be no doubt, I think, that Sinope must be provided with a water supply, so long as the town can meet the expense out of its own resources. It will contribute a great deal to the health and happiness of the people.

92. Pliny to the Emperor Trajan

The free and confederate city of Amisus enjoys, with your permission, the privilege of administering its own laws. I am sending with this letter a petition handed to me there which deals with the subject of benefit societies, so that you, Sir, may decide whether and to what extent these clubs are to be permitted or forbidden.

93. Trajan to Pliny

If the citizens of Amisus, whose petition you send with your letter, are allowed by their own laws, granted them by formal treaty, to form a benefit society, there is no reason why we should interfere: especially if the contributions are not used for riotous and unlawful assemblies, but to relieve cases of hardship amongst the poor. In all other cities which are subject to our own law these institutions must be forbidden.

94. Pliny to the Emperor Trajan

Suetonius Tranquillus, Sir, is not only a very fine scholar but also a man of the highest integrity and distinction. I have long admired his character and literary abilities, and since he became my close friend, and I now have an opportunity to know him intimately, I have learned to value him the more.

There are two reasons why he needs the privileges granted to parents of three children: his friends could then effectively express their recognition of his merits, and, as his marriage had not been blessed with children, he can only look to your generosity, at my suggestion, for the benefits which the cruelty of fortune has denied him. I know, Sir, what a favour I am asking, but I remember your kindness hitherto in granting my wishes; and you may judge how much this means to me by the fact that I should not make such a request during my absence abroad did I not have it much at heart.

95. Trajan to Pliny

You are certainly well aware, my dear Pliny, that I grant these favours sparingly, seeing that I have often stated in the Senate that I have not exceeded the number which I said would meet my wishes when I first addressed its distinguished members. I have, however, granted your request and issued instructions that it is to be officially recorded that I have conferred on Suetonius Tranquillus the privileges granted to parents of three children, on the usual terms.

96. Pliny to the Emperor Trajan[1]

It is my custom to refer all my difficulties to you, Sir, for no one is better able to resolve my doubts and to inform my ignorance.

I have never been present at an examination of Christians. Consequently, I do not know the nature of the extent of the punishments usually meted out to them, nor the grounds for starting an investigation and how far it should be pressed. Nor am I at all sure whether any distinction should be made between them on the grounds of age, or if young people and adults should be treated alike; whether a pardon ought to be granted to anyone retracting his beliefs, or if he has once professed Christianity, he shall gain nothing by renouncing it; and whether it is the mere name of Christian which is punishable, even if innocent of crime, or rather the crimes associated with the name.

For the moment this is the line I have taken with all persons brought before me on the charge of being Christians. I have asked them in person if they are Christians, and if they admit it, I repeat the question a second and third time, with a warning of the punishment awaiting them. If they persist, I order them to be led away for execution; for, whatever the nature of their admission, I am convinced that their stubbornness and unshakeable obstinacy ought not to go unpunished.

1. See bibliography and notes in A. N. Sherwin-White's *Letters of Pliny*.

There have been others similarly fanatical who are Roman citizens. I have entered them on the list of persons to be sent to Rome for trial.

Now that I have begun to deal with this problem, as so often happens, the charges are becoming more widespread and increasing in variety. An anonymous pamphlet has been circulated which contains the names of a number of accused persons. Amongst these I considered that I should dismiss any who denied that they were or ever had been Christians when they had repeated after me a formula of invocation to the gods and had made offerings of wine and incense to your statue (which I had ordered to be brought into court for this purpose along with the images of the gods), and furthermore had reviled the name of Christ: none of which things, I understand, any genuine Christian can be induced to do.

Others, whose names were given to me by an informer, first admitted the charge and then denied it; they said that they had ceased to be Christians two or more years previously, and some of them even twenty years ago. They all did reverence to your statue and the images of the gods in the same way as the others, and reviled the name of Christ. They also declared that the sum total of their guilt or error amounted to no more than this: they had met regularly before dawn on a fixed day to chant verses alternately amongst themselves in honour of Christ as if to a god, and also to bind themselves by oath, not for any criminal purpose, but to abstain from theft, robbery, and adultery, to commit no breach of trust and not to deny a deposit when called upon to restore it. After this ceremony it had been their custom to disperse and reassemble later to take food of an ordinary, harmless kind; but they had in fact given up this practice since my edict, issued on your instructions, which banned all political societies. This made me decide it was all the more necessary to extract the truth by torture from two slave-women, whom they call deaconesses. I found nothing but a degenerate sort of cult carried to extravagant lengths.

I have therefore postponed any further examination and hastened to consult you. The question seems to me to be worthy of your consideration, especially in view of the number of persons endangered; for a great many individuals of every age and class, both men and women, are being brought to trial, and this is likely to continue. It is not only the towns, but villages and rural districts too which are infected through contact with this wretched cult. I think though that it is still possible for it to be checked and directed to better ends, for there is no doubt that people have begun to throng the temples which had been almost entirely deserted for a long time; the sacred rites which had been allowed to lapse are being performed again, and flesh of sacrificial victims is on sale everywhere, though up till recently scarcely anyone could be found to buy it. It is easy to infer from this that a great many people could be reformed if they were given an opportunity to repent.

97. Trajan to Pliny

You have followed the right course of procedure, my dear Pliny, in your examination of the cases of persons charged with being Christians, for it is impossible to lay down a general rule to a fixed formula. These people must not be hunted out; if they are brought before you and the charge against them is proved, they must be punished, but in the case of anyone who denies that he is a Christian, and makes it clear that he is not by offering prayers to our gods, he is to be pardoned as a result of his repentance however suspect his past conduct may be. But pamphlets circulated anonymously must play no part in any accusation. They create the worst sort of precedent and are quite out of keeping with the spirit of our age.

98. Pliny to the Emperor Trajan

Amongst the chief features of Amastris, Sir, (a city which is well built and laid out) is a long street of great beauty. Throughout the length of this however, there runs what is called a stream, but is in fact a filthy sewer, a disgusting eyesore which gives off a noxious stench. The health and appearance alike of the city will benefit if it is covered in, and with your permission this shall be done. I will see that money is not lacking for a large-scale work of such importance.

99. Trajan to Pliny

There is every reason, my dear Pliny, to cover the water which you say flows through the city of Amastris, if it is a danger to health while it remains uncovered. I am sure you will be active as always to ensure that there is no lack of money for this work.

100. Pliny to the Emperor Trajan

We have discharged the vows,[1] Sir, renewed last year, amidst general enthusiasm and rejoicing; and have made those for the coming year, the soldiers and provincials vying with one another in loyal demonstrations. We have prayed the gods to preserve you and the State in prosperity and safety, and to show you the favour you deserve for your many great virtues, and above all for your sanctity, reverence and piety.

101. Trajan to Pliny

I was glad to hear from your letter, my dear Pliny, that the soldiers and provincials, amidst general rejoicing, have discharged under your direction their vows to the immortal gods for my safety, and have renewed them for the coming year.

102. Pliny to the Emperor Trajan

We have celebrated with due solemnity the day[2] on which the security of the human race was happily transferred to your care, commending our public vows and thanksgiving to the gods to whom we owe your authority.

103. Trajan to Pliny

I was glad to hear from your letter that the day of my accession was celebrated under your direction by the soldiers and provincials, with due rejoicing and solemnity.

104. Pliny to the Emperor Trajan

Valerius Paulinus, Sir, has left a will which passes over his son Paulinus and names me as patron of his Latin freedmen.[3] On this occasion I pray you to grant full Roman citizenship to three of them only; it would be unreasonable, I fear, to petition you to favour all alike, and I must be all the more careful not to abuse your generosity when I have enjoyed it on so many previous occasions. The names of the three are

---

1. 3 January 113; see x: 35.   2. 28 January; see x: 52.

3. Freedmen whose rights were limited because they had been freed in conditions which failed to comply with the *lex Aelia Sentia*.

Gaius Valerius Astraeus, Gaius Valerius Dionysius, and Gaius Valerius Aper.

105. Trajan to Pliny

Your desire to further the interests of the freedmen entrusted to you by Valerius Paulinus does you very great credit. To speed your purpose I have issued instructions that it is to be officially recorded that I have granted full Roman citizenship to the persons mentioned in your letter, and I am prepared to do the same for any others for whom you may ask it.

106. Pliny to the Emperor Trajan

Publius Accius Aquila, Sir, a centurion in the sixth cohort in the auxiliary cavalry, has asked me to send you a petition begging your interest in his daughter's citizen status. It was difficult to refuse, especially as I know how readily you give a sympathetic hearing to your soldier's requests.

107. Trajan to Pliny

I have read the petition which you forwarded on behalf of Publius Accius Aquila, centurion of the sixth cohort of cavalry, and have granted his request. I have accordingly given his daughter Roman citizenship and am sending you a copy of the order to hand to him.

108. Pliny to the Emperor Trajan

I pray you, Sir, to tell me what legal rights you wish the cities of Bithynia and Pontus to have in regard to the recovery of money owed to them from contracts for hire or sale, or for any other reason. I find that several of the senatorial governors allowed priority to civic claims, and that this privilege has come to acquire the force of law.

I think, however, that it would be sound policy for you to make some permanent regulation to secure their interests for all time; for any previous concession, however wisely granted, remains only a temporary expedient unless confirmed by your authority.

109. Trajan to Pliny

The legal rights of the cities of Bithynia and Pontus to recover money owed to them for any reason, can only be determined by reference to their individual laws. If they already possess the privilege of priority over other creditors, it must be maintained; if not, I have no right to grant them it against the interests of private creditors.

110. Pliny to the Emperor Trajan

The public prosecutor of Amisus, Sir, has brought a claim before me against Julius Piso, for the sum of 40,000 denarii granted to the defendant twenty years previously by joint vote of the local senate and assembly. He based his claim on your instructions which forbid donations of this kind. Piso, on the other hand, declared that he had spent large sums of money on his city and had almost exhausted his means. He also pleaded the lapse of time since the grant, and argued that he should not be compelled to refund what had been given him so long ago for his many public services, since it would mean the ruin of his remaining fortunes. I therefore thought that I ought to adjourn the whole case until I could ask you, Sir, for directions on what line to take.

111. Trajan to Pliny

It is true that I have issued instructions forbidding public grants of money, but grants made a long time previously ought not to be revoked nor rendered invalid, lest we undermine the position of a great many people. Let us then leave out of consideration any features of this case which date back twenty years, for in every city the interests of individuals are as much my concern as the state of public funds.

112. Pliny to the Emperor Trajan

Bithynia and Pontus, Sir, are subject to the code of law drawn up by Pompey, which makes no provision for payment of entrance fees by those elected to the local senate by the censors; but in certain cities, where persons in excess of the legal number have been nominated by your special permission, they have been paying fees of one or two thousand denarii. Subsequently the governor, Anicius Maximus, made it a rule (though only in a very few places) that persons elected by the censors should also pay an entrance fee, which varied from city to city.

It remains then for you to consider whether from now on all persons elected senators should pay a fixed sum as entrance fee; for it is only fitting that a ruling which is to be permanent should come from you, whose deeds and words should live for ever.

113. *Trajan to Pliny*

It is impossible for me to lay down a general rule whether everyone who is elected to his local senate in every town of Bithynia should pay a fee on entrance or not. I think then that the safest course, as always, is to keep to the law of each city, though as regards fees from senators appointed by invitation, I imagine they will see that they are not left behind the rest.

114. *Pliny to the Emperor Trajan*

The code of Pompey, Sir, permits the cities of Bithynia to confer their citizenship on anyone they choose, provided that it is not someone who is already a citizen of another Bithynian city. The same law sets out the reasons for which the censors may remove senators from office. Certain censors have therefore asked my opinion whether or not it is their duty to expel a senator who is a citizen of another city.

But although the law states that such people may not be elected senators, it says nothing about removing them from the senate for this reason. I therefore felt that I must ask you for your instructions, especially as I am informed that every city has several senators who hold citizenship elsewhere, and many individuals and cities will be seriously affected by the enforcement of a section of the law which by general consent has long since fallen into disuse. I am sending the relevant sections of the law with this letter.

115. *Trajan to Pliny*

You had good reason, my dear Pliny, to be uncertain what answer to give to the censors' question whether senators who are citizens of other cities in the same province should retain their seats in the senate. The authority of the law on the one hand, and the long-established practice against it on the other, would influence you in opposite directions. My own view is that we should compromise; we should make no change in the situation resulting from past practice, so that citizens of any city may remain senators even if their election was not strictly legal; but in future the law of Pompey must be observed. If we tried to enforce it in retrospect it would inevitably lead to great confusion.

116. Pliny to the Emperor Trajan

It is a general practice for people at their coming-of-age or marriage, and on entering upon office or dedicating a public building, to issue invitations to all the local senators and even to quite a number of the common people in order to distribute presents of one or two denarii. I pray you to let me know how far you think this should be allowed, if at all. My own feeling is that invitations of this kind may sometimes be permissible, especially on ceremonial occasions, but the practice of issuing a thousand or even more seems to go beyond all reasonable limits, and could be regarded as a form of corrupt practice.

117. Trajan to Pliny

You have every reason to fear that the issuing of invitations might lead to corrupt practices, if the numbers are excessive and people are invited in groups to a sort of official present-giving rather than individually as personal friends. But I made you my choice so that you could use your good judgement in exercising a moderating influence on the behaviour of the people in your province, and could make your own decisions about what is necessary for their peace and security.

118. Pliny to the Emperor Trajan

The winning athletes in the Triumphal Games,[1] Sir, think that they ought to receive the prizes which you have awarded on the day they are crowned for victory. They argue that the actual date of their triumphal entry into their native towns is irrelevant; the date which matters is that of the victory which entitled them to the triumph. On the other hand, I point out that the name refers to 'triumphal entry' and so I am very much inclined to think that their date of entry is the one we could consider.

They also claim awards for previous victories won in Games to which you have subsequently given triumphal privileges, arguing that if they receive nothing in Games which have lost these privileges after their victories it is only fair that they should have something for Games which afterwards acquire them. Here, too, I very much doubt whether any retrospective claim should be allowed and feel that they

1. Games in which the winners were privileged to drive in triumph into their native towns, and afterwards received a civic pension.

should not be given anything to which they were not entitled at the time of victory. I pray you, therefore, to think fit to resolve my difficulties and make it clear how your benefactions are to be bestowed.

119. *Trajan to Pliny*

In my opinion, awards in these Games should date from the winner's triumphal entry into his city and not before. Prizes awarded in Games to which I have granted triumphal privileges must not be given retrospectively where no such privileges existed previously. Nor does it assist the athletes' claim if they can gain no more awards in the Games from which I have removed triumphal privileges since their victories, for though the Games are now held under different conditions they are not required to hand back prizes previously won.

120. *Pliny to the Emperor Trajan*

Up to now, Sir, I have made it a fixed rule not to issue anyone a permit to use the Imperial Post unless he is travelling on your service, but I have just been obliged to make an exception. My wife had news of her grandfather's death and was anxious to visit her aunt. I thought it would be unreasonable to deny her a permit when promptitude means much in performing a duty of this kind, and I felt sure that you would approve of a journey made for family reasons.

I am writing thus because I should feel myself lacking in gratitude if, among your many acts of kindness, I did not mention this further instance of your generosity whereby I was given confidence to act without hesitation, as if I had asked your permission: but had I waited to receive it, I should have been too late.

121. *Trajan to Pliny*

You were quite right, my dear Pliny, to feel confident of my response. You need not have had any doubts even if you had waited to ask me if you could expedite your wife's journey by making use of the permits which I issued to you for official purposes; it is her duty to make her visit doubly welcome to her aunt by her prompt arrival.[1]

1. Pliny must have died before 18 September, as there are no further formal birthday greetings to Trajan like those of x: 88.

Appendix A: Inscriptions

THERE are a few fragmentary inscriptions referring to Pliny, the longest of which (C.I.L.v. 5262) is known only from a fifteenth-century copy and one fragment remaining in Milan. The whole had evidently stood over the baths at Comum, but was afterwards cut up to make a tomb and sent to Milan in the middle ages, where it was found in the church of St Ambrose.

Gaius Plinius Caecilius Secundus, son of Lucius of the tribe Oufentina, consul: augur: praetorian commissioner with full consular power for the province of Pontus and Bithynia, sent to that province in accordance with the Senate's decree by the Emperor Nerva Trajan Augustus, victor over Germany and Dacia, the Father of his Country: curator of the bed and banks of the Tiber and sewers of Rome: official of the Treasury of Saturn: official of the military Treasury: praetor: tribune of the people: quaestor of the Emperor: commissioner for the Roman knights: military tribune of the Third Gallic legion: magistrate on board of Ten: left by will public baths at a cost of ... and an additional 300,000 sesterces for furnishing them, with interest on 200,000 for their upkeep ... and also to his city capital of 1,866,666 2/3 sesterces to support a hundred of his freedmen, and subsequently to provide an annual dinner for the people of the city. ... Likewise in his lifetime he gave 500,000 sesterces for the maintenance of boys and girls of the city, and also 100,000 for the upkeep of the library. ...

The following fragment can still be seen, built into the wall of Como Cathedral (C.I.L.v. 5263).

To Gaius Plinius Caecilius Secundus, son of Lucius of the tribe Oufentina, consul: augur: curator of the bed and banks of the Tiber and sewers of Rome. ...

The following inscription was found at Fecchio, a small village near Como, and sent to the Brera Museum in Milan (C.I.L.v. 5667):

To Gaius Plinius Caecilius Secundus, son of Lucius of the tribe Oufentina, consul: augur: curator of the bed and banks of the Tiber and sewers of Rome: official of the Treasury of Saturn: official of the military Treasury: . . . quaestor of the Emperor: commissioner for the Roman knights: military tribune of the Third Gallic legion: magistrate on board of Ten: priest of the deified Emperor Titus: dedicated by the citizens of Vercellae.

This is the only reference we have to a priesthood which must have been held in Pliny's native Comum; another inscription records that Calpurnius Fabatus held a similar one.

Appendix B: Pliny's House at Laurentum

A reconstructed plan taken from Clifford Pember's model in the Ashmolean Museum, Oxford.

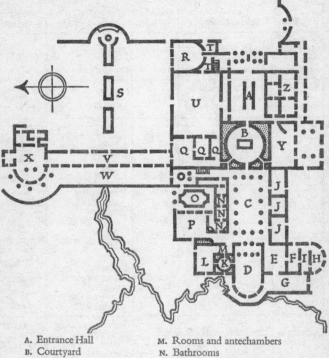

A. Entrance Hall	M. Rooms and antechambers
B. Courtyard	N. Bathrooms
C. Inner hall	O. Heated swimming-bath
D. Dining-room	P. Ball court
E. Bedroom	Q. Suite with upper storey
F. Bedroom	R. Dining-room, with stores above
G. Gymnasium	S. Garden with vine pergola
H. Bedroom	T. Rooms behind dining-room
I. Bedroom	U. Kitchen garden
J. Slaves' rooms	V. Covered arcade
K. Bedroom	W. Terrace
L. Small dining-room	X. Pliny's private suite
	Y-Z. Kitchens and storerooms, not mentioned by Pliny

AD	Events in Roman History		Events in Pliny's Career (Capitals indicate change of rank)		References to Letters
60	April 68 June 68 Dec. 69	Revolt of Vindex Death of Nero Accession of Vespasian	Late 60 or early 61	Pliny born	VI : 20 II : 1; VI : 10
70	24 June 79 24 Aug. 79	Death of Vespasian Accession of Titus Eruption of Vesuvius		Death of Elder Pliny	VI : 16 and 20
80	13 Sept. 81	Death of Titus Accession of Domitian	81	Begins career at Bar Marries first wife Defends Junius Pastor in Centumviral Court DECEMVIR STLITIBUS IUDICANDIS TRIBUNUS MILITUM of 3rd Gallic legion in Syria SEVIR EQUITUM ROMANORUM	V : 8 I : 18 Inscription I : 10; III : 11; VII : 31; VIII : 14 Inscription
	89	Domitian banishes philosophers from Rome (III : 11)	88 or 89	QUAESTOR AUGUSTI with Calestrius Tiro	VII : 16
90	Autumn 93	Domitian banishes philosophers from Italy and executes Stoic leaders	91 93	TRIBUNUS PLEBIS PRAETOR with Tiro Prosecutes Baebius Massa with Herennius Senecio	I : 23; VII : 16 III : 11; VII : 11 VI : 29; VII : 33
	18 Sept. 96	Death of Domitian Death of Corellius Rufus (I : 12)	94–96	PRAEFECTUS AERARII MILITARIS	Inscription
	Jan. 97	Death of Verginius Rufus (II : 1)	97	Death of second wife Speech in vindication of Helvidius Priscus	IX : 13 IX : 13
	25 Jan. 98	Death of Nerva Accession of Trajan	98–100	PRAEFECTUS AERARII SATURNI with Cornutus Tertullus	X : 3a

APPENDIX C: TABLE OF EVENTS

Events in Roman History	Events in Pliny's Career (Capitals indicate change of rank)		References to Letters
	Jan. 100	Prosecutes Marius Priscus	II : 11 and 12
	Sept.–Oct.	CONSUL with Cornutus Tertullus	III : 13 and 18
		Marries third wife, Calpurnia	IV : 19, VII : 5
	(in 98)	Granted *ius trium liberorum* by Trajan	X : 2
	100–101	Prosecutes Caecilius Classicus	III : 9
101–2 First Dacian War of Trajan (VI : 27)			
?102 Death of Martial (III : 21) Death of Silius Italicus (III : 7)	Winter 102–3	Defends Julius Bassus	IV : 9
?103 Death of Frontinus (IV : 8)	103	Elected AUGUR	IV : 8; X : 13
	104–6	Elected CURATOR ALVEI TIBERIS ET RIPARUM ET CLOACARUM URBIS	Inscription; V : 14; VII : 15
105–6 Second Dacian War, and defeat of Decibalus (VIII : 4)	Winter, 106–7	Defends Varenus Rufus	V : 20; VI : 5 and 13; VII : 6 and 10
	17 Sept. 111	Arrives in Bithynia	X : 17b
	Between 28 Jan. and 18 Sept. 113	Presumed death of Pliny	

Appendix D: Key to Technical Terms

CENTUMVIRAL COURT: The Chancery Court of Rome; a civil court of justice consisting of 180 members who normally sat in four panels and dealt with the more important cases concerning wills and inheritances.

CLIENT: Roman society still retained the old relationship of a client dependent upon a patron, with moral and legal mutual obligations. Freedmen (ex-slaves) were automatically clients of their former masters.

CONSUL: This was still the highest office in the State; the two consuls now held office for considerably less than a full year, so that the honour could be widely distributed. All ex-consuls enjoyed the privileges of consular rank, and the possibility of being elected governor of one of the most important provinces.

DECEMVIR STLITIBUS IUDICANDIS: One of the ten magistrates who presided over the panels of the Centumviral Court.

IMPERIAL POST: Under the Empire official dispatches were carried by special messengers travelling usually by carriage, and changing horses at recognized posting-houses. Private letters had to be entrusted to hired couriers or to friends making a journey, and only in special circumstances were permits issued to private individuals enabling them to use the Imperial Post.

KNIGHTS: This Order ranked next to the Senate, and had originally been the rank of citizens from whom horsemen were drawn for the army. They came to represent business and commercial interests outside the Senate; all knights had to have a minimum property qualification of 400,000 sesterces. They held important posts in the

Emperor's service in Rome and in the provinces, and from them and his personal freedmen the Emperor developed an efficient Civil Service.

PRAETOR: The State office next in rank to the consulship; the praetors had lost much of their judicial authority, but provided officials for the Treasury and other administrative posts, and most provincial governors were ex-praetors.

PROCURATOR, IMPERIAL: A knight or an imperial freedman serving on the Emperor's staff in Rome or in the provinces for which he was responsible; some minor provinces were given procurators as governors.

QUAESTOR: The lowest post in the senator's official career; quaestors served as financial officials, usually in the provinces, or as *quaestores Augusti* were assigned to the Emperor to convey his wishes to the Senate.

SENATE: Its members had to have the minimum property qualification of a million sesterces and were limited to 600. They were recruited from the sons of senators, from new quaestors, and from individuals nominated by the Emperor. Though the Senate's powers as supreme Council of State were now limited, it had important judicial authority and was still active as a deliberative body.

SESTERCE: At this period the sesterce was the unit for reckoning sums of money, though the coin in common use was the silver denarius, worth four sesterces or sixteen bronze asses. As there were twenty-five denarii (a hundred sesterces) to the gold aureus, most Victorian editors and some modern translators have tried to give an English equivalent by dividing by a hundred and referring to pounds or gold sovereigns. This has no relevance in 1963, but most of us would like to visualize what a capital of 400,000 or a tip of twelve sesterces meant to the possessor. One way to do so is to list some known sums of money, large and small, and see how they compare. Juvenal twice says that he could live comfortably as a single man on the income from 400,000 invested capital, plus a few slaves and silver plate. Assuming that his income would be five per cent of his capital, if a sesterce were equivalent to a modern 6d. then he would have £500 a year tax free, and, with much less to spend money on in first-century Rome than in a modern capital city, he could surely do quite well. Then the twelve-sesterce tip is 6s. This is of course pure conjecture and readers can make their own guesses. The *relative* values remain constant.*

The table below suggests that the Civil Servants' salaries (the procurators) fall into the £1,500–£7,500 range, and a member of the bar could expect £250 for a case. The senators' unearned income would be augmented by salaries from short-term appointments such as Pliny held. If we compare his fortune with the enormous sums quoted by Suetonius for real extravagance (Vitellius's banquets could cost 400,000 or £10,000 apiece) then Pliny's claim to be only moderately rich is more understandable.

TREASURY, MILITARY: This was financed largely by estate duties and sales taxes to provide pensions for discharged soldiers. It was administered by three praetors nominated by the Emperor.

TREASURY, OF SATURN: Originally the main State Treasury, this had declined in importance by competition with the Emperor's *fiscus*, or privy purse; it was administered by two senators appointed by the Emperor.

TRIBUNE, MILITARY: A young officer, who usually did not intend to pursue his military service beyond the prescribed six months before starting on a senatorial career.

TRIBUNE OF THE PEOPLE: This office still existed as a stage in the senator's career, though its powers as representative of the *plebs* had vanished. Its popular associations made the Emperors choose annual 'tribunician power' as the distinctive mark of their authority.

* The introduction of decimal coinage and progressive inflation have made nonsense of money values suggested in 1963, though the table of relative values can still be applied. A figure of 25 sesterces to the debased £ sterling of 1974 has been suggested, but this too may be outdated by the time this reprint (planned for the end of 1975) appears.

Table of Relative Money Values

	Sesterces	(Conjectural) Value) Sesterce = 6d.	References
Senator's Census	1,000,000	£25,000	
Senator's income at five per cent	50,000	£1,250[1]	
Knight's census	400,000	£10,000	
Knight's income	20,000	£500	
Top salaries: Pro-consuls of Asia and Africa, Prefect of Egypt, senior legates	400,000	£10,000	
Procurator's salaries	60,000– 300,000	£1,500–£7,500	
Legionary's pay *per annum*	1,200	£30	
Legionary's bonus on discharge	12,000	£300	
Largess to public given by Emperor (*congiarium*)	300	£7–10	
State price for grain, a peck	3	1s. 6d.	Annals, XV:39
Daily cash dole (*sportula*) for clients	6¼	3s. 1½d.	Juvenal, I: 120
Admission to public baths	1/16	less than ½d.	Juvenal, VI: 446
Martial's new book	20	10s.	Martial, I: 117

Reference in Pliny			
1. Income from property at Tifernum	400,000	£10,000	X: 8
2. Value of small farm	100,000	£2,300	VI: 3
3. Tip to member of *claque*	12	6s.	II: 14
4. Cash gift to person at receptions in Bithynia	4–8	2s.–4s.	X: 116
5. Entrance fees paid by senators in Bithynia	4,000–8,000	£100–£200	X: 112
6. Municipal councillor's census	100,000	£2,500	I: 19
7. Permitted fee to counsel after case	10,000	£250	V: 9
8. Purchase price of property near Comum	3,000,000	£75,000	III: 19
9. Pliny's estimated fortune	15–20,000,000	£375–500,000	
10. Regulus's fortune	60,000,000	£1,500,000	II: 20

1. Nearly all senators had means well above this figure, and many were extremely wealthy.

Central and Northern Italy

Comum
Vercellae
TRANSPADINI Vicentia VENETIA
Mediolanum
Ticenum Brixia Verona Patavium Altinum
R.Po
LIGURIA GALLIA CISALPINA

0 English Miles 100
0 Kilometres 160

UMBRIA
ETRURIA
PICENUM
Arretium
Tifernum
Perusia Firmum
Asisium
Hispellum
Ameria
L.Vadimon Narnia
Ocriculum SAMNIUM
Centumcellae Tibur
Alsium Rome
Praeneste
Ostia Tusculum
Laurentum
LATIUM CAMPANIA
Formiae
Baiae Naples Mt
Misenum Vesuvius
Pompeii
Caprea Stabiae

Nola
Baiae Naples
Misenum Mt Vesuvius
Herculaneum
Pompeii
Stabiae
Surrentum
Capreae 0 Miles 10

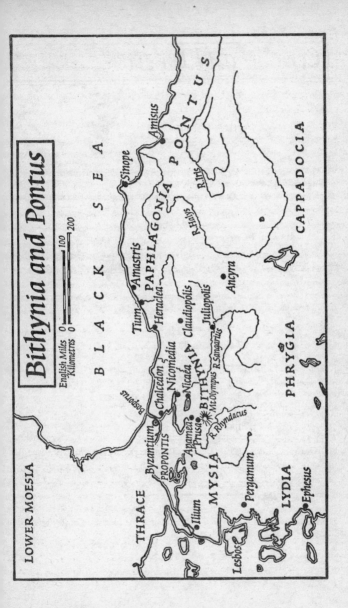

Select Bibliography

TEXTS

R. A. B. Mynors: *Letters I–X.* Oxford, 1963 (Oxford Classical Text)

A. M. Guillemin: *Lettres I–IX* (with notes and French translation), 3 vols. Budé edition, Paris, 1927–8

M. Durry: *Lettres X et Panégyrique* (with notes and French translation). Budé edition, Paris, 1959

COMMENTARIES

E. G. Hardy: *Pliny's Correspondence with Trajan.* London, 1889

A. M. Guillemin: *Notes in Budé edition* (see above)

A. N. Sherwin-White: *The Letters of Pliny.* Oxford, 1966

Fifty Letters of Pliny. Oxford, 1966

The following lists are selective, containing generally accessible books and recent articles in which information relative to Pliny can be found.

BOOKS

Cambridge Ancient History Vol. XI: *The Imperial Peace.* Cambridge, 1936 (esp. Ch. V by R. P. Longdon 'Nerva and Trajan')

J. Carcopino: *Daily Life in Ancient Rome.* London, 1941 (Penguin Books, 1962)

G. E. F. Chilver: *Cisalpine Gaul.* Oxford, 1941

J. Crook: *Consilium Principis.* Cambridge, 1955

H. Dessau: *Inscriptiones Latinae Selectae.* Berlin, 1892, 1916

A. M. Guillemin: *Pline et la Vie littéraire de son Temps.* Paris, 1929

G. Highet: *Juvenal the Satirist.* Oxford, 1954

A. H. M. Jones: *The Greek City.* Oxford, 1940

H. Mattingly: *Catalogue of Roman Coins in the British Museum.* Vol. III, Nerva-Trajan. 1936

M. McCrum and A. G. Woodhead: *Documents of the Flavian Emperors.* Cambridge, 1961

A. N. Sherwin-White: *Roman Citizenship.* Oxford, 1939

Roman Society and Roman Law in the New Testament. Oxford, 1963

E. M. Smallwood: *Documents of Nerva, Trajan and Hadrian.* Cambridge, 1966

R. Syme: *Tacitus.* 2 vols. Oxford, 1958

ARTICLES

P. A. Brunt: 'Charges of Provincial Maladministration'. *Historia* X, 1961

R. T. Bruyère: 'Tacitus and Pliny's Panegyricus'. *Class. Phil.* XLIX, 1954

A. Cameron: 'The Fate of Pliny's Letters in the Late Empire'. *C. Q.* XV, 1965

R. Duncan-Jones: 'The Finances of the Younger Pliny'. *P.B.S.R.* XXXIII, 1965

G. P. Gould: Review of O.C.T. of *Letters*. *Phoenix* XVIII, 1964

J. C. Hainsworth: 'Verginius and Vindex'. *Historia* XI, 1962

M. Hammond: 'Pliny the Younger's views on government'. *Class. Phil.* XLIX, 1954

T. F. Higham: 'Dolphin Riders'. *Greece & Rome* VII, 1, 1960

S. Jameson: 'Cornutus Tertullus and the Plancii of Perge'. *J.R.S.* LV, 1965

C. J. Kraemer: 'Pliny and the early church service'. *Class. Phil.* XXIX, 1934

H. Last: 'The study of the persecutions'. *J.R.S.* XXVII, 1937

R. P. Longdon: 'Notes on the Parthian campaigns of Trajan'. *J.R.S.* XXI, 1931

S. L. Mohler: 'Bithynian Christians'. *Class. Phil.* XXX, 1935

B. Radice: 'A fresh approach to Pliny's letters'. *Greece & Rome* IX, 2, 1968
'Pliny and the Panegyricus'. *Greece & Rome* XV, 2, 1968

G. E. M. de Ste Croix: 'Why were the Early Christians Persecuted?' *Past and Present*, 26, 1963
'Rejoinder to A. N. S-W's Amendment'. *Past and Present*, 27, 1964

A. N. Sherwin-White: 'The date of Pliny's Praetorship'.[1] *J.R.S.* XLVII, 1957
'Trajan's replies to Pliny: authorship and necessity'. *J.R.S.* LII, 1962
'Early persecutions and the Roman Law'.[2] *J. Theol. Studies*, N.S. III (2), 1952

    1. Appendix IV in *Letters of Pliny*
    2. Appendix V in *Letters of Pliny*

S. E. Stout: 'The Coalescence of the Two Plinies'. *Trans. Am. Phil. Ass.* LXXXVI, 1955

F. A. Sullivan, S.J.: 'Pliny *Epistulae* VI, 16 and 20 and modern Volcanology'. *Class. Phil.* LXIII, 3, 1968

R. Syme: 'The Imperial Finances of Domitian, Nerva and Trajan'. *J.R.S.* XX, 1930
'The Friend of Tacitus'. *J.R.S.* XLVII, 1957
'The Lower Danube under Trajan'. *J.R.S.* XLIX, 1959
'Pliny's less Successful Friends'. *Historia* X, 1961
'Pliny and the Dacian War'. *Latomus* XXIII, 1964

G. B. Townend: 'The Hippo Inscription and Career of Suetonius'. *Historia*, X, 1961.

H. W. Traub: 'Pliny's Treatment of History in Epistology Form'. *Trans. Amer. Phil. Ass.* LXXXVI, 1955

K. W. Waters: 'The Character of Domitian'. *Phoenix* XVIII, 1964

Index of Proper Names and Places

Some names which have a single passing reference are not included